For *Daisy Houston Whitlock*
(1883–1954), who always listened
when her young, movie-crazy
grandson re-told the motion
pictures he'd just seen.

THE GOLDEN AGE OF "B" MOVIES

Doug McClelland

BONANZA BOOKS

ACKNOWLEDGMENTS

For their help, my thanks to Gene Andrewski; David Barnes; Eric Benson; DeWitt Bodeen; Bradley Beach Public Library; Bruco Enterprises; Carol K. Carey, Museum of Modern Art; Gary Collins, Universal 16; Irwin Danels, Harris Mislansky and Lynne Vetrano, Columbia Pictures; Eddie Brandt's Saturday Matinée; William K. Everson; Joe Judice; Miles Kreuger; William Lacey, CBS Television; Kenneth G. Lawrence, Movie Memorabilia Shop of Hollywood; Library of Lincoln Center: The Theater Collection; Leonard Maltin and *Film Fan Monthly;* Alvin H. Marill; Memory Shop; Movie Poster Service; Movie Star News; James Robert Parish; Robert Scherl; Ted Sennett; Chris Steinbrunner, WOR Television; Murray Summers and *Filmograph;* Wence Torres, Metromedia Television; Lou Valentino; and particularly John Cocchi, one of the best friends the movies—and authors on the movies—ever had.

Special billing and thanks to Evelyn Ankers for writing the introduction to this book and, more important, for brightening so many "B" movies in the forties with her beauty and talent.

CONTENTS

The "B" and I
EVELYN ANKERS

"B" movies had their heyday during Hollywood's so-called Golden Age. They were quickly made, cheaply produced but popular little films; hence, their sobriquets as "quickies" or "cheapies."

Acting in them, as I did almost continually throughout the 1940s, was hard, exhausting, frustrating work. Yet, as I look back on those years—I must admit, a bit nostalgically—from our present home on Maui, Hawaii, it seems that there were more good than bad times. The "fun," however, depended upon the cast, the crew, the director, and whether or not we were on schedule.

But let's begin at the beginning.

After appearing in several English plays and films, I made my American debut in 1940, in the hit Broadway thriller *Ladies in Retirement*. Right after the opening, Twentieth-Century Fox, Warner Brothers, and Universal Pictures all wanted to sign me to a long-term contract. In those days, a long-term contract meant seven years or more with the infamous six-month option clause. Every six months the studio had the right to decide to use the contract player in a film, change the terms of the contract (cut our salary, for example), or drop us completely. We had no recourse—our agents were practically powerless. If the studio suggested a salary cut, we had no choice but to go along with their demands, unless, of course, we could stand the shame of being dropped. My agent, Louis Schurr, suggested we suspend negotiations until the play went to Hollywood after the New York run, which we did.

I signed with 20th-Century Fox and prepared for my first Hollywood assignment, *Scotland Yard,* in which I was typecast as a British girl opposite George Sanders. Finally, wardrobe and script were ready; next, title, cast, producer, director and starting time were announced. At the last minute, however, Mr. Sanders refused to do the film because he felt the story was derogatory to England, especially Scotland Yard. The studio suspended him. Now they had a problem—they couldn't use me with their only

1

other English contract player, John Loder, because neither of us were big enough stars to carry the picture singly or together. They hired another contract actress, American Nancy Kelly, to appear with Mr. Loder. This left me in an awkward position, since they didn't have anything else lined up in which they could use an English actress. Meanwhile, Universal wanted to feature me with Bud Abbott and Lou Costello in *Hold That Ghost,* so I signed a seven-year contract with them on Jan. 8, 1941.

I didn't know, however, that I was to play an American girl, least of all one with a Brooklyn accent, especially when they had so many American players under contract. That's Hollywood for you, I guess—or *was.* Well, that first American movie was a chore for all concerned. I had to cut down those broad A's I was used to. There were quite a few extra takes when I'd say *new* or *dew* instead of *nu* or *du.* I had trouble, too, saying *recurd* instead of *rec-cord.*

Abbott and Costello thought me stuffy because I was so "English"; they just loved to tease me with their vaudeville tricks, which were too off-color to relate here. Suffice it to say I was always glad to find a wall to stand against, or a chair to sit in, between takes on *Hold That Ghost.*

By the time I'd finished my fourth consecutive American part, and my accent was no longer a problem, they cast me as the English heroine in *The Wolf Man.* I had to reverse the entire procedure and broaden all my A's again! Next came a Western role, then two English, one American, two English—I was starting to feel like a yo-yo. Eventually, I played fourteen American parts in a row before the English *The Pearl of Death.*

Another early American film of mine was a "B" called *Hit the Road,* with the Little Tough Guys (who had split from the Dead End Kids). They were terribly difficult to work with. I felt they couldn't act and were just playing themselves—hoodlums. It was very hard on poor Joe May, the director, who was very conscientious and trying to do a good job. He came to me once and begged me to talk to the boys, who wouldn't stop clowning and get to work. The

Richard Denning, Evelyn Ankers in *Black Beauty*
(20th Century-Fox Pictures, 1946)

film was over schedule, yet no matter how Mr. May pleaded with them to be serious, they just ignored him. I went back on the set with him and gave them a good, stern bawling-out (not the first that day). As long as I stayed around they worked, but they didn't seem to have any respect for Mr. May—why I don't know. Maybe because he had a European accent or because he was a father figure to them.

I remember one long, rough day on *Hit the Road*. The last shot was a close-up of me. I think it was just to placate me, since Mr. May had undoubtedly kept me around all afternoon just to keep the Little Tough Guys in line. I had a date that night with my "steady," actor Glenn Ford. I removed my make-up and changed clothes and thought I was the last one to leave the set, but on my way out I bumped into "little tough guy" Huntz Hall (acne and all). He put his arms around me so that I couldn't get away and asked me for a kiss. I said, "No! Leave me alone, please—I'm late and I have a date." He persisted. I implored him, "Let go of me or I'll hurt you. I mean it!" He only laughed and tried to force me to kiss him. I responded as my Dad had taught me to—I let him have it with my knee right between his legs. He fell to the ground yelling bloody murder (I knew then he had survived the kick) and I took off. This was perhaps the reason the boys listened to me above everyone else on the set: I was the only one who gave them some of their own medicine.

Both before and during production of "B" pictures we often got daily script changes (each on different colored paper). If we were lucky, a studio messenger delivered the script changes to us sometime over the weekend. By Monday morning we were supposed to know all our dialogue and have all the accessories ready for each costume. If necessary, the studio would supply us with accessories, but I preferred to use my own comfortable shoes, gloves, hats, and jewelry. (Usually what was furnished by the wardrobe department didn't fit or look very good anyhow.) If neither the studio nor I had what was needed, someone would be sent to shop for me—which was fine, as long as the costume didn't include hats—or I would shop for myself. I dreaded this because it was so time-consuming and fatiguing, particularly after working hard all day. We weren't paid for that time either, and I much preferred to be home working on my script, inserting and relearning that day's changes and "blocking out" the part.

Sometimes I had to change some of my dialogue, if it were in a specific British accent such as Cockney, Mayfair, high- or middle-class,

**Lon Chaney, Jr., Evelyn Ankers in *The Wolf Man*
(Universal Pictures, 1941)**

north country—even Irish or Scotch. The script writer, unless he was English, didn't know the many different idioms, slang, and provincial sayings associated with the various accents and lilts of the English language spoken on the British Isles. To give the part credibility, therefore, I had to add all these things myself—search for them mentally, as there was never any time to do any creative research for a character or role in a "B" or "B-plus" picture. Not when you were under contract, that is.

Usually, I just made notes of any changes on my script in pencil, hoping the director would have time for a rehearsal for the actors alone (excluding rehearsals for lighting and camera). Then, one could discuss the changes with the director, script girl (for timing and matching purposes), or dialogue director (if there was one, which was very seldom on a "B") plus fellow actors, so you could give them any changes in cues or dialogue affecting them and run through it with them.

What could happen without adequate preparation is exemplified by an experience I had on

The Great Impersonation, in which I co-starred with Ralph Bellamy.

John Rawlins was our director, although he was known in the industry primarily as a film cutter. One day, I was called onto the set by the assistant director. Mr. Bellamy was already there, seated at one end of a sofa where the make-up man was checking him. At that time, he was one of my idols, but I had never met him. The director, whom I also had never met, came up to me and said, "Hi, are you ready to shoot?"

I replied, "Oh—you must be the director, Mr. Rawlins."

He answered that he was the director and guided me over to the empty seat next to Mr. Bellamy, who was now looking in his mirror examining his appearance while the hairdresser fiddled with his hair. Then Mr. Rawlins walked away and looked into the camera to see how we looked. I was waiting for him to return and introduce me to Mr. Bellamy, as I was most anxious to rehearse. This was a long, involved key scene in which I had to lean over and kiss

Evelyn Ankers, Carleton Young in *Queen of Burlesque* (Producers Releasing Corp. Pictures, 1946)

him—in a vampy, Mata Hari style.

When the hairdresser left Mr. Bellamy, I was about to introduce myself and ask him if he would care to rehearse when suddenly I heard, "OK—silence, please—action!"

There was deathly silence as we both just sat there looking at each other with our mouths open, wondering if we were dreaming. We hadn't even been informed where the director wanted to start or finish the scene, as this was set up as a two-shot and only *part* of the whole scene—which hadn't even been shot yet!

Mr. Rawlins finally yelled "Cut!" and came over to ask us what the problem was. I managed to stutter, "First, I would like to meet my leading man, as I have never kissed a man before without first being introduced to him. Second, it would help us both, I'm sure, if we knew where you wanted to start and end the scene." Mr. Bellamy heartily agreed, interjecting, "It would also help a lot if we could have a rehearsal. If not for your benefit at least for ours."

Other directors, such as my favorite, Felix Feist, who directed *All by Myself,* my favorite film (because it gave me a rare chance at lighter characterization), had us rehearse long enough so we could usually do the master scene all the way though in the first take without any major mistakes. Felix would then do another take for security and print them both. Then he would come in for a two-shot and, finally, close-ups. Felix also would call the leading players in before shooting started for a "read-through" of our scenes together. That way, we could estab-

lish our characters in relation to each other. This also gave us an opportunity to change, add, or delete any dialogue that would tighten the scene, make it flow better or be more believable. Aside from the obvious advantages, it was also great for the players to get to know one another and thereby feel at ease on the actual shooting day.

At Universal, Vera West, head of the studio's wardrobe department, generally designed all my clothes, presenting the initial sketches to the studio executives and myself for approval. Exceptions to this were parts or scenes that called for a simple costume such as tailored suits, sleepwear, bathing suits, character or old clothes, and show costumes. The show or dance costumes for *Bowery to Broadway, Queen of Burlesque,* and *The Lone Wolf in London* all came from Western Costume Company, as did the uniforms in *Eagle Squadron* and *Ladies Courageous,* the Western outfits for *The Texan Meets Calamity Jane* and the "period" clothing in *North to the Klondike, Black Beauty, Last of the Redmen,* and *Spoilers of the*

Ralph Bellamy, Evelyn Ankers in *The Great Impersonation* (Universal Pictures, 1942)

North. (My handsome actor husband Richard Denning, whom I married on Sept. 6, 1942, and stayed married to, appeared with me in *Black Beauty.* For this reason it is one of my favorite pictures.) At Universal, I also used my own clothes when it was more convenient for me, because fittings were very time-consuming and tiring.

The "B" pictures took from seven days to three weeks to make—including Saturdays. (Whereas the more expensive "A" pictures could be in production for months, sometimes even a year.) This did not count rehearsals, shopping, wardrobe and wig fittings, and hair and make-up tests. (I had always been a natural blonde until the late forties, when I did *Tarzan's Magic Fountain.* My hair was dyed dark brown for that picture so that when my character in the story grew old, it would show gray. I then bleached my hair back to blonde. Almost immediately, I went up for *The Texan Meets Calamity Jane,* and the producer asked me, "What happened to your brown hair?" I explained the situation, but he said Calamity Jane had had

dark hair and asked if I would go brunette again. I did, but both my daughter and husband hated me with dark hair, so it was back to blonde for good after the film.) We also had sittings for production stills in the still gallery after each picture, which supplemented the photographs taken on the set every day, and conferences with the publicity people.

In June and July of 1944, I worked on two pictures at once, *Bowery to Broadway* and *The Frozen Ghost,* a "B." I remember it well because I was about six months pregnant with my beautiful daughter, Diana Dee (Dee Dee). The Universal executives didn't know about my condition, and I wanted to keep working and receive my salary as long as possible, because my husband was in the Navy, and I knew they would fire me as soon as they found out. I managed to fool Vera West for a while by telling her that I had "female problems" which made me hungry all the time and caused the weight gain, assuring her that the problem would be taken care of as soon as I could get some time off. By the time *Frozen Ghost* started, however, she had caught

Basil Rathbone, Evelyn Ankers in *Sherlock Holmes and the Voice of Terror* (Universal Pictures, 1942)

on but was willing to go along and helped me by providing veils and muffs to hide the tell-tale tummy.

During *Bowery to Broadway,* while I was doing the 1890s "striptease" number, the un-born baby unexpectedly kicked vigorously, which made me gasp out loud. I explained, "It must have been a gas pain causing my 'female problem' to act up." Before long, nearly every-one on the set knew that I was expecting a baby but didn't talk about it so the front office wouldn't find out.

Tala Birell, who was also in the cast of *Frozen Ghost,* did not know, however, and she couldn't understand why they had hired such a portly leading lady. The cameraman's assistant used to mark our ultimate feet positions on the set floor in chalk outlines, and when he drew my feet he put two tiny baby feet between them. Believe it or not, poor Tala could never figure out why he marked mine like that, or why we all laughed so much each time she asked.

After my daughter was born, I freelanced so I could be with her and Dick whenever I wanted to be.

I am often asked why I was put into so many horror films. Perhaps it was because Universal needed a younger version of Fay Wray (it had been almost ten years since she had done *King Kong),* someone who could do realistic, blood-curdling screams and react in a modern style to modern monsters. When things got dull or I got a little too big for my shoes, the crew would bring me down a peg or two by calling me "the poor man's Fay Wray," or "Ankers aweigh," which was their favorite quip.

Once an elderly extra told me she had been with Universal since its inception, dubbing all the screams for actresses as they were chased by monsters—including Fay Wray—because their screams were never realistic enough. I said I was sorry I had deprived her of her job, but she replied that she really didn't mind because I helped save her throat.

I had no idea that some of the horror films I made would acquire the cult status they have today. I eventually did realize they would be released over and over again, because many of them were *period films* or set in foreign climes, and were therefore relatively dateless. But, be-cause The Screen Actors Guild set 1948 as the starting date for television residuals on the old films, I only received residuals on the last three or four films I made.

A somewhat embarrassing incident occurred in connection with one of these horror films, *The Ghost of Frankenstein.* On a promotional tour for the film, I found myself engaged in

Patric Knowles, Evelyn Ankers in *All by Myself* (Universal Pictures, 1943)

conversation with a charming, cultivated man, quiet-mannered and a little shy. We talked about Hollywood, motion pictures and life in general, and before parting, the gentleman informed me that he had enjoyed working in the picture with me. I uttered a vague thank-you and only later learned that I had been talking to Bela Lugosi, who, completely disguised by his make-up, had played a wicked, bearded hunchback in the picture. (He also appeared with me in *The Wolf Man*).

It was a pleasure, too, to know George Zucco, David Bruce, and Millburn Stone, with whom I worked in *The Mad Ghoul*. All three were great troupers and, best of all, they were gentlemen, quite a unique characteristic in Hollywood in those days.

I remember an incident relative to this that happened when I was working on *The Wolf Man*. Just before I started the film, the front office called me in to tell me they liked my work and were rewarding me with a plush, new dressing room which I would share with Anne Gwynne, also under contract to Universal. Natu-

rally I was thrilled. On the first day of shooting, Lon Chaney, Jr., my leading man, said to me, "So you're the gal who swiped my dressing room. You took it away from Broderick Crawford and me—I think that was a hell of a thing to do!" Since I was going to have to work with this man (over and over again, as it turned out), I agreed. When I asked the front office about it, they told me Lon had been warned that this would happen if he didn't stop "misbehaving." Soon after, I found out just what "misbehaving" meant. Someone told me that every Friday or Saturday night, Lon and Brod Crawford would take bottles into their dressing room, get loaded, and, then somehow manage to hang the furniture from the ceiling and brawl. On Monday, the cleaning crew was treated to a sight resembling a World War II battlefield.

Lon Chaney, Jr., enjoyed nothing more than a good donnybrook. Right after he and I had finished *Son of Dracula*, I think, the studio invited the major magazines to a dinner party on the lot to meet all the horror stars. Everybody was there—Boris Karloff, Bela Lugosi, and

Jon Hall, Evelyn Ankers in *Last of the Redmen*
(Columbia Pictures, 1947)

George Zucco. Lon, seated near my husband and me, proceeded to direct a number of rude, uncalled-for remarks toward Dick. Being a gentleman, Dick ignored them. Until. . . .

"How come," I recall Lon saying to Dick, "you're in the Navy and still in Los Angeles?"

Dick replied, "It's a lot better than not being in the service at all during wartime,"—which was Lon's situation.

A while later, Lon said, "I've got a little ice cream on my sleeve," and wiped it on Dick's dress blues. That did it. Dick took his ice cream—which was pistachio green, in keeping with the horror motif—and pushed it in Lon's face. With all that green dripping from his face, he looked as if he were back in make-up for one of his monster characters. Lon was about to heave his coffee at Dick, thus starting one of the brawls he so dearly loved, when I intervened and quieted things down. Then we all had to troop into the next room to have our pictures taken!

About six months later, Dick was transferred to submarines, where he spent the next three years.

To get back to *The Mad Ghoul* (not Lon Chaney, but the movie of that title)—I was very disappointed that I never got to sing in the picture as originally planned. (A few years before, in Buenos Aires, I had had my own radio program as a singer). I rehearsed for weeks but didn't have any time off when the recording studio and orchestra were free. Consequently, when it came time for me to sing, there was no recording for me to sing (or mouth) to, except stock recordings made by other artists. Naturally I was very upset and felt it would be much more advantageous for me to do the number live. They explained that there was no orchestra available in the recording studio, and that even in "A" pictures it was not practical to record while actually doing the scene. I had to mouth it to someone else's voice since we were, as always, behind schedule.

I was later told by an employee that they already had those numbers in the library and intended to use them before they ever asked me to rehearse and sing them, and they didn't want to move the orchestra from another picture they were working on because they would have had to pay the musicians overtime.

I made some valued friends while working in pictures, although, as in any other business, you don't feel like fraternizing with the same people you've been working with all day. The producer would usually give the cast a party on the last night of a picture. Often, I would wait and observe the people I liked best at that time, then possibly get together with them later when we

Lon Chaney, Jr., Evelyn Ankers in *The Wolf Man*

were on "lay-off." At Universal, the contract people were without work and pay for six weeks of every six-month period, unless we were working on loan-out to another studio. This "lay-off" period was always used by the publicity department for photo sessions and interviews. If we were lucky, we could sneak off to the Racquet Club in Palm Springs for the weekend—maybe.

I did become very close to Anne Gwynne, the actress with whom I appeared in *Weird Woman* and *Ladies Courageous*. The studio sent us on many publicity junkets together (along with Maria Montez, Marie McDonald, and Jane Frazee), and we spent much time together helping out at the USO and the Hollywood Canteen during World War II. In fact, I introduced Anne to my attorney, Max Gilford, whom she soon married. Their daughter, Gwynne, and son, Gregg, grew up with our daughter, Dee Dee—mostly in our pool.

Weird Woman was my first "heavy" part, and not of my own choosing. This was a new field for me, and I found it very difficult to feel comfortable or convincing. Reggie LeBorg, the director, sensed something was wrong, and on the first day, after each scene, asked, "Evie, what's the problem? It's not believable." I answered, "I know why—I'm miscast. I don't feel a bit mean and I don't want to hurt Anne because she's my best girlfriend." He answered, "Well, this time forget all that. Think of something mean she must have said or done to you and try it again." He then would say "Action!" and I would sort of squint or narrow my eyes, even attempt to flare my nostrils in desperation—trying to work myself up to appearing evil—then turn my head and look Anne in the eye threateningly. Bang, we

would become hysterical with laughter, and so would the whole company watching us.

This happened time and time again, until we were absolutely exhausted. It was not only ridiculous but also costly in time as well as money, not to mention poor Reggie's patience. We felt so sorry for him, even when he tried to get angry with us, which only made it worse. How we ever finished that picture, I'll never know. Universal got the message and never cast me as a villainess again.

Anne and I were in *Ladies Courageous* together, but when the picture ran too long, our roles were cut to near-bit parts. I believe it was shot before *Weird Woman*, since we didn't have any trouble working together on this.

Around that time, MGM wanted to borrow me for the Cockney maid in *Gaslight*, a supporting part similar to the one I created on the stage in *Ladies in Retirement*. But Universal needed me to play the Dutch girl in *Ladies Courageous*, which was planned as an "A," so newcomer Angela Lansbury became MGM's maid—and won an Academy Award nomination. A few years before, back in England, I was being considered for the role of Mrs. Chips in MGM's *Goodbye, Mr. Chips*. This part finally went to yet another newcomer—Greer Garson—who also received an Oscar nomination. Both these pictures could have turned the tide in my career, but apparently the good Lord had other plans for me and knew that eventually I'd be much happier away from it all on our beautiful Maui.

Two films in which I was featured have endured: *Sherlock Holmes and the Voice of Terror* and *The Pearl of Death*. It was always fun working with Basil Rathbone—or Rasil

Bathbone, as I called him—and Nigel Bruce, who played Dr. Watson. Much good-natured teasing was exchanged between us. Nigel, who liked to take a nip now and then, often had gout and had to sit with his foot up, which we razzed him about.

In *The Pearl of Death,* I had to assume several disguises, one of which was a poor old match woman. After I had done her quavering, squeaky voice for the scene and the director had called "Cut!", the teddibly British Nigel said to me, "Do tell me, Eeva-lyn, deah, what *was* that? You sounded like a little billy goat!"

For another impersonation in the same picture, I had to use an Irish accent. We were rushed for time, and I worried after we shot the scene that I didn't have it exactly right. But our director, Roy William Neill, said that since the girl was supposed to be faking it anyway, it didn't have to be letter-perfect. When I walked over to Basil and Nigel, Nigel remarked, "That was the damndest Irish-Scotch accent I ever heard!"

I had the feeling Nigel used to put on his own huffy-puffy old-school-tie British accent a little. (He was really Scottish.) Basil once said to him, "Nigel, if you were any more British we couldn't understand you!"

Nigel could also be naughty. Although he was getting on in years, he loved to flirt and would put his arm around me tightly and try to "wolf" me, saying, "You're the most beautiful girl I've ever seen." Once I warned him that he had better be careful, because my husband would be coming home from the Navy soon and would visit the set and catch him.

"Is he big?" asked Nigel.

"Over six feet," I replied.

One day Dick did visit the set, and Nigel spent the whole day hiding in the corner. I had been kidding, of course, but he took me seriously. The crew knew the story and laughed along with Dick, Basil, and me.

Perhaps the film of mine that people remember best is *The Wolf Man*. I have many memories of making it—but only some of them are pleasant. There was Lon Chaney, Jr., for exam-

ple. He would come on the set about an hour after everyone else because of the long make-up job required for his Wolf Man appearance. It became his particular kick to creep up behind me, tap me on the shoulder so I would turn around and then, with his face about an inch from mine, bare his fangs and put his horrible hairy arms and claws around me. He had to hold me, or I would have ended up in the rafters.

After a while I overcame this by sitting with my back against the wall (à *la* my experience with Abbott and Costello), but he would still catch me sometimes if I were working. What a way to earn a living!

Another time I was in a scene which called for me to be chased through a dark and eerie forest. The prop men used the fog machines beforehand to make a low blanket of fog, about a foot from the ground. Something is chasing me. I turn as it gets closer and see it is the Wolf Man. I scream and faint as directed, falling into the layer of fog which covers me completely. He creeps *very* slowly toward me (for suspense) and bends over me. They pan in closer. Then the director shouts "Cut!" and everyone gets to work breaking down the set and getting ready for the close-up—everyone except me. I was out cold after inhaling all the chemical fog I'd been lying in from almost the beginning of the action. Finally, somebody remembered I had been in the scene, too. It would have been a short career if they hadn't tripped over me at last.

I shudder in the same way when I recall one of the Gypsy scenes. Lon Chaney and I were strolling through the camp arm-in-arm when we came upon a Gypsy holding a huge, live bear on a chain. We stopped and looked, then moved on. The bear, however, decided that he wanted to get to know me better. I was unaware of what was happening behind me. The next thing I knew Lon took off, as did everybody else. I turned, wondering what the commotion was all about and where my leading man had gone, and saw the bear coming after me!

I never ran so fast in all my life. With the bear coming close behind me, I shot up a ladder into the rafters, where an electrician grabbed my hand and pulled me onto his platform. He then blinded the bear with a hot floodlight. The trainer finally caught up with the animal, retrieved his chain, reprimanded him, and gradually got him back down onto the stage. After I scrambled down myself (it was much harder going down, believe me), they told me I had *flown* up! Of course, we had to do the scene over many times, but they would come in to a close-up of Lon and me whenever possible so that no one would see our knees knocking.

With all that, it was a pleasure and an honor to work with the marvelous players we had in *The Wolf Man.* Besides Lon, there were Claude Rains, Ralph Bellamy, Warren William, Patric Knowles, Maria Ouspenskaya and Bela Lugosi—surely one of the best casts a "B" movie ever had. This picture was one of the almost thirty I made in less than four years at Universal Pictures alone. When it was over, I was relieved and happy that the gray hairs didn't show among the blonde.

EVELYN ANKERS

The "B" Movie:
"ELEMENTARY, MY DEAR WATSON"

To many movie-goers, the forties mean: Humphrey Bogart saying to Ingrid Bergman, "Here's looking at *you,* kid." . . . Greer Garson catching a Nazi in her kitchen. . . . Bing Crosby singing "Too-Ra-Loo-Ra-Loo-Ra" to Barry Fitzgerald. . . . Jane Wyman saying *The Lord's Prayer* in sign language. . . . Judy Garland taking the trolley to the World's Fair. . . . Larry Parks boasting, "You ain't heard nothin' yet." . . . Twelve-year-old Elizabeth Taylor winning the Grand National Steeplechase. . . . Ray Milland hiding his whiskey bottle in the chandelier. . . . Betty Grable's legs. . . . Carmen Miranda's hats. . . . Al Jolson's booming voice. . . . Spencer Tracy meeting Katharine Hepburn. . . . John Wayne winning both the West and World War II. . . . Lana Turner dropping her lipstick and watching it roll over to John Garfield. . . . Cary Grant composing "Night and Day." . . . Victor Mature pushing down the temple columns. . . . Gregory Peck turning Jewish. . . . Jeanne Crain turning black. . . . James Cagney shouting, "Top of the world, Ma!" as the gas tank beneath him exploded. . . . Claudette Colbert going to war. . . . Irene Dunne going to Siam. . . . Bette Davis, Olivia de Havilland, Joan Crawford, Susan Hayward, Eleanor Parker, and Ida Lupino going berserk.

These were the "A" movies, expensively produced and duly heralded. And then we had. . . . Basil Rathbone telling Nigel Bruce, "Elementary, my dear Watson." . . . Joan Davis getting laughs with a quip or a fall on her rump. . . . Scarfaced Peter Lorre falling in love with blind girl Evelyn Keyes. . . . Laurel and Hardy safeguarding a new explosive. . . . The two faces of schizophrenic Phyllis Thaxter in mortal combat. . . . Red Skelton wailing, "Ah-wooooo, I'm the Fox!". . . Judy Canova and Susan Hayward going to school together. . . . Nils Asther aging sixty years before Helen Walker's horrified eyes. . . . Anthony Quinn's horse winning the Kentucky Derby. . . . Keenan Wynn and Frank Morgan as father and son ghosts. . . . Mabel Paige running the

13

gamut from mother to menace. . . . Erich von Stroheim hypnotizing his way into infamy. . . . Charlie Chan streamlining Confucius. . . . Billy Lee and Sharyn Moffett loving their dogs. . . . The Andrews Sisters singing. . . . Ann Miller dancing. . . . Evelyn Ankers screaming. . . . George Zucco salivating. . . . Leon Errol walking. . . . Hugh Herbert's "Woo-woo's!" . . . Dennis O'Keefe's double takes. . . . Ann Savage shriveling strong men with her glare. . . . Ann Harding menacing nine girls. . . . The Wolf Man, the Mummy, the Mad Ghoul, the Ape Man, the Creeper, and the Ritz Brothers going berserk.

These were the "B" movies, inexpensively produced and usually unheralded—except by movie-goers, who often found more to enjoy in these bottom-rung quickies than in the ballyhooed epics their profits supported.

Sometimes, as with Paramount's *The Biscuit Eater,* a "B" even stepped out to become an award winner. But it wasn't easy, because reviewers—guided by the studios—concentrated on the "A"-line products, usually not even bothering to see the also-rans. If a company suspected that it had released a "sleeper" (or surprise hit), it quickly alerted the critics, who often as not didn't respond. Occasionally an enterprising reviewer such as the late James Agee, a "B" booster, would act on his own judgment, and because of his review, the company would find itself with a hit, such as *Detour,* from Producers Releasing Corporation.

"B" movies began to proliferate in the midthirties when distributors felt that "double features" might be just the ticket to lure increasingly frugal Depression audiences back into theaters. It became expedient to produce quickly made, cheap, and simple "co-features" for the big-drawing Clark Gable or Fred Astaire-Ginger Rogers attractions, generally sans big-name stars and short in running time (usually about an hour). These were also sometimes referred to as "program fillers" or "programmers." The "B" designation might have stood for "bread and butter" or possibly "block booking," the term describing the method by which the major studios coerced theaters into accept-

The Andrews Sisters in *Give Out, Sisters* (Universal Pictures, 1942)

ing their total output at a given time. All of the big studios produced "B" films, previously the specialty of such small, independent "Poverty Row" studios as Majestic, Mayfair, Chesterfield-Invincible (companies which would be gone after the forties), Republic, and Monogram.

During the 1940s, the last decade of the screen's Golden Age, when wartime escape-seekers helped to raise movie attendance to an all-time high, the "B" movie reached full bloom as both a business and an entertainment—despite the fact that the majors made many of them solely as write-offs for studio overhead. Each studio had its particular "B" movie style. Metro-Goldwyn-Mayer, which "Hollywood Rajah" Louis B. Mayer made into the richest of the Hollywood studios, made "B"s that often resembled "A"s, employing glossy sets and an impressive roster of stars. Warner Brothers, noted for its tough and realistic "A"s, produced quickies of widely divergent quality, often rescued by fine casts. Twentieth-Century Fox and, especially, Paramount issued a variety of respectable and often sophisticated "B" features.

Universal Pictures turned out a "B" a week until 1946, films which were short on story but spotlighted pleasant players and, more often than not, a scattering of musical numbers. Additionally, its horror films set an industry-wide trend that has yet to abate. Meanwhile, producer Val Lewton's enormously creative economy horror unit at RKO Pictures was responsible for some of the most distinguished films of the decade, in any category.

Of all the leading studios, however, Columbia Pictures, run by Harry ("King Cohn") Cohn, had the best track record for turning out quality "B"s. Excelling in melodrama, the lot also went on producing quickies after most of the other studios had stopped. In fact, Columbia's low-budget product frequently had more compelling stories than the studio's "A" releases that regularly featured such stars as Rita Hayworth or Glenn Ford.

The most visibly independent studios during this active decade were Republic, Producers Releasing Corporation (PRC), and Monogram Pictures, in order of diminishing importance. Their product was nearly always "B," usually action or comedy. Sometimes the action got so rough-and-tumble (particularly at PRC or Monogram, where the pictures occasionally were called "Z") that audiences were treated to the sight of quaking cardboard sets.

The major studios found their low-budget productions a good way to groom new talent, and many future "A" stars got their start in "B" movies, as did many writers and directors.

Cecil Kellaway, Frank Morgan, Audrey Totter, Marshall Thompson, Gladys Cooper in *The Cockeyed Miracle* (Metro-Goldwyn-Mayer, 1946)

Basil Rathbone, Evelyn Ankers, Nigel Bruce in *The Pearl of Death* (Universal Pictures, 1944)

Sometimes, too, young actors starting their careers in the "B"s would pass older actors on their way down. In addition, as director-producer William Castle, who made some of the period's better quickies, wrote in his recent autobiography, "The low-budget 'B' picture in the 1940s—before the advent of television—was a training ground for talented young directors who were forced to use their imagination in lieu of money. Many famous producers and directors graduated from this school"—Dore Schary, Robert Wise, Mark Robson, Fred Zinnemann, Edward Dmytryk, Anthony Mann, and Castle himself.

There was no pressure on the "B" movies to succeed, and as a result they were often able to experiment with themes that might then have seemed too chancy for bigger budgeted productions. Long before "A"s would popularize them, the "B"s offered "adult" Westerns such as Columbia's *Thunderhoof* and sympathetic Indians such as those in Allied Artists' (Monogram) *Black Gold*. Devil worship was pivotal in RKO's *The Seventh Victim*, twenty-five years before *Rosemary's Baby*, and multiple personality was the subject of MGM's *Bewitched* twelve years before *The Three Faces of Eve* and thirty-one years before television's *Sybil*.

After the World War II entertainment boom, "B" production began to wane. The federal government forced movie companies to relinquish ownership of movie theaters, a practice which for years had allowed a number of them to control booking policy. More and more, two "A"s were paired on the same bill. Television was absconding with a hefty share of the movie audience, and studios hoped (in vain) to get them back with bigger fare. Gradually, many of the studios went out of business, leaving television, with its hour-long series and movies-of-the-week, to take over the equivalent of "B" production. The quality of these television surrogates, though, has been considerably below that of the "B"s during their forties heyday. Just why this should be so is a mystery to confound the Falcon.

At Columbia, Samuel Briskin, Harry Cohn's second-in-command, would take prospective studio writers to an office where a large blackboard announced the titles of forthcoming "B" features, such as (hypothetically) *Boston Blackie's Tryst* or *Two Senoritas from Sheboygen*. The writer would pick a title that intrigued him, then go off and write the first ten pages of a script around one of the blackboard titles. If Briskin then approved, the writer completed the script and got the opportunity to stay around the lot a while and maybe shoot for bigger game.

Singer-actress Jane Frazee, who was to "B" movie musicals then what Judy Garland was to the "A"s, recently reminisced about those hectic years. "We'd hit Make-up at 6 A.M. I always ran into Anne Gwynne there—she probably made more pictures at Universal than I did. Anne'd say, 'What picture are you doing?' and I'd say, 'I don't know.' "

Whatever they were doing, they were doing it right. The following personal selection of fifty representative "B" movies from the Golden Age of the forties is proof of that.

Doug McClelland

AMONG THE LIVING

(Paramount Pictures, 1941)

Credits

Producer, Sol C. Siegel
Director, Stuart Heisler
Screenplay, Lester Cole, Garrett Fort
Story, Brian Marlow, Cole
Music, Gerard Carbonara
Camera, Theodor Sparkuhl
Editor, Everett Douglas
Running Time: 68 minutes

Cast

ALBERT DEKKER (John Raden/Paul Raden)
SUSAN HAYWARD (Millie Pickens)
Harry Carey (Dr. Ben Saunders)
Frances Farmer (Elaine Raden)
Gordon Jones (Bill Oakley)
Jean Phillips (Peggy Nolan)
Maude Eburne (Mrs. Pickens)
Frank M. Thomas (sheriff)
Harlan Briggs (judge)
Archie Twitchell (Tom Reilly)
Dorothy Sebastian (woman in café)
William Stack (minister)
Kit Guard (worker)
Ella Neal (first mill girl)
Catherine Craig (second mill girl)
George Turner, Harry Tenbrook (mill workers)
Patti Lacey, Roy Lester, Ray Hirsch,
    Jane Allen (jitterbug dancers)
Delmar Watson (newsboy)
Eddy Chandler (motorcycle cop)
Richard Webb (hotel clerk)
Mimi Doyle (telephone operator)
John Kellogg (reporter)
Blanche Payson (woman at trial)
Ethan Laidlaw (first guard)
Charles Hamilton (second guard)
Frank S. Hagney, Lane Chandler (neighbors)
Lee Shumway (scissors grinder)
Clarence Muse (waiter, Riverbottom Café)
Len Hendry (drugstore clerk)
Besse Wade (bit)
Rod Cameron (first man)
Keith Richards (second man)
Abe Dinovitch, Jack Curtis, Chris Frank (bits)

Paramount's *Among the Living* was a high point in the careers of both its principal players, now deceased, Albert Dekker and Susan Hayward. The beautiful Hayward had been cast in a couple of colorless ingenue roles during her two years at the studio, but it wasn't until this exceptional "B" that producers realized that the red-haired "Brooklyn Bombshell" was not to be denied bigger vehicles. Dekker had been relegated mostly to supporting roles since entering pictures a few years earlier; if *Among the Living* did not exactly change this caste, it did provide the burly actor with what was possibly his meatiest screen opportunity.

A low-budget bellwether in the forties trend of psychological thrillers, *Living* achieved a remarkably high standard of quality for *any* level of filmmaking. Besides the two dynamic leads, credit was mainly due to Los Angeles' own Stuart Heisler, an immensely talented director who never received the renown he deserved, and scenarists Lester Cole and Garrett Fort. Aided by cinematographer Theodor Sparkuhl, Heisler created a nightmarish visual chiaro-scuro, artfully utilizing some whooshing camera effects and fast-cut collages that would not gain wide usage for years. Writers Cole and Fort knew just when to lighten the melodrama with humor.

The setting was a poor Southern mill town. Dekker portrayed a dual role: a sane business-man married to Frances Farmer, and his homi-cidally mad, incarcerated twin. As the story opened, the latter murdered his keeper (Ernest Whitman) and escaped. He moved into a room-ing house run by frowzy old Maude Eburne, who told him, "I had one of them Frenchmen living here last year. Honest to goodness *every* time you'd turn 'round that Frenchman was a-grab-bing for your hand and kissing until he'd like to pull the skin off." The maniac soon began dating Eburne's mercenary, enticing young daughter (Hayward).

"Say," Hayward exclaimed, eyeing his bank-roll, "if I had a wad of folding dough like that I'd go right out and buy an outfit that would knock this neighborhood cockeyed!"

As they left one afternoon for a round of what

Susan Hayward, Kit Guard, Albert Dekker, Frank M. Thomas, Gordon Jones, Maude Eburne (center foreground)

looked like the flirtatious girl's *second* favorite sport, shopping, her mother waved them off the stoop and muttered approvingly, "Us Pickneses always had a weakness for refineness." Then she cranked to her feet and turned to go in, pulling a sticking housedress away from her behind.

In a particularly effective sequence, the crazed Dekker found his next victim. Wandering about Skid Row, past poolrooms and a legless man selling puppies, he straggled into an almost surreally swinging waterfront café. As he sat with a B-girl (Jean Phillips), the place became a whirling inferno of laughing doxies, arguments and jitterbugging couples, who created an ominous atmosphere. The frenzy climaxed in a dark alley where, triggered by her screams, Dekker strangled Phillips, pressing her hands tightly against her ears in death, as he had his previous victim. (He had been traumatized in childhood by the screams of his mother as his father repeatedly beat her.)

Later, as Dekker and Hayward were involved in buying Hayward a gift, the store radio proclaimed that there was now a five thousand dollar reward for him, dead or alive. The unsuspecting girl's already bright eyes beamed. "I could get a fur coat, I could get outa this town!"

That night she dug up an ancient gun and told him they were going out to his deserted family estate to look for the fiend.

"You're not afraid—at all?" gawked the fiend.

"For five thousand dollars I'm not afraid of anything, not even death!" she declared—almost prophetically. Luckily, the rest of the town was equally venal and, virtually en masse, trooped by the cobwebby old house in time to save her life.

"My Millie got him!" a mercurial Ma Eburne yelped. "It was that dirty Mr. Paul, my new boarder!" A kangaroo court was set up on the spot, and Hayward did her best to arouse the mob to violence. In the fracas, the insane Dekker was shot and died by his mother's grave.

Although Dekker had the showier role(s), the late-entering Hayward's eager, banister-hopping incandescence almost stole the picture. She was raw talent of stunning proportions, as four Academy Award nominations plus one win (for 1958's *I Want to Live!*) eventually would attest. Right on her heels, though, was that rubber-faced harridan Maude Eburne. Perhaps the most consistently droll character actress in my ken, she never failed to rise above often meager material and had one of her better chances as Hayward's "refined" mother. The tragic Frances Farmer, who a few years earlier had been a beautiful and promising Paramount star, was near the end of her movie tether as,

Gordon Jones, Maude Eburne, Albert Dekker, Susan Hayward

still young, she began a decade of harrowing alcoholism and mental illness. Farmer, also now deceased, had little to do here except look frightened and emit a dubbed scream or two.

Among the Living, released in 1941, was the last "B" picture the cocoon-bursting Susan Hayward would appear in, but it was superior to several of the "A"s she would get as a superstar.

Only in her fifties, she died in 1975 after months of agonizing illness (brain cancer), and the light of the world grew dimmer forever. The feisty lady's fortitude throughout the long ordeal—and, indeed, throughout her whole life—recalled to me a conversation alleged to have taken place between the dying Revolutionary soldier-author Ethan Allen and his doctor, but which might well have been Susan Hayward and hers.

"General, I fear the angels are waiting for you," said the physician.

"Waiting, are they? Waiting, are they?" answered Ethan Allen. "Well, damn 'em, let 'em wait!"

Albert Dekker, Frances Farmer

BEAUTIFUL BUT BROKE

(Columbia Pictures, 1944)

Credits
Producer, Irving Briskin
Director, Charles Barton
Original story, Arthur Houseman
Screenplay, Monte Brice
Art director, Lionel Banks
Music director, M.W. Stoloff
Songs, L. Wolfe Gilbert and Ben Oakland;
   James Cavanaugh and Walter G. Samuels;
   Jimmy Paul, Dick Charles and Larry
   Markes; Mort Greene and Walter
   Donahue; Phil Moore
Camera, L.W. O'Connell
Editor, Richard Fantl
Running Time: 72 minutes

Cast
JOAN DAVIS (Dottie Duncan)
JANE FRAZEE (Sally Richards)
John Hubbard (Bill Drake)
Judy Clark (Sue Ford)
Bob Haymes (Jack Foster)
Danny Mummert (Rollo)
Byron Foulger (Maxwell McKay)
George McKay (station master)
Ferris Taylor (mayor)
Isabel Withers (Mrs. Grayson)
John Eldredge (Waldo Main)
Grace Hayle (Birdie Benson)
John Tilson (Putnam)
Willie, West and McGinty (specialty)
Emmett Vogan (hotel manager)
Ben Taggart (pullman conductor)
Helen Ireland, Gloria Campbell, Janice
   Simmons (saxophone players)
Marguerite Campbell, Laura Gruver,
   Genevieve Durah (trumpet players)
Dorothy Prons (trombone player)
Lorraine Paige (drums)
Gerald Pierce (elevator boy)
Joseph Palma, Brian O'Hara, Kernan
   Cripps (defense workers)
George Bronson (shy soldier)
John Tyrrell (sergeant)
Lew Kelly (huckster)

Until it slipped into redundant slapstick, Columbia's *Beautiful But Broke* was one of the decade's most enjoyable romps. It actually was a showcase for that remarkable but neglected clown, Joan Davis, who had one of her best workouts (in *every* way) in this often hilarious gem of a film. This was the first of two 1944 movies to team Davis and songstress Jane Frazee—the second was *Kansas City Kitty.*

The early half of *Beautiful But Broke* was a fast-paced model "B"-movie comedy that deserves re-evaluation.

The zany, sketch-like, somewhat improvisational "story" concerned the efforts of Davis and her two pals (in pompadours), Frazee and Judy Clark, to make a go of an all-girl orchestra.

There was scarcely an early frame that was not successfully used for comic effect. When the straight vocalizing of a frumpy all-girl trio threatened to stall things, there was ringside Joanie playing a chicken leg as if it were a harmonica. During Frazee's train solo—a tune protesting war protestors called "Take the Door to the Left"—an attentive Davis crossed her legs and then couldn't uncross them. While Clark tore into "Mama, I Want to Make Rhythm," Davis, leading the orchestra, pranced around and backed into a Clark kick. Davis' co-players may have been less than amused by all this, but the comedienne was playing to her audiences. Today, when her films show up (usually on television), we continue to be grateful.

(Coincidentally, fifteen years later Davis' daughter, Beverly Wills, was featured in the most famous film about an all-girl orchestra, *Some Like It Hot*, as a member of Sweet Sue's Society Syncopators.)

Beautiful But Broke opened with Davis practicing the violin, sundry office noises persistently interrupting to pop the musical weasel for her. Dissolve to Davis, close-up, in one of those tearful service farewells so familiar to World War II moviegoers—but Davis' tears, came the two-shot, were for her Canine Corps-bound dog. When John Eldredge, head of the theatrical agency that employed her, also joined up, idea-girl Davis, was made owner of the clientless operation. Her "pigeon" (John Dilson) was

Jane Frazee, Judy Clark

promised an all-girl (because of the war) orchestra for his nightclub.

She enlisted Frazee and Clark, struggling music publishers-songwriters-singers (that war again), to help gain time until she could get a band together. With Dilson in earphones, Davis told him the band he was about to hear was playing at a ship's launching. In another room, Frazee and Clark sneaked on a band recording.

"How many engagements has the band played?" Davis was asked.

"Several thousand," she ventured.

Suddenly, her prospect exclaimed, "That's a record!"

The jig apparently up, Davis slapped on her hat—but was stopped when he explained, "Not many bands have played that many engagements."

Inevitably, while Clark was singing along, the record in the other room got stuck; and in the scramble the girls' watercooler was knocked over.

"The launching," said Davis.

The client agreed to hire the group. Talking it over, Davis informed him that her name was Dottie Duncan, quipping, "as in coffee and doughnuts." He went on to reveal, "I never make advances." Oh, Davis sobered, she could see he wasn't that kind of man. The deal clinched, her visitor said, "Well, goodbye, Miss Coffee."

Another one of Davis' schemes had Frazee and Clark masquerading as the Bartokis Sisters,

a Greek singing act sporting Carmen Miranda accents and introduced by Davis as "the mademoiselles." Davis' jive-jargon monologue directed to stout, elderly matron Grace Hayle—who responded with, "I dig your jive, honey"—was a very funny compendium of 1940s hepcat blat.

Later a band was finally put together and on its way across country to its booking. The girls—led by Davis, who had stuck someone else with the agency—were stranded, taking refuge in a deserted house that turned out to be a target for Army missile tests. Awakened by the noise, Davis and the girls turned on the radio and heard, "This is the beginning of the duck season." Satisfied with this explanation, they returned to bed. Then a large cannon shell glided through a window. Said (I think) Frazee, "What kind of ducks have they *got* around here?!" The girls rushed for a closet which, when the smoke cleared after the big blast, was all that was left of the house—perched up in a tree.

The jokes weren't really that fresh in 1944, but they were rendered with such shameless vim

John Eldredge, Joan Davis

Jane Frazee, John Hubbard, Judy Clark, Bob Haymes, Joan Davis

and vigor that even today they seem funny, perhaps even more so with the contemporary free-wheeling approach to film style. At the time *Variety* called *Beautiful But Broke* "a commonplace 'B' entry"—that surfeit of Golden Age riches.

Joan Davis was magnificent, even when her pratfalls grew repetitious, as in an interminable building routine with Willie, West, and McGinty. Judy Clark was Poverty Row's Betty Hutton, actually seeming to imitate the Huttontot's frantic style.

Between these two, Jane Frazee was pretty much the straight woman, albeit a charming, agreeably sensible one—qualities that were the essence of her ubiquitous screen image in general. And—besides the material previously mentioned—she did get to sing (with Clark) one of the big hit tunes of the day, Phil Moore's "Shoo-Shoo Baby," plus the solo number, "We're Keeping It Private (Me and Private Jones)." Formerly partnered in vaudeville and radio with her sister Ruth as the singing Frazee Sisters, Jane had become Hollywood's "Queen of 'B' Musicals," exercising her warm "pop" contralto in almost all her pictures, effortlessly and smilingly.

John Hubbard was Frazee's somewhat epicene love interest in *Beautiful But Broke,* Bob Haymes (Dick's brother) Clark's understandably cowed swain.

Joan Davis, ever and unjustly self-deprecating (and deprecated), wound up literally falling for a precursor of Dennis the Menace played by little Danny Mummert (Alvin Fuddle of the Blondie series)—which was better than not falling at all.

Center: Jane Frazee, Judy Clark, Joan Davis, Lew Kelly

BEHIND GREEN LIGHTS

(20th-Century Fox Pictures, 1946)

Credits

Producer, Robert Bassler
Director, Otto Brower
Original screenplay, W. Scott Darling, Charles G. Booth
Music director, Emil Newman
Camera, Joe MacDonald
Editor, Stanley Rabjohn
Running Time: 64 minutes

Cast

CAROLE LANDIS (Janet Bradley)
WILLIAM GARGAN (Lt. Sam Carson)
Richard Crane (Johnny Williams)
Mary Anderson (Nora Bard)
John Ireland (Sgt. Oppenheimer)
Charles Russell (Arthur Templeton)
Roy Roberts (Max Calvert)
Mabel Paige (Flossie)
Stanley Prager (Ruzinsky, the milkman)
Charles Tannen (Ames)
Fred Sherman (Zachary)
Don Beddoe (Dr. Yager)
Bernard Nedell (Walter Bard)
Tom Moore (Metcalfe)
Harry Seymour (Kaypee)
Jimmy Cross (King)
Charles Arnt (Daniel Boone Wintergreen)
Lane Chandler (Det. Brewer)
Russ Clark (radio operator)
Jack Davis (Webster)
William Forrest, Jr. (Dr. Hastings)
Steve Olsen (morgue attendant)
Larry Blake (ambulance officer)
Harry Tyler (Bill, crematorium attendant)
Robert Adler, Ted Jordan, Reginald Simpson (men)
Jack J. Ford (Capt. Mike O'Shea, photo)
Dolores Boucher, Beverly Ruth Jordan (girls)
John Glennon, Ralph Hodges, George McDonald (boys)
Perc Launders, Lee Phelps, Barney Ruditsky, Clarence Straight (cops)
Nicodemus Stewart (black man)
J. Farrell MacDonald (McNally)

Twentieth-Century Fox's *Behind Green Lights,* dramatizing a single night's events in a big city police station, preceded by several years Paramount's *Detective Story.* While it was not really in the same class with that powerful "A" production, *Behind Green Lights* was a thoughtful, professionally made little melodrama that packed a lot of story into its sixty-four minutes. And it did get there first.

Furthermore, its depiction of our law enforcers as fallible but reasonably intelligent, hard-working, well-intentioned human beings was balm for the many who complained then that movies of this period generally portrayed cops as bungling clowns or crooks.

Lieut. William Gargan was the mainspring of the police station and the action, a good cop torn between ethics and ambition. We saw the night shift begin. A mother with a child whose head was stuck in a goldfish bowl had come to the station for aid . . . underage teenagers arrested in a "hot spot" were dismissed with a scolding . . . eager young reporter Richard Crane started his first night on the "police run."

Then a car rolled up on the sidewalk in front of the station and notorious blackmailing private detective Bernard Nedell fell out, dead. His address book yielded the name of Carole Landis, socialite daughter of the reform candidate running for mayor. Brought in, she told Gargan that Nedell had been blackmailing her over some incriminating papers he possessed, and she had gone to his apartment that night to ask him to accept $10,000 instead of the $20,000 he'd demanded. He refused. She got the papers back at gun point, but swore she did not kill him.

Don Beddoe, the news-leaking coroner, informed yellow journalism publisher Roy Roberts that the mayoralty candidate's daughter was being held. Roberts, backing the incumbent, then suggested to Gargan that he book Landis for the murder so he could discredit her father in his papers. "How'd you like to be chief?" he asked Gargan, who had to admit he'd like it fine.

Also visiting Nedell that fatal night, Gargan learned, were his estranged wife (Mary Anderson, in a mannered, theatrical performance)

William Gargan, John Ireland, Charles Russell, Mary Anderson

and her attorney-fiancé (Charles Russell), both angry because Nedell refused to give her a divorce. Suspect, too, was elderly flower woman Mabel Paige, who hated Nedell because he never paid for the flowers he took. More and more, however, it began to look as if Gargan would have to book Landis, for whom he was forming a romantic attachment and who cynically recognized his stressful predicament.

Roberts continued his insidious pressure of Gargan: "I don't want to see you go back to pounding a beat."

Finally, Paige, who had been hanging around the station to collect the "dollar six bits" the dead man owed her, revealed that she too had gone to his apartment that night to collect her money and, while warming her fanny over a radiator on the stairway, had spied coroner Beddoe furtively leaving the apartment. When Gargan confronted him, he pulled a gun and they fought.

"Help! Police!" screamed Paige, ducking down behind the police lieutenant's desk.

The killer apprehended, Roberts' plan thwarted, and Gargan's conscience intact, as dawn broke the lieutenant and Landis left the station together.

Some of the picture's motivations were a little fuzzy. Why had Russell shot Nedell after he obviously was dead from poison? Why was Landis being blackmailed? Why had Beddoe killed Nedell? With these questions unanswered, and Gargan's incredibly quick affection for Landis, the W. Scott Darling-Charles G. Booth screenplay—with its myriad of characters and incidents—gave the impression that it might originally have been drafted as an "A," then whittled down (for whatever reason) to the standard short "B" running time.

Joe MacDonald's photography had unusual nuance, with its tilting angles (as when the car carrying the dead man drifted onto the sidewalk in front of the station) and—considering the general confinement of the story—its expressive images (as when the frantic figure of Beddoe, trying to escape, was pilloried by the camera at the far end of a long shadowy hall).

Director Otto Brower's steady hand helped make *Behind Green Lights,* as Otis L. Guernsey, Jr., in the *New York Herald Tribune* wrote, "more sensible and real than most extravagantly fictional crime melodramas." He astutely went on to say, "This film depends more on pique of curiosity and a close interplay between characters than on florid melodrama; as a result it is an interesting, if not boldly thrilling, murder mystery."

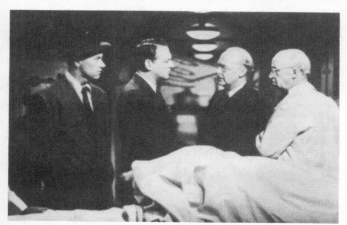

John Ireland, William Gargan, Don Beddoe,
J. Farrell MacDonald

William Gargan, John Ireland, Carole Landis

Gargan was generally believable as the be-sieged lieutenant, but Carole Landis, a once promising, sexy blonde starlet, was strictly a Hollywood producer's idea of a junior leaguer. Her curves concealed in a forties suit with quarterback shoulder pads, she was still un-mistakably someone more likely to have passed through Earl Carroll's portals than Vassar's. She was not an untalented actress, and when not miscast was often a pleasing actress with a seductively warm speaking voice (and what ever happened to *those*?). This was her next to last film for 20th, and the studio which never really took advantage of her popularity with audiences obviously had lost all interst in her. Despite top billing, she spent most of the picture off-screen in the police station waiting room. In 1948, despondent over her affair with the married Rex Harrison and hardly cheered by her declining career, the twenty-nine-year-old Landis commit-ted suicide.

The scene-stealer in *Behind Green Lights* was Mabel Paige as Flossie, the dogged, white-haired flower seller who had two words for the whole affair: "Bird seed!" In her pert feathered hat and bulky old sweater fastened by a large safety pin, and with her spry manner and cries of "That stiff died owin' me!", she was someone who could only have been bested by better actors than this picture possessed.

BEHIND THE EIGHT BALL

(Universal Pictures, 1942)

Credits

Associate producer, Howard Benedict
Director, Edward F. Cline
Screenplay, Stanley Roberts, Mel Ronson
Original story, Stanley Roberts
General music director, Charles Previn
Songs, Don Raye and Gene DePaul
Dances, Eddie Prinz
Gowns, Vera West
Camera, George Robinson
Editor, Maurice Wright
Running Time: 60 minutes

Cast

AL RITZ, JIMMY RITZ, HARRY RITZ
  (The Three Jolly Jesters)
Carol Bruce (Joan Barry)
Dick Foran (Bill Edwards)
Johnny Downs (Danny)
William Demarest (Police Chief McKenzie)
Sonny Dunham and His Band (themselves)
Grace McDonald (Babs)
Richard Davies (Clay Martin)
William Ruhl (Officer Flynn)
Kernan Cripps (Officer Doyle)
Lew Kelly (Hank, the stagehand)
Ray Kellogg (Dunham vocalist)
Russell Hicks (Harry B. Kemp)
Jack Arnold, a.k.a. Vinton Haworth
  (Bobby Leonard, MC)
Johnnie Berkes (bearded man)
Claire Whitney (society woman No. 1)
Ruth Lee (society woman No. 2)
Duke York (first hood)
Bob Barron (second hood)
Mickey Simpson (third hood)
Emmett Lynn (Charlie, the undertaker)
Hal Belfer (Wally Raymond)
Jane Cowan (debutante)
Henry Hall (grandpa)
Eddie Coke (grandson)
Forbes Murray (husband)
William Cabanne (young man)
Charles Sullivan (waiter)
Jack C. Smith (cop)
Ethan Laidlaw (tough man in audience)
Eleanor Counts (cigarette girl)

30

Behind the Eight Ball was the first picture on a three-year contract for The Three Ritz Brothers that would wind up, for many years, their middling film career that had begun at 20th-Century Fox in the thirties. Succeeding Universal vehicles for Al, Jimmy and Harry were *Hi' Ya Chum* and *Never a Dull Moment,* and with Abbott and Costello and Olsen and Johnson already on the same lot, the studio needed another comedy act like—to use a worn phrase that miraculously escaped being a Universal title—a hole in the head.

If the boys' material was too often less than fresh, they never gave less than their screwloose, uninhibited all, and led by the eyerolling Harry Ritz (who several major comedians today say inspired their own styles), they frequently managed to be amusing with their unpretentious foolishness. *Behind the Eight Ball* was more entertaining than subsequent Ritz showcases at Universal because it not only had an agreeable score and cast, but a plethora of plot—a murder mystery—squeezed into its astonishingly brief one hour running time.

The main setting was a barn theater in the Berkshire Mountains where Carol Bruce was presenting a pre-Broadway musical comedy in which two guest stars on two successive evenings were shot and killed during the performances. "Somebody doesn't want you around here," said police chief William Demarest to Bruce. He then ordered everybody, including the audience, to return on Saturday night when a new guest act would take over, and, Demarest hoped, he would catch the murderer. Naturally, no one would touch the place—except the Three Jolly Jesters (the Ritz Brothers), New York nightclub men's-room attendants trying to break into show business and unaware, at first, of their predecessors' fates.

"They look so young," sighed the show's lead dancer (Johnny Downs).

When the boys learned the truth, they hit the road.

"Imagine them calling the show *Fun for All,*" grumbled one Ritz.

"I'm glad we got out of there before they called it *Three Men in a Hearse,*" replied Harry,

William Demarest, Hal Belfer (on floor), Johnny Downs, Grace McDonald

who usually got the best lines.

Demarest retrieved them, however, and after a pep talk by Bruce they stayed. A couple of other attempted murders took place, and throughout the movie a weirdly suspicious, bearded local character (Johnnie Berkes) kept peering into windows.

At one point, all the lights in the barn theater went out—it was only Harry, who had plugged his electric shaver into the stage lighting controls and was giving himself a shave. Bedding down in the dark barn that night, a shaking Harry told his equally miserable brothers, "Mom was right. We should have gone straight instead of becoming actors."

First, Downs was suspected of the crimes, then Carol Bruce's boyfriend (Dick Foran), a farmer-scientist and co-owner with Bruce of the theater (they'd inherited equal shares from their parents). Eventually, an Axis short-wave radio set was found in a secret room and, during the Ritzes' big number on opening night, Richard Davies, a member of the featured Sonny Dunham Band, was exposed as the killer. (He had been hired only for this engagement, leader Dunham hastened to assure.) The gun in Davies' clarinet was fixed to fire when he hit high C. Mysterious peeper Berkes wrapped up the mystery when he finally approached impresario Bruce—and asked if she needed another hoofer.

Direction was wisely entrusted to Edward F. Cline, who had helmed two of W.C. Fields' best for the studio, *My Little Chickadee* and *The Bank Dick. Behind the Eight Ball* was not in their league, but Cline kept the action moving. He also achieved the properly sinister atmosphere, with stormy opening nights at the barn theater and well-timed lightning flashes. If Cline telegraphed the murderer's identity by giving Davies' seemingly irrelevant character excessive attention, he atoned for this with an effective climax. This occurred when the barn audience was let in on something the Ritz Brothers did not know, namely that the clarinet the Greek tunic-clad boys were using as a prop in their finale piece, "Bravest of the Brave," was actually a loaded gun. As the assemblage ducked or departed, the Ritzes continued their knock-about stage antics with the lethal musical instrument in a classic screen moment that Alfred Hitchcock might have elaborated upon for one of his thrillers. (The gun finally went off, hitting only a light.)

The original Don Raye-Gene DePaul songs were above average for a "B" musical and included one Hit Parade topper, "Mr. Five by

The Ritz Brothers

The Ritz Brothers

Five" ("Fifteen chins and a ton of jive"), sung by Grace McDonald with the swinging Dunham band. Universal's busiest female dancer, McDonald (whose "style" consisted of clutching her knee-length skirts when she tapped) teamed for dance and romance with eternal collegian Johnny Downs. Their big number—"Don't You Think We Ought to Dance?"—was a pleasant, easy old vaudevillelike turn. Bruce's musical high point was her warmly wistful vocal reminiscent of "Thanks for the Memory," "Wasn't It Wonderful?" This song had an offbeat bittersweet quality that depicted the marriage of Bruce and Downs in the show-within-the-show, surrounded by bridesmaids in white, followed a year later by divorce, the bridesmaids now in black, and then reconciliation.

The Ritz Brothers' peak in this outing was probably their bodybuilding satire opener, "Atlas" ("Charles Atlas did it!"). Featuring Harry, his bowlegged physique limp and bristly in a print tiger skin and shoes and socks, it was a funny "tribute" to the famed physical culturist. The boys also proved themselves adept and energetic hoofers in the finale.

The Hollywood Reporter's careful but fair review of Behind the Eight Ball was nevertheless among the rare positive evaluations. "Entertaining with their usual violence, the Ritzes knock themselves out to be amusing and, where they are popular, will give this lesser musical considerable bounce," the paper wrote. "The Howard Benedict production has one of the most tuneful musical scores in the long line of dance band featured attractions Universal has been turning out as moneymakers."

Al Ritz, the eldest, died in 1965, but Harry and Jimmy continue to work. Today, they at last seem on the verge of general recognition for their dizzy, anything-for-a-laugh galvanism.

BEWITCHED

(Metro-Goldwyn-Mayer, 1945)

Credits

Producer, Jerry Bresler
Director-scenarist, Arch Oboler
From Oboler's original story, *Alter Ego*
Music, Bronislau Kaper
Camera, Charles Salerno, Jr.
Editor, Harry Komer
Running Time: 65 minutes

Cast

PHYLLIS THAXTER (Joan Alris Ellis)
Edmund Gwenn (Dr. Bergson)
Henry H. Daniels, Jr. (Bob Arnold)
Addison Richards (John Ellis)
Kathleen Lockhart (Mrs. Ellis)
Francis Pierlot (Dr. George Wilton)
Sharon McManus (little girl at zoo)
Gladys Blake (Glenda)
Will Wright (Mr. Herkheimer)
Horace McNally, a.k.a. Stephen McNally
  (Eric Russell)
Oscar O'Shea (Capt. O'Malley)
Minor Watson (governor)
Virginia Brissac (governor's wife)
The voice of Audrey Totter (Karen)

A dozen years before Eleanor Parker appeared in *Lizzie* and Joanne Woodward in *The Three Faces of Eve,* both films based on case histories of women with multiple (three) personalities, MGM released Phyllis Thaxter's *Bewitched,* in which two totally different people living within Thaxter fought for control of her body.

No, it was not "B" budget restrictions that kept Thaxter down to only two personalities, and yes, one of them was good and one of them was bad.

Otherwise, *Bewitched* was a stunningly inventive little film melodrama that, as élite critic James Agee wrote in *The Nation,* achieved "The first persuasive imitations of stream of consciousness I know of in a movie."

Bewitched also marked the first film for radio wizard Arch (*Lights Out*) Oboler, who never quite realized the success on the screen that he had in radio. He directed, as well as adapted for pictures, his own radio drama which had starred Bette Davis. It was called *Alter Ego* (meaning "other self" and the movie's much better—but perhaps too intellectual—other title during production). The result was a "B" still discussed today.

And it couldn't have been easy. Aside from the obvious problems of visually dramatizing the conflict inside a person's mind, MGM plainly had little faith in the project. This was evident when Jerry Bresler, formerly head of the short subjects division, was named producer, and when Oboler's budget was slightly more than that allocated to a short subject. This was highly unusual for the mighty Metro where even the "B" 's generally had the posh veneer of an "A" at any other studio. Parsimony was evident not only in the obviously painted backdrop used for the lawn of Thaxter's home but also by the noticeable shortage of extras, unusual during those still affluent years. Streets were empty; a concert performance had practically no audience; a busy hotel's cigar counter was photographed repeatedly with close-ups on the principals only; and a supposedly crowded courtroom used extras only in tight shots clustered around the leads.

Oboler overcame these difficulties, however, by using his imagination. A fearlessness nurtured in radio, a medium in which anything was possible, freed him to try many new things in the film, and most of them worked. It was one of the rare instances when radio and film techniques

Henry H. Daniels, Jr., Phyllis Thaxter, Horace (Stephen) McNally

cohabited successfully. Only occasionally did a radio drama background mitigate against Oboler in the film—such as when a succession of the major characters faced the cameras to ask, "why-why-why?"

He was fortunate to have MGM contract player Phyllis Thaxter as the lead. For the pretty, natural, almost demure actress this was only her second film (the first: 1944's *Thirty Seconds Over Tokyo*). Her winsome vulnerability made Joan Ellis' plight matter to viewers of the film, and Thaxter's extensive stage training made harrowingly effective her descents into the feral recesses of the girl's mind.

The film began auspiciously, and did not disappoint later. A tower clock set in an urban nightscape pealed 11 P.M. as the credits unwound, Bronislau Kaper's music building suspensefully. "There was apparently nothing abnormal about the girl," dictated psychiatrist Edmund Gwenn to his secretary in the first scene. A narrator's voice then intoned, "In fifty-nine minutes she would be dead." Next a shot of the young Thaxter taciturnly awaiting execution, followed by a flashback to an earlier scene of the advantaged, well-loved girl laughing with young fiancé Henry H. Daniels, Jr., on the patio outside her home. Inside, their engagement party perked along.

Sobering, she asked Daniels, "Bob, do you hear—someone talking?"

She had been hearing voices for some time, had fainted at least once, and had her parents (Kathleen Lockhart, Addison Richards) and family doctor (Francis Pierlot) bewildered. When Daniels left her alone for a moment, clouds covered the full moon, casting the young woman in shadows. "Joan . . . Joan . . . Joan," called a female voice. "I've been fighting with you all of your life. . . . Listen, you, I've waited a long time for this. You've gotta let me live! . . . I won't go back in the dark. I'll live! I'll live!"

Unseen, unbilled, and unpublicized, former radio actress Audrey Totter provided the voice of Thaxter's alter ego—called Karen. With at least as much dialogue as the lead actress herself, Totter etched a chilling portrait of the evil personality living inside Thaxter. Totter's dialogue was especially iniquitous as she strained—sometimes sounding out of breath from the effort—to dominate the body in which she was trapped.

That night, cinematographer Charles Salerno, Jr.'s camera tracked a deserted, damp city street, locating the terrified Thaxter hovering in a doorway. "Did you think you could run away?" persisted the voice. "Why don't you let me take over now?" She promised she would never talk again if Thaxter would just go away—alone. "What do you want Bob for? You want a *man!*" Totter jeered. After seeking refuge in a concert hall where a soprano was in the middle of "Nobody Knows the Trouble I've Seen," and hearing Totter's voice call her "crazy" again and

Edmund Gwenn, Phyllis Thaxter, Horace (Stephen) McNally

Horace (Stephen) McNally, Phyllis Thaxter

again, Thaxter ran away to New York.

Working at a hotel cigar counter, she met young attorney Horace McNally, who, bringing her flowers every day, finally persuaded her to go out with him. On a ferry ride up the Hudson, he noted, "I've never seen you laugh." She told him she had just recovered from an illness. McNally proposed, but as they embraced Totter's voice oozed from Thaxter's mouth. "I'm alive! Hold me. No, don't talk," she implored McNally, kissing him ravenously.

Later, Daniels, the home-town fiancé, came to take Thaxter back with him. "I've got what I want," raved Totter. "His [McNally's] arms! I'll make your body sing and cry! The scissors. Pick them up. Kill him! Lift your arm. Higher . . . higher . . . higher. Now—strike!" Thaxter stabbed Daniels in the back, killing him. As she cried out, her whole murder trial flashed through her mind in a montage behind a close-up of the actress' frozen horrified face.

McNally defended her in court, claiming self-defense, but she refused to say a word on her own behalf. As she sat on a bench in jail awaiting the verdict, motionless, her head bent, an off-camera guard's voice complained, "I'm supposed to be having a spaghetti dinner at six. Why don't they make up their mind?" In court, just as the jury's decision was about to be rendered, Totter's voice returned to boast exultantly that she would live and win McNally. Thaxter screamed, "I did it! I killed him!"

On the night of her execution, psychiatrist Edmund Gwenn and McNally convinced governor Minor Watson to have her sent to his house for an experiment. "Once in many, many millions of births," explained Gwenn, "a body can have two divergent personalities living in the same brain." The subsequent full-length shot of Thaxter's sudden appearance in the governor's doorway, a long black coat draped over the shoulders of her light prison uniform, strikingly crystallized the almost fantastic dichotomy of her situation: she was at once sinister and pathetic.

Hypnotizing her, Gwenn was unsuccessful at first when he asked, "Why do you want to die? . . . Who will die when you die?" She merely mumbled incoherently.

Suddenly, she threw her head back and laughed hysterically, then tried to kiss the stunned McNally.

Gwenn prepared to begin his exorcism, determined that the good personality's only hope was total obliteration of the bad. "You won't be able to see them," he informed the governor and McNally, "but they'll see each other for the first time," adding firmly, "The execution will take place as scheduled."

The audience soon saw two special effects created, two wraithlike Phyllis Thaxters rise from the chair—one, warm and gentle Joan, the other, evil and destructive Karen, memorably incarnated by the actress with dark lipstick, heavy eye make-up, and a fixed licentious defiant smile.

"Joan, use your strength for us," beseeched Gwenn. "There must be no compromise with evil. It must die!" Gradually, under the psychiatrist's relentless hypnotic probing and suggesting, the almost demonic alter ego disappeared. "Joan, come back," instructed Gwenn. "You are free forever."

The governor said he would appoint a commission to study the facts, the implication being that Thaxter would be free at last of both mental and physical incarceration.

McNally and Gwenn offered earnest, convincing portrayals. Bewitched acting honors, however, went to its two feminine leads—one visible (Phyllis Thaxter), the other invisible (Audrey Totter). The latter's bravura soundtrack characterization of the monstrous Karen drew virtually no mention from the reviewers of the period. Since Totter was not identified in the picture's credits, the critics evidently didn't know that the voice was not the leading lady's own. The realization of Totter's participation does not diminish Thaxter's contribution, though. The two actresses' work—comparable only to the recent The Exorcist (featuring Linda Blair and Mercedes McCambridge's voice)—was one of the most unusual tandem performances in film history.

Despite its oversimplified Freudian explanations and facile solution, Arch Oboler's Bewitched was a fascinating "B." Few novice film directors have had as promising a debut.

THE BIG NOISE

(20th-Century Fox, 1944)

Credits:
Producer, Sol M. Wurtzel
Director, Mal St. Clair
Original screenplay, W. Scott Darling
Music director, Emil Newman
Music score, David Buttolph, Cyril J. Mockridge
Camera, Joe MacDonald
Editor, Norman Colbert
Running Time: 74 minutes.

Cast
STAN LAUREL and OLIVER HARDY
  (themselves)
Doris Merrick (Evelyn)
Arthur Space (Alva P. Hartley)
Veda Ann Borg (Mrs. Mayme Charlton)
Bobby [Robert] Blake (Egbert Hartley)

Frank Fenton (Charlton)
James Bush (Jim Hartman)
Phil Van Zandt (Dutchie Glassman)
Esther Howard (Aunt Sophie Manner)
Robert Dudley (Hartley's father)
Edgar Dearing (motorcycle officer)
Selmer Jackson (Manning)
Harry Hayden (Digby)
Francis Ford (attendant at train depot)
Jack Norton (drunk)
Charles Wilson (train conductor)
Ken Christy, Sarah Edwards, Emmett Vogan,
  Billy Bletcher (bits)
Beal Wong (Japanese military officer)
Louis Arco (German military officer)
Del Henderson (man in upper berth)
George Melford (Mugridge, the butler)
Julie Carter (cab driver)

I stand practically alone in my affection for Laurel and Hardy's *The Big Noise,* one of their last screen features.

The critical consensus was pretty well summed up by Archer Winsten in the *New York Post:* "They have hit bottom with the most witless screenplay of their long careers." Although the press always had been cool to the team, the public had not. But by 1944—when moviegoers had begun to fancy themselves more sophisticated—the team's sight gags and slapstick comedy routines seemed passé. (They had worked together in films since 1926.) In his book about Laurel and Hardy, William K. Everson referred to the movie as "probably the worst of all the full-length Laurel and Hardy films."

Yet the picture always makes me laugh, a reaction I do not have to other, more highly regarded Laurel and Hardy vehicles. "Fat and Skinny" can often be annoyingly repetitive and long-winded in their comedy routines; it is understandable to hear some complain that a little of their shenanigans goes a long way. Still, Stan Laurel (feather of brain as well as of weight) and Oliver Hardy (a hippopotamus with a "tea pinkie") were unique, endearing stylists who left an indelible mark on the history of comedy and today are revered more by the critics than when they were alive.

The Big Noise, one of several early-forties 20th-Century Fox films in which Laurel and Hardy starred, displayed their faults as well as a preponderance of their virtues. We saw them take pointless pratfalls, unknowingly climb a recently painted pole, crowd into a single, upper berth on a train. Yet Laurel and Hardy performed their familiar feats with relish, as if for the first time. And when the film is shown on television today (which it often is), to many young viewers it *is* for the first time. There was enough new material and an interesting supporting cast to make the film's poor reputation something of a mystery.

Far from being "witless," the movie's rousing *March of Time* opening with a shot of Washington, D.C., followed by a close-up of a sign reading "Patent Office," seemed a lampoon of

James Bush, Veda Ann Borg, Phil Van Zandt, Frank Fenton

the semi-documentary FBI testimonials in which 20th specialized during the forties. It was quickly shown that eccentric inventor Arthur Space was pestering the department again. He had invented such "wacky" devices, revealed patent executive Harry Hayden, as a motorized toothbrush (which, in considerably modified form, has proved to be not such a crazy idea). Now he was offering the war effort his powerful new explosive, which he called "the Big Noise."

Disguising his voice by means of a clothespin on his nose, his bratty son (Bobby Blake) pretended to phone from Washington, telling Space the government wanted the bomb and to guard it carefully.

Space called a detective agency, and the phone was answered by janitors Laurel and Hardy, who were studying nights to become detectives. Mistaking them for super sleuths, Space hired them and told them to come right over to his house. On arrival, the two bunglers, toying with Space's paint-remover invention, reversed it and smeared white paint all over his favorite painting, which Space called "The Heighth [sic] of Spring." Consoled Laurel, "You could call it 'The Depth of Winter.'" Laurel and Hardy grew apprehensive, though, when Space, in the throes of a dizzy spell, took a hammer and cracked himself on the head several times to get rid of the seizure. "Another of my inventions," he remarked.

Hardy explained to Laurel that all inventors were eccentric. "You know," he whispered,

flicking his wrist *just so,* "twisted."

Space's family also included Esther Howard, the flirtatious middle-aged sister of Space's dead wife who giddily wondered what the two detectives would look like. Meanwhile Robert Dudley, Space's aged father, honked a horn as he whizzed about in a motorized wheelchair and admonished Howard, "You'd think a woman with five husbands would want to take a rest." Next door, a gang of thieves (Frank Fenton, Veda Ann Borg, Phil Van Zandt, James Bush) prepared to steal Howard's jewels.

"I'm famished," said Hardy, sighting dinner preparations.

"We'll start with the turkey," said Space, uncovering a tray holding several pills. "Will you have white meat or dark?"

Dumbfounded, the boys watched him plunk pills—and only pills—for a full-course meal on their plates. Laurel asked, "Could I have another joint?"

"Won't you sit down," Howard advised the pair, "and eat the turkey before it gets cold."

"Here you are, Junior," said Space, handing

Oliver Hardy, Stan Laurel, Esther Howard

Oliver Hardy, Stan Laurel

Bobby Blake his allotment of pills.

"Gee, the neck as usual," sulked the youngster. "I'm capsule-happy *now.*"

Popping pills, Grandpa Dudley coughed. "I got a bone stuck in my throat," he explained.

"Don't bolt your food, Grandpa. He always does that, especially when we have fish," the widow Howard told Laurel and Hardy.

This scene in its entirety was perhaps the highlight of the movie, a clever and consistently funny poke at the burgeoning vitamin-pill industry. There was also a droll tussle with a push-button bedroom that, too, had a sharper technology-gone-mad satirical thrust than might have been expected of Laurel and Hardy. The whole picture, moreover, can be looked on as something of a send-up of the detective movie genre so popular then. Maybe *The Big Noise* was ahead of its time. If the film had come along a couple of years later, its title and other similarities might have seemed a spoof of the classic *The Big Sleep* (1946)—in which a wheelchair-confined old man (Charles Waldron) called a private detective (Humphrey Bogart) to his home to hire him for a case involving his two daughters, one widowed (Lauren Bacall), one wayward (Martha Vickers).

Temporarily fouling up the plans of the crooks next door was the surprise arrival of Veda Ann Borg's innocent niece (Doris Merrick), who first went to Space's house by mistake. Attracted to the young woman, Space offered to escort her next door, blowing the whistle Hardy had given him for emergencies. The boys suddenly materialized from nowhere. "Let's go, sister," said Hardy toughly, grabbing the startled girl. Space had only wanted them to carry her bags.

When Washington called to say they could use Space's bomb after all, thieves Van Zandt and Bush decided to steal the explosive on their own. Laurel and Hardy took off for Washington with the bomb, the villains in close pursuit. They wound up parachuting from a remote-controlled plane and dropping the bomb on an enemy submarine. The last scene saw them sitting on a crate in the middle of the ocean, Laurel playing "Mairzey-Doats" on his concertina as Hardy smilingly conducted a school of fish that danced on the water to that nonsense hit tune of the day.

Directed by Mal St. Clair, Laurel and Hardy drew great support from Arthur Space, a minor actor who had one of his largest roles as the hammer-happy inventor. (This may have been partial payment for the excision of his entire part from the boys' previous vehicle, *The Dancing Masters.*) Robert Dudley as his cranky old father; Esther Howard, delightful as the frequently merry and almost as frequently widowed in-law; tough blonde Veda Ann Borg, today, for some reason, a "camp" heroine, playing pretty Doris Merrick's very young Auntie Mame; Jack Norton, spotted on a train doing his celebrated drunk bit; and little Bobby Blake, now Robert Blake of *Baretta* fame on television. All helped to make *The Big Noise* an underrated blast—not merely "another fine mess" for the comedy stars.

THE BISCUIT EATER

(Paramount Pictures, 1940)

Credits

Producer, Jack Moss
Director, Stuart Heisler
Screenplay, Stuart Anthony, Lillie Hayward
Based on a short story by James Street
Music, Frederick Hollander
Camera, Leo Tover
Editor, Douglas Everett
Running Time: 81 minutes

Cast

BILLY LEE (Lonnie McNeil)
CORDELL HICKMAN (Text Lee)
Richard Lane (Harve McNeil)
Lester Matthews (Mr. Ames)
Helene Millard (Mrs. McNeil)
Snowflake, a.k.a. Fred Toones (Sermon)
Tiverton Invader (Promise)
William Russell, Earl Johnson (field judges)

". . . And knowing man's need of a friend God gave him a dog—"

Paramount's modest-budgeted, starless *The Biscuit Eater* opened with this anonymous legend written on the screen. Its thesis was substantiated by a film that was one of the most moving boy-and-his-dog stories ever filmed and, surprisingly for a "B," one of the most critically esteemed. *Life* named it "Movie of the Week," describing the production "fresh and unpretentious." The New York *Times* found it a "heartwarming pastoral of the Georgia hunting country," Kate Cameron's New York *Daily News* review described *The Biscuit Eater* as "a picture that must be seen by all dog-fanciers, which takes in a pretty large part of the human race. . . . Billy Lee is as natural as a child can be on the screen."

Capping all this, the National Board of Review named the picture one of the year's ten best.

While *The Biscuit Eater* seems a bit less fresh now than it did in 1940, it still remains a poignant, skillful dramatization with rare appreciation of the special love between child and pet, plus the wondrous adventure of childhood. Director Stuart Heisler took his company on location to Albany, Georgia, the heart of the South's hunting country, to shoot most of the film. The result was some lovely Leo Tover-photographed rural scenes that could never have been duplicated in Hollywood.

There were the magnificent natural tableaux of bird dogs in the field holding their points in motionless majesty. "Bird dogs been known to hold a point a full hour," explained trainer Richard Lane.

And there were the vividly visualized plot turns, an outstanding episode being the journey into an eerie swamp by little Billy Lee, Lane's son, and black friend Cordell Hickman to retrieve Billy's dog. Stealthily wending their way, the frightened children were suddenly stopped in their tracks by great dark wings reflected in the water; looking up, they saw that the horrific image was actually caused by a mass of vines clustered overhead. A real crocodile appeared, then the tall, zombie-like black hermit of the

Richard Lane, Billy Lee, Tiverton Invader

swamp. Looking at his own trembling legs, Hickman—a pint-size version of black comedian Mantan (''Feets-do-yo'-stuff'') Moreland—said, ''You can shake, doggone it, but I'm a-takin' you with me!''

In an era when even big box office filmmaker Cecil B. DeMille did most of his outdoor epics on studio sound stages at Paramount, it was almost unheard of for a ''B'' to be filmed at such a far location. In addition, *The Biscuit Eater* had notably little rear projection process work, a blight on many far more expensive productions of the day with abundant exterior scenes.

Richard Lane played a veteran bird dog trainer worried about his job because new boss Lester Matthews was thinking of selling the dogs and turning the place into a horse ranch. When Matthews promised Billy that he could have one puppy from a soon-to-be-born litter, the ecstatic child went to sleep and dreamed that puppies were crawling all over him in his bed as he laughed hysterically.

Equally charming was the birth scene: Billy's little neighboring friend (Cordell Hickman), hoisted to peer over the barn door, reported each new puppy's arrival as Billy, near-bursting with excitement below, hugged himself with joy. Matthews gave him the runt of the litter—''You know, the promise,'' he said. Billy named the dog Promise.

As the animal grew, he showed the dreaded traits of a ''biscuit eater.'' Explained Lane, ''That's what we call a dog too sorry to hunt anything 'cept his own food.'' Promise took to sucking eggs in the hen house, later jumped over a high fence to impregnate one of the farm's prize dogs. Lane ordered Promise off the property. Secretly, Billy decided to train him for the annual field trials thereabouts—''Then nobody, not even Papa, can call you a no-account biscuit eater.'' Promise was winning the trials, too, until Billy learned that if his father's dog didn't take the prize, owner Matthews would convert the ranch to horses and Lane would be out of a job. At a crucial moment, Billy called Promise a biscuit eater, causing him to lose and his father's dog to win.

Promise's performance did not go unnoticed, however. ''I was wrong about that dog all along,'' admitted Lane. Matthews said, ''It's easy to see how enough love and faith can outclass a whole kennel of thoroughbreds.''

One night while trying to visit his own litter of new puppies, Promise was shot by a hired hand (Snowflake). ''Ya gotta try to forgive me,'' sobbed Billy, the puppies joining the mournful wail as Promise died in his master's arms. Lane and Matthews had overheard Billy explaining to the

Billy Lee, Tiverton Invader

Richard Lane, Billy Lee, Helene Millard, Cordell Hickman, Lester Matthews, Tiverton Invader

dying animal why he had caused him to lose the field trials. "Very few of us have the honor to die for something," commented Matthews. The film ended as Billy's mind flashed back to scenes of Promise's early training in the fields.

Nine-year-old Billy Lee totally immersed himself in the part of the "little boy who became a man." A one-time Indiana farm child in real life, the youngster was a thoroughly believable country sprig, more than meeting the demands of a role with an emotional range that would have taxed a Barrymore. He and the ingratiating Cordell Hickman worked together nicely. *The Biscuit Eater* was the high point in both careers.

The picture also presented a subdued Richard Lane, who played the father with stern, quiet authority. His portrayal surprises those of us who thought of the actor only as the fast-talking urban inspector of the Boston Blackie screen series or as the roller derby broadcaster on Los Angeles TV in the 1970s.

The dog cast as Promise was, in fact, a prize-winner named Tiverton Invader. He, too, was extremely well-directed by Stuart Heisler; an affective and disarming bit had the dog drop his head whenever the term biscuit eater was used.

The story, written by James Street for the *Saturday Evening Post,* was redone in 1972 by Walt Disney Productions as a vehicle for young Johnny Whitaker. This version, given a happy ending, made no ten-best lists. Paramount's 1940 telling remains the definitive screen *Biscuit Eater*—a film that awakened everyone to the heights "B" movies could reach.

Cordell Hickman, Billy Lee, Tiverton Invader, Lester Matthews, Richard Lane, Helene Millard

BLACK GOLD

(Allied Artists, 1947)

Credits

Producer, Jeffrey Bernard
Director, Phil Karlson
Screenplay, Agnes Christine Johnson
Story, Caryl Coleman
Music director, Edward J. Kay
Art director, E.R. Hickson
Camera, Harry Neumann
Editor, Roy Livingston
Color, Cinecolor
Running Time: 90 minutes

Cast

ANTHONY QUINN (Charley Eagle)
KATHERINE DeMILLE (Sarah Eagle)
Elyse Knox (Ruth Frazer)
Kane Richmond (Stanley Lowell)
Ducky Louie (Davey)
Raymond Hatton (Bucky)
Thurston Hall (Col. Caldwell)
Alan Bridge (Jonas)
Moroni Olsen (Dan Toland)
H.T.Tsiang (Davey's father)
Charles Trowbridge (Judge Wilson)
Jack Norman (Monty)
Darryl Hickman (schoolboy)
Clem McCarthy, Joe Hernandez (themselves)

Black Gold was Anthony Quinn's first starring role after more than a decade in films, and it can be said to have launched him as a major screen performer. Indeed, it may have set the pattern for some of the later, more ambitious Quinn portrayals in such "A"s as *La Strada, Requiem for a Heavyweight,* and *Zorba the Greek.* As Charley Eagle, an illiterate but idealistic, warm-hearted Indian who dreamed of winning the Kentucky Derby, and frequently shouted "Chi-hua-hua!", he gave a rewarding performance in a film that treated the American Indian with dignity long before it became the fashion.

Black Gold also marked Quinn's one and only picture with his then wife, Katherine De-Mille, the adopted daughter of famed producer-director Cecil B. DeMille. She complemented Quinn's bravura with a moving delineation of the Indian wife, serene Sarah Eagle, once a reservation schoolteacher who dedicated her life to her family and home. DeMille, in the best role of her sporadic career, almost stole the film with her sensitive restraint, creating a woman of quiet strength and great dignity, outwardly a bit

of a stoic whose face, in moments of meditation or sudden joy, could radiate with love. She was a swarthily attractive woman, with black eyes and a strong face and voice, and it is the film medium's loss that it never again made adequate use of this unusual actress. In *Black Gold,* Katherine DeMille gave one of the most affecting characterizations ever to grace a "B" movie.

The next most important role went to a Chinese youngster, Ducky Louie, who didn't quite live up to his name. He did, in fact, have an extraordinarily difficult part as the lad orphaned when white men murdered his father (H.T.Tsiang) and later adopted by Charley and Sarah Eagle. A considerable range of emotions was required as his bitterness was dissolved by the love that enveloped him, and the inexperienced Ducky Louie was not quite up to it all.

In the desert near the Texas-Mexico border, outlaws had just killed Louie's father while pretending to help him illegally enter the United States. Quinn took the distraught lad with him to Mexico where he planned to race his mare, Black Hope. There they encountered an old

Ducky Louie, Jonathan Hale, Kane Richmond, Elyse Knox, Anthony Quinn

horse trainer friend of Quinn's, Raymond Hatton, as well as Moroni Olsen, an unscrupulous horse owner whom Hatton called "the biggest unhung crook south of the border."

When asked by Olsen how an Indian came to own such a fine horse, Quinn explained, proudly, "I drive mules six months up north."

True to form, Olsen tricked the ignorant red man into entering his horse in a claiming race and when he won, Olsen claimed the animal for a mere $500. That night Quinn stole the horse, leaving Olsen's money in the empty stable.

Around a campfire, he told his young companion, who blamed all whites for his loss, "White man kill my father, too. White man crazy drunk. They put him in jail—six months. . . . But I know anger no good. America big place. Plenty room for Indian and Chinese boy. Now my ranch is biggest on reservation."

Quinn took Louie back to his modest farm. His wife, busy at her chores, greeted him with a calm "Hello, Charley. Your dinner's on the stove."

"How come you always know when I'm coming home?" he wondered.

"Maybe I hear it in the wind," she replied.

It was then established that he had gone away months before in the middle of the night—"The old ways speak to me," he explained.

Louie was adopted by the couple, and at DeMille's insistence was enrolled in school where pretty blonde Elyse Knox was the understanding teacher. He had his problems there with schoolmate Darryl Hickman, who taunted him with questions like "Are you yellow all over?" But Louie overcame.

After a while, oil was discovered on Quinn's land, intensifying the Indian's dreams of winning the Kentucky Derby. With the aid of Hatton, back on the scene, and Louie, he set about training Black Hope's colt—whom he named, appropriately, Black Gold—for the big race.

"Black Hope's colt wins Kentucky Derby—not just for Charley—for all Indians," he said.

Black Hope's sudden death was another hurdle for the Chinese youth, who worshipped the horse.

Wealthy now, Quinn and his family moved to a large new house where they entertained dignitaries. Quinn began to have heart attacks, and one day, in his old clothes and wearing a back pack, he left home once again—to die in the wilderness. This time, his wife, son, and horse sought him out in the hills.

"You win Kentucky Derby for me, eh?" the dying Quinn entreated Black Gold.

"For the first time I wish I were a white

Anthony Quinn, Ducky Louie, Katherine DeMille

Ducky Louie, Anthony Quinn

woman," said DeMille.

"Why?" asked Quinn, sinking.

"So I could cry."

Louie rode Black Gold in the Derby and won. Afterward, at the presentation stand, the black-clad, ever-sedate, radiant DeMille told the crowd, "I want to thank everyone who is here and one who is not. Chi-hua-hua!"

The end frame bore the legend "Suggested by the winning of the 1924 Kentucky Derby by the horse Black Gold"; apparently the picture was based on an actual event, or events.

Black Gold was not without its imperfections. The Cinecolor (which got second billing after Quinn) tended toward orange. Nevertheless, this was still one of the better examples of that inferior tint process which cropped up for a few years in tightly budgeted productions. Some of the characters, too, seemed at times to be merely sketched in by the screenplay, and occa-sionally the generally melodic, Indian-themed background score grew oppressively sticky.

Overall, *Black Gold,* sensitively directed by Phil Karlson, was a significant production far beyond its modest "B" budget as well as a charming and touching one. Quinn gave a strong performance. His Charley Eagle was an endearing, even noble figure. The actor (actu-ally of Irish-Mexican descent) was especially impressive in the death scene, as was Canadian-born Katherine DeMille, whose occasional ex-pressions of emotion were all the more effective because the character she played was generally impassive. Raymond Hatton, too, made a track-wise but refreshing old codger; it was almost as if he'd never seen a Walter Brennan movie.

At the finish line, *Black Gold,* with its sensitive insights into the mystique of a misunderstood people, did almost everyone connected with it proud.

THE BODY DISAPPEARS

(Warner Brothers Pictures, 1941)

Credits

Associate producer, Ben Stoloff
Director, D. Ross Lederman
Screenplay, Scott Darling, Erna Lazarus
Based on the story *Black Widow*
    by Scott Darling and Erna Lazarus
Special effects, Edwin A. DuPar
Camera, Allen G. Siegler
Editor, Frederick Richards
Running Time: 72 minutes

Cast

JEFFREY LYNN (Peter De Haven)
JANE WYMAN (Joan Shotesbury)
Edward Everett Horton (Prof. Shotesbury)
David Bruce (Jimmy Barbour)
Herbert Anderson (George ''Doc'' Appleby)
Marguerite Chapman (Christine Lunceford)
Craig Stevens (Robert Struck)
Willie Best (Willie)
Ivan Simpson (Dean Claxton)
Charles Halton (Prof. Moggs)
Wade Boteler (Insp. Deming)
Sidney Bracy (Barrett, the butler)
Natalie Schafer (Mrs. Lunceford)
Michael Ames, a.k.a. Tod Andrews (Bill)
DeWolfe Hopper, a.k.a. William Hopper
    (Terrence Abbott)
John Hamilton (judge)
Frank Ferguson (Prof. McAuley)
Romaine Callender (Prof. Barkley)
Vera Lewis (Mrs. Moggs)
Paul Stanton (prosecutor)
Stuart Holmes (waiter)
Charles Drake (Arthur)
Jack Mower, Jimmy Fox (clerks)
Peggy Diggins, Lorraine Gettman,
    a.k.a. Leslie Brooks (bridesmaids)
Hank Mann (porter)
Creighton Hale (Prof. Edwards)
Harry Lewis (elevator boy)
Wedgwood Nowell, Houseley
    Stevenson, Sr. (professors)
Mary Brodel (Norah)
George Meader (Prof. Ponsonby)
Georgia Carroll (telephone girl)
Tom Stevenson (James)
Eddy Chandler (desk sergeant)
John Dilson (Dr. Jasper)
Frank Sully, Sol Gores (attendants)
Eddie Kane (stage manager)
Thornton Edwards (motorcycle cop)
Ann Edmonds, Juanita Stark,
    Paula Francis (co-eds)

The Invisible Man and the *Topper* series had already explored the dramatic and farcical possibilities of the special-effects department's ability to make actors dematerialize (and vice versa) on camera. Then Warner Brothers' *The Body Disappears* appeared to prove there was still life in the old gimmick yet.

Although Jeffrey Lynn received top billing, he was invisible most of the time, leaving the burden of the acting on the shoulders of leading lady Jane Wyman, Edward Everett Horton, and black comedian Willie Best. They, as much as anything, were responsible for the film's respectable laugh quotient. Edwin A. DuPar's special effects contributed the careening cars driven by invisible men, visible underwear on bodyless women, unseen simians, and valises transported without carriers. Still, it was the reactions of the talented comic troupers that evoked the biggest guffaws.

The story had millionaire sportsman Lynn pass out at his bachelor dinner on the eve of his wedding to Marguerite Chapman. As a practical joke, his collegiate chums (including David Bruce and Herbert Anderson) put him in a dissecting room of their medical school. Meanwhile, wacky campus professor Horton and his frightened assistant Best were busy in the laboratory inventing a life-restoring serum. But they needed a dead body. Mistaking the unconscious Lynn for a corpse, they stole him.

"This one's got a lily in his hands. He may be dead but he's neat about it," said Best, quaking at being alone in the morgue late at night. "They must have embalmed him in Scotch and soda," Best went on, hoisting Lynn through a window. "He's so saturated if a breeze hit him he'd ripple."

The serum made Lynn invisible. "Oh, my head," he groaned, coming to without a visible one. He was allowed to stay at the professor's house until an antidote could be devised, to the delight of Horton's slick-chick daughter (Jane Wyman), who had had a crush on Lynn since she spied him at a golf tournament. Learning that his fiancée was only after his money, Lynn switched his affections to Wyman.

And who wouldn't have? Jane Wyman, a

David Bruce, Natalie Schafer, Sidney Bracy, Marguerite Chapman, Peggy Diggins, Lorraine Gettman (Leslie Brooks)

former chorus girl, was one of the prettiest, perkiest of blonde actresses. Seven years later she would win the best-actress Academy Award for (as she put it in her acceptance speech, "keeping my mouth shut for once") her role as the deaf-mute in *Johnny Belinda.* She then did a turnabout and sang (with Bing Crosby) the Oscar-winning "In the Cool, Cool, Cool of the Evening" in *Here Comes the Groom,* establishing herself as perhaps the cinema's most versatile artist and a brunette forevermore.

Wyman was still serving her lengthy apprenticeship in *The Body Disappears,* but it was evident that those days were drawing to a close. She brought a saucer-eyed charm and vivacity to her ingenue role—making something humorous out of the simple act of impatiently shutting the door on a date she didn't particularly like, and registering droll persistence when Jeffrey Lynn dematerialized as they were kissing. She was winsome, too, exclaiming to doubting authorities after her father was put in a sanitarium (and then realizing her gaffe), "My father did make a man invisible. I've *seen* him!"

Horton's timing was a joy. His highpoint was a long, difficult scene with an invisible pet monkey, conversing and shaking hands with it on his shoulder, then chasing the undetectable, escaped simian all over the grounds to the horror of onlooking neighbor Charles Halton. In the closing courtroom scene, Horton and Judge John Hamilton watched Lynn and Wyman clinch. "Isn't she beautiful? Looks just like her mother," observed widower Horton. "She must," answered the judge. Then Willie Best sat on Horton's hypodermic needle filled with serum and, realizing his worst fears, turned invisible.

And comedian Best lived up to his name, doing the scared-of-his-own-shadow bit with such dexterity that he ought to have taken a patent out on the routine. Anyone tempted to dismiss this familiar forties actor as just another black exploited by the movies should see *The Body Disappears.* Best proved himself a skilled comic player of no small resources. His reactions were a howl in the back seat of a speeding, apparently driverless car as he suddenly found himself wearing the now invisible Wyman's cast-off bra around his head. He was even funnier, certainly more inventive, in a jailhouse pantomime as he counted a large amount of bail money, licking each finger, savoring the taste, and going on to shoot imaginary craps as he continued the count.

D. Ross Lederman's direction allowed but a few lags, and his expert cast was almost able to

Jeffrey Lynn, Jane Wyman

Edward Everett Horton, Jane Wyman

gloss over those, helping immeasurably to make *The Body Disappears* a cheerful comic fantasy.

A postscript. During World War II, actor-Army captain Ronald Reagan and his bride Jane Wyman were the sweethearts of Hollywood fan magazines. In article after article they were the epitome of all war-separated couples. Looking at *The Body Disappears* today, it is easy to understand both Jane Wyman's popularity and why war, for Ronald Reagan, was hell.

Willie Best, Jeffrey Lynn, Edward Everett Horton

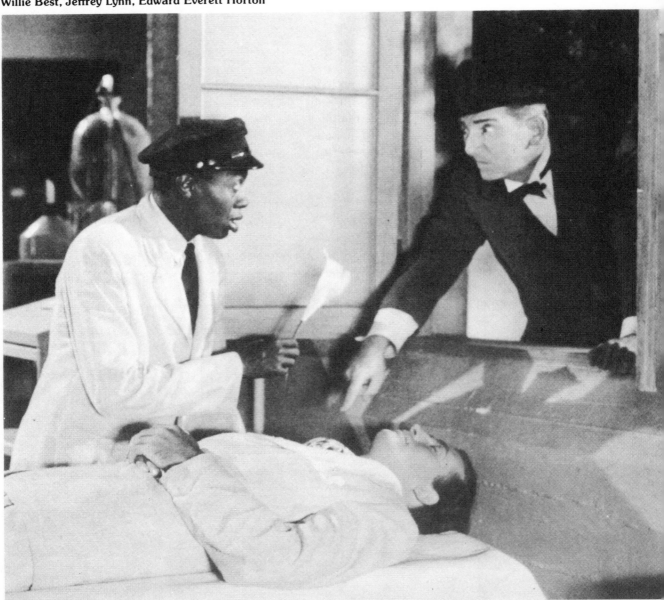

CHARLIE CHAN AT THE WAX MUSEUM

(20th-Century Fox, 1940)

Credits

Associate producers, Walter Morosco,
   Ralph Dietrich
Director, Lynn Shores
Original screenplay, John Larkin
Based on the character created by
   Earl Derr Biggers
Music director, Emil Newman
Camera, Virgil Miller
Editor, James B. Clark
Running Time: 66 minutes

Cast

SIDNEY TOLER (Charlie Chan)
Sen Yung, a.k.a. Victor Sen Yung (Jimmy Chan)
C. Henry Gordon (Dr. Cream)
Marc Lawrence (Steve McBirney)
Joan Valerie (Lily Latimer)
Marguerite Chapman (Mary Bolton)
Ted Osborn (Tom Agnew)
Michael Visaroff (Dr. Otto von Brom)
Hilda Vaughn (Mrs. Rocke)
Charles Wagenheim (Willie Fern)
Archie Twitchell, a.k.a. Michael Branden
   (Carter Lane)
Edward Marr (Grenock)
Joe King (Insp. O'Matthews)
Harold Goodwin (Edwards)
Robert Shaw (bit)
Jimmy Conlin (Barker)
Marjorie Cooley (bit)
Charles Trowbridge (judge)
Stanley Blystone (court attendant)
Emmett Vogan (district attorney)

Of all the many Charlie Chans to be seen on the screen through the years, from Warner Oland to Sidney Toler to Roland Winters, I have always preferred Toler's delineation of the beloved Chinese detective.

Toler seemed to possess, to a greater degree than his colleagues, the natural sense of humor intended by Chan's creator, author Earl Derr Biggers. Toler's Charlie uttered fractured interpretations of Confucius that often sounded more as if they should be intoned over matzoball soup rather than won ton. More than any of the other actors who played the Honolulu-based sleuth, Toler—Caucasian and Missouri-born—evidenced sly relish and expert timing in tossing off such aphorisms as (in *Charlie Chan in Panama*), "Bad alibi like dead fish—cannot stand test of time." His bon mots continue to delight Chan fans, whose numbers grow with the years.

Most of the Chan movies, unlike dead fish, *do* stand the test of time, especially the eleven films with Toler that were made at 20th-Century Fox from 1938 to 1942. At Monogram Studios, where Roland Winters finally took over after Toler's death in 1947, the series deteriorated. An example of vintage Toler-Fox-Chan is *Charlie Chan at the Wax Museum,* which promised all sorts of dark doings and delivered enough of them to make the visit worthwhile in the mystery that unfolded.

Boasting a group of intricately interrelated suspects, the picture opened with the escape of gangster Marc Lawrence, whom Chan had helped convict for murder. Vowing vengeance, Lawrence hid out at the wax museum of discredited doctor C. Henry Gordon, famous for his plastic surgery on the faces of wanted criminals. After Gordon operated on Lawrence, Lawrence convinced Gordon to invite Chan to a

Sidney Toler, Marguerite Chapman, Ted Osborn, Joan Valerie

weekly radio broadcast emanating from the museum—a program that revealed solutions to previously unsolved crimes. His plan: to kill Charlie Chan.

Chan accepted. He was joined there by several characters, including his meddling Number Two son (Sen Yung, later Victor Sen Yung) who was playing hooky from college; reporter Marguerite Chapman; the radio program host (Ted Osborn); criminologist Michael Visaroff; and Hilda Vaughn, peculiar widow of Lawrence's executed associate who had been framed by another ex–Lawrence confrere, a presumed-dead murderer now known to be alive and (disguised by plastic surgery) somewhere in their midst. Other suspects congregated on this stormy night were dotty old night watchman Charles Wagenheim and the doctor's blonde assistant (Joan Valerie).

The first murder victim was Visaroff, killed during the broadcast by a poison dart from a blow gun (a singularly popular murder weapon in mystery films of the era); and later, before he got the chance to do away with Chan, the fugitive Lawrence was killed.

Chan's detecting eventually exposed the culprit as Ted Osborn, the radio show's host. Osborn, in reality the renovated racketeer, had killed Visaroff and Lawrence to make certain that his new identity would be kept secret.

Chan's first clue had been Osborn's quick radio sign-off after the first murder; a genuine reporter, Chan deduced, would have continued broadcasting the details of the crime no matter what had happened.

As usual in the Chan series—and this was one of their strong points—the murderer was one of the least suspected characters. (The picture tried to throw suspicion on the watchman by giving him far more footage than his importance to the story merited. And Charles Wagenheim, in the part, was clearly made up to be much older than he actually was.) Placing the cast in the somewhat claustrophobic main museum setting (although hidden rooms and a secret basement provided some variety) was effective. Also, it is particularly pleasant to encounter a young, pretty Marguerite Chapman a couple of years before she became one of Columbia Pictures' most attractive leading ladies.

Sidney Toler, C. Henry Gordon, Joan Valerie

Sidney Toler

The sinister atmosphere was well-sustained by director Lynn Shores. Wax figures in evidence represented not only Jack the Ripper, Bluebeard and a murdered, negligée-clad "Broadway Butterfly," but a replica of Charlie Chan himself, which of course Number Two son mistook for his father at one point. In the final moments, however, by then fed up with wax figures, Chan's son kicked the statue in the seat of the pants—of course, it turned out to be the real Charlie.

For fans wanting more subtle humor, there was the wit and wisdom of Chan the man. Asked "Haven't you ever been surprised, Charlie?", the detective answered, "Only when honorable wife announce she expect thirteenth child." My favorite example from *Charlie Chan at the Wax Museum,* though, is this Chan maxim: "Only very foolish mouse make nest in cat's ear." Who would dispute it?

THE COCKEYED MIRACLE

(Metro-Goldwyn-Mayer, 1946)

Credits
Producer, Irving Starr
Director, S. Sylvan Simon
Screenplay, Karen deWolf
Based on the play *But Not Goodbye* by
   George Seaton
Music, David Snell
Camera, Ray June
Editor, Ben Lewis
Running Time: 81 minutes

Cast
FRANK MORGAN (Sam Griggs)
KEENAN WYNN (Ben Griggs)
GLADYS COOPER (Amy Griggs)
AUDREY TOTTER (Jennifer Griggs)
Richard Quine (Howard Baker)
Marshall Thompson (Jim Griggs)
Cecil Kellaway (Tom Carter)
Leon Ames (Ralph Humphrey)
Morris Ankrum (Dr. Wilson)
Arthur Space (Amos Spellman)
Jane Green (Mrs. Lynne)
Naomi Childers, Howard Mitchell (visitors)
Guy deWolf (boy)
Susan Simon (girl)
Robert Anderson (boy)
Douglas Madore (bit)
Billy Chapin (boy)
Crete deWolf (girl)

The Cockeyed Miracle was a novel 1946 comedy-fantasy about two clowning, argumentative ghosts "embodied" by Frank Morgan and Keenan Wynn. When their dialogue occasionally descended to the "Stop, you're killing me" level of banter, a parade of outstanding mummers recruited from the luminous MGM stock company managed to inject some charm and warmth into the proceedings.

The fresh gimmick was this: turn-of-the-century New England shipbuilder Morgan, age sixty-three, died of heart trouble and was fetched for the Heavenly journey by his long-deceased father, Wynn, a ne'er-do-well dandy who had died at age thirty-six when crowned by a whiskey bottle ("I was launched"). Most of the jokes sprang from the fact that son Morgan was a white-haired, elderly gent, while his "Pa" Wynn was still a youthful–looking blade with an eye for the ladies.

A number of problems faced Morgan's family when he succumbed, so he convinced Wynn to stay with him on earth awhile to help them out, although—per regulation in these films—neither had any substance nor could they be seen. The oddly matched, ghostly couple had difficulties communicating with each other as well.

"All you left Ma and me was a fifteen-dollar saloon bill," reminded Morgan.

"I'll thank you," admonished Wynn, "to treat your father with more respect."

Morgan's riposte: "Why, I'm twice as old as you are!"

Among the dilemmas facing the ethereal loiterers was the static romance of Morgan's anxious daughter (Audrey Totter) and her absent-minded, rock-collecting professor swain (Richard Quine—years later to become a well-known director), who was preparing to join a Western university. Her problem was solved when Wynn, exercising other-wordly powers, caused a rainstorm while the couple was buggy-riding, forcing them to take shelter in a barn. Then nature took over.

Watching Totter quickly exchange her wet dress for a provocative blanket, Wynn asked Morgan, "What does she do?"

"She's a librarian."

Keenan Wynn, Frank Morgan

"Must read a lot," gibed Wynn.

Quine proposed to Totter, asking her to accompany him west.

Then there was Morgan's son (Marshall Thompson), who needed money to leave tyrannical uncle Leon Ames' "fish factory" (as Morgan called it) and go to England to carry on the family tradition of shipbuilding. Unfortunately, shortly before his death Morgan secretly had invested the entire family bank account in real estate that his partner Cecil Kellaway—in whose name the deal was made—was having a hard time selling. When the family discovered the money had mysteriously disappeared, both Totter and Thompson prepared to sacrifice themselves to stay home and care for their now widowed mother (Gladys Cooper).

Aided by another Wynn-storm, the cove property in question was proved safe enough to satisfy potential purchaser Arthur Space and was immediately sold. Kellaway, however, learning that his silent partner had died, decided to keep the entire sum for himself. Wynn clouded up again; in the ensuing torrent Kellaway was struck by lightning. The check for Morgan's share of the cove's sale was found on Kellaway's body and turned over to Gladys Cooper.

Based on a briefly run 1944 Broadway play by George Seaton starring Harry Carey, the film had a sturdier framework than most "B"'s could boast. The screen version sometimes lapsed into the banal and heavy-handed, but expert trouping managed to keep it from sinking.

Wynn, Metro's busiest young character actor, and the venerated ex-Wizard of Oz Morgan—a clever bit of dual contract casting, clearly the movie's *raison d'être*—were an incongruously amusing father and son.

"Look, Pa, no hands!" exclaimed Morgan as he walked through his first wall.

"Just as easy as I used to go through a week's pay," observed Wynn.

The special effects were kept to a minimum, with the best sight gag being Morgan's and Wynn's trip upstairs in the former's house—levitating right through the ceiling.

Audrey Totter, gaining notice as a specialist in contemporary hard-bitten women, had a rare ingenue part—in wasp-waisted period costume, yet—which she played prettily. The ever-lovely, distinguished Gladys Cooper made Morgan a brave, sensible, devoted wife. Cecil Kellaway, one of the great character actors, subtly managed to prepare viewers for the treachery of Morgan's "lifelong friend" by effecting throughout a furtive little scurry.

The Cockeyed Miracle got more attention

Frank Morgan, Audrey Totter, Keenan Wynn

Keenan Wynn, Frank Morgan, Marshall Thompson, Leon Ames, Gladys Cooper

from reviewers than was normal for a "B," probably due to the then still mighty roar of Leo the Lion. Frank Quinn of the *New York's Daily Mirror* chose it "Mirror Movie of the Week" in the Sunday edition, singling out Frank Morgan and Keenan Wynn as "a pair of hilarious ghosts." *Variety* liked it, too: "Cast names are mostly familiar and dependable, the production good and the direction [by S. Sylvan Simon] neatly valued to get the best from the material."

No *Topper* or *Here Comes Mr. Jordan*, this lower-berth production still kept audiences entertained while awaiting the main MGM feature on the program which that year may have starred Judy Garland or Katharine Hepburn, Lana Turner or Esther Williams.

CONFESSIONS OF BOSTON BLACKIE

(Columbia Pictures, 1942)

Credits

Producer, William Berke
Director, Edward Dmytryk
Original screenplay, Paul Yawitz
Story, Yawitz, Jay Dratler
Based on the character created by Jack Boyle
Music director, M.W. Stoloff
Camera, Philip Tannura
Editor, Gene Milford
Running Time: 65 minutes

Cast

CHESTER MORRIS (Boston Blackie)
HARRIET HILLIARD (Diane Parrish)
Richard Lane (Insp. John Farraday)
George E. Stone (The Runt)
Lloyd Corrigan (Arthur Manleder)
Joan Woodbury (Mona)
Walter Sande (Sgt. Mathews)
Ralph Theadore (Joe Buchanan)
Walter Soderling (Joseph Allison)
Billy Benedict (ice-cream man)
Mike Pat Donovan (cop)
Jack Clifford (motorcycle cop)
Eddie Laughton (express man)
Jack O'Malley (taxi driver)
Al Hill (police-desk sergeant)
Ralph Dunn (Officer McCarthy)
Harry Hollingsworth (plainclothesman)
Budd Fine (express man's helper)
Martin Spellman (Jimmy Parrish)
Harry Bailey, Betty Mack, Dorothy
    Curtis (bidders)
Bill Lally (Sgt. Dennis)
Julius Tannen (Dr. Crane)
Eddie Kane (auctioneer)
Herbert Clifton (Albert, the butler)
Jessie Arnold (first nurse)
Lorna Dunn (second nurse)
Gwen Kenyon (third nurse)
Harry Depp (Mr. Bigsby)
Stanley Brown (intern)
Eddie Fetherstone (taxi driver)

Boston Blackie, the thief-chasing ex-jewel thief hero of Columbia Pictures' long-running crime series, actually made no confessions in *Confessions of Boston Blackie,* the second film in the collection. But the picture—directed by Edward Dmytryk who also guided such "A"s as *Crossfire* and *The Caine Mutiny*—was so fast, so action-packed and well-acted, that no one seemed to notice.

The late Chester Morris played the glib amateur detective in all thirteen Columbia entries in the series, which began in 1941 and ended in 1949, and he was one of their biggest assets. A New York-born, seasoned actor from a show business family, Morris' breezy, flip personality, and lightning movements made him an ideal "B" hero, especially *this* quickie hero, whose adventures were usually at least as mirthful as they were mysterious. No matter what the crisis, a quip or a gag was never far off, and Morris' Blackie was both assisted and hindered by a handful of regulars who were particularly deft at levity: Richard Lane, as Inspector Farraday, ever-suspicious of Blackie's motives; George E. Stone, "the Runt," Blackie's eager, nebbish sidekick; and Lloyd Corrigan, Blackie's wealthy, crime detection-meddling friend.

The heroine of *Confessions of Boston Blackie* was none other than Harriet Hilliard, of Ozzie and Harriet (and David and Ricky) fame. A pretty damsel in distress, she had a valuable statue which she put up for auction to send her tubercular kid brother (Martin Spellman) to the country for his health. The auction gallery she chose was crooked, with a secret basement workshop where fake copies of costly items were made. At the auction of her statue, she recognized the copy, and when one of the bosses (Ralph Theadore) shot at her from the back of the room as she was about to expose them, he accidentally killed their sculptor (Walter Soderling). Morris, in attendance with Corrigan, had fired at the killer but was arrested by Lane for shooting at Hilliard.

Meanwhile, Theadore secreted the dead man's body into the statue's false back. Only later did he realize that the combination to the safe containing the real statue was in the

Walter Sande, Richard Lane, Chester Morris, Lloyd Corrigan

corpse's pocket. Corrigan bought the bogus statue, and the rest of the picture was primarily devoted to Morris, who had escaped custody, as he eluded the police and apprehended the criminals Ralph Theadore and Kenneth McDonald, who were trying to get the statue back.

The exciting climax took place in the workshop basement of the gallery, where, after running down the culprits, Morris and friends—in best cliff-hanger fashion—were trapped in the air-tight quarters. It took Morris only seconds to think of lighting a fire in the ventilator shaft. The smoke filtering out to the street soon brought rescuers.

There was also a rather overdone subplot involving sinister-looking Joan Woodbury, Morris' castoff girlfriend who, after totaling his apartment in a rage, looked less like the spurned woman than a straitjacket case.

In general, the film's light touch prevailed. As always, it was especially evident in the love-hate (or hate-love) relationship of Morris and Lane, the inspector.

"I wouldn't trust you as far as I could throw one of those statues," said Lane at one point.

"Those lousy cigars you smoke are ruining your wind," answered Morris.

Another time, Lane complained to Morris, disguised as a doctor, that he had these pains in his fingers occasionally.

"Soak them five times a day in boiling water and mustard. And go heavy on the mustard,"

advised Dr. Morris.

Later, at a party given by Corrigan (carrying a cadelabra he accidentally had handcuffed himself to), someone asked Lane what had happened to his hand.

"Oh," he mumbled, "a little mustard burn."

The jokes sped by. As "Runt" George E. Stone pursued Harriet Hilliard who was being driven off by one of the villains; he was stopped by a motorcycle cop and asked what he was doing.

"I'm chasing a woman," he confessed.

"A woman, eh? Someday you'll thank me for this," asserted the officer, arresting Stone for going through a red light.

Confessions of Boston Blackie was not art, but its headlong pace and sense of its own ridiculousness could give some of today's filmmakers a lesson. There was no "Method" involved in this madness. After all, in a 65-minute movie could hapless ice-cream vendor Billy Benedict, stiff after being locked in his freezer by Chester Morris, have time to ponder how it actually *felt* to be a human popsicle?

Richard Lane, Chester Morris

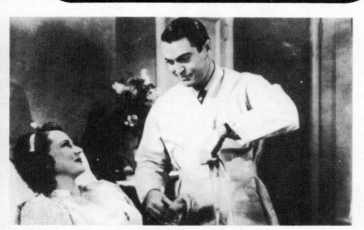

Harriet Hilliard, Chester Morris

CRIME BY NIGHT

(Warner Brothers Pictures, 1944)

Credits

Associate producer, William Jacobs
Director, William Clemens
Screenplay, Richard Weil, Joel Malone
From the novel *Forty Whacks*
   by Geoffrey Homes
Camera, Henry Sharp
Editor, Doug Gould
Running Time: 72 minutes

Cast

JANE WYMAN (Robbie Vance)
JEROME COWAN (Sam Campbell)
FAYE EMERSON (Ann Marlowe)
ELEANOR PARKER (Irene Carr)
Charles Lang (Paul Goff)
Stuart Crawford (Larry Borden)
Cy Kendall (Sheriff Max Ambers)
Charles C. Wilson (D.A. Hyatt)
Juanita Stark (Maisie, switchboard operator)
Creighton Hale (Horace Grayson)
George Guhl (Harry, jailer)
Hank Mann (Mr. Dinwiddie)
Bill Kennedy (hospital attendant)
Dick Rich (Fred, chauffeur)
Fred Kelsey (Dad Martin)
Bud Messinger (bellboy)
Jack Cheatham, Eddie Parker,
   Jack Stoney, Frank Mayo (deputies)
Jack Mower (tenant)
Roy Brant (Roy, waiter)

66

Warner Brothers' *Crime by Night* was spun out with a little more élan than most of the studio's "B"'s, but the main reason it rates attention today is because it featured three budding contract actresses: Jane Wyman, Eleanor Parker, and Faye Emerson.

Although Wyman got top billing, the pleasantly offhand little mystery really focused on Jerome Cowan, a supporting player continually typecast as a shyster lawyer. He portrayed Sam Campbell, a private detective who, with his pert secretary Wyman as Robbie Vance ("Guaranteed no relation to Philo," she quipped), was hired by ex-pianist Stuart Crawford to investigate the axe murder of his former father-in-law, a wealthy industrialist-publisher. The locale was a studio-set lakeside resort. Crawford was concerned because before his death, the murdered man had caused his premature retirement from the concert stage when he chopped off Crawford's hand with an axe. He felt suspicion for the murder would naturally fall on him, and he was right.

Others involved were Eleanor Parker, Crawford's ex-wife and daughter of the late millionaire; Faye Emerson, Crawford's former manager; Charles Lang, Parker's new boyfriend, a singer at the lodge whom Emerson managed; and Cy Kendall, the bullying local sheriff.

Before long, the caretaker on the dead man's property and Lang were murdered also, then there was a considerable ruckus about a missing chemical formula used at the war plant owned by Crawford's late father-in-law. Emerson ultimately was unmasked as the killer and head of a spy ring when Cowan tricked her into attempting to kill a bogus eyewitness (Fred Kelsey), who

Charles C. Wilson, Jane Wyman, Eleanor Parker, Cy Kendall, Jerome Cowan

turned out to be blind.

The unfailingly likable Jane Wyman was detective Cowan's wisecracking assistant-girlfriend. Halfway through the film, she was off-screen for quite a while and when she was on camera, her dialogue was lugubriously unwitty—"You and I are gonna stick so close together we could wear the same suspenders," she advised Cowan as they did some furtive reconnoitering. Nevertheless, the personable actress was a snappy sight in her upsweep hairdo covered by pillbox hats, and did have one good confrontation with Faye Emerson, who had been dallying with Cowan.

"We have a lot in common, don't we?" Emerson snidely explained to Cowan when he found the two girls hissing.

"Common is right," smiled Wyman.

Cowan, slicking his hair down for his brief leading man status yet still no threat to Robert Taylor, was an agreeably breezy, woman-and-money-minded addition to the burgeoning private eye contingent. He returned immediately to the ranks of supporting actors, but did so with the knowledge that—except for his cloying habit of referring to Wyman as "Candy-lamb"—he had brought off this star assignment in jaunty style.

A very young Eleanor Parker, who would soon be recognized as one of the finest, and most beautiful, actresses in Hollywood and, like Wyman, say farewell to "B"s, was spotted here and there, with little of interest to do. Faye Emerson's wily villainess role was a little more colorful and she had fun with it.

Detective films in which a woman turned out to be the culprit were numerous in the forties. Sometimes, they almost seemed the rule. There were *The Maltese Falcon* (which probably started the femme fatale trend, and in which Jerome Cowan was the first victim); *Murder, My Sweet; The Brasher Doubloon; Lady in the Lake* and *Out of the Past*, to name a few of the more notable examples. *Crime by Night*, occasionally bogging down in its novel-like exposition, did not make their class, but it entertained. The title of the original Geoffrey Homes book was more to the point, however: *Forty Whacks*.

Jerome Cowan, Jane Wyman, Stuart Crawford

Cy Kendall, Stuart Crawford, Jane Wyman, Jerome Cowan

CRIME DOCTOR'S MAN HUNT

(Columbia Pictures, 1946)

Credits
Producer, Rudolph C. Flothow
Director, William Castle
Screenplay, Leigh Brackett
Based on the radio program by Max Marcin
Story, Eric Taylor
Music director, Mischa Bakaleinikoff
Camera, Philip Tannura
Editor, Dwight Caldwell
Running Time: 61 minutes

Cast
WARNER BAXTER (Dr. Robert Ordway)
ELLEN DREW (Irene Cotter/Natalie Cotter)
William Frawley (Insp. Manning)
Frank Sully (Rigger)
Claire Carleton (Ruby Farrell)
Bernard Nedell (Waldo)
Jack Lee (Sgt. Bradley)
Francis Pierlot (Gerald Cotter)
Myron Healey (Philip Armstrong)
Olin Howland (Marcus Leblanc)
Ivan Triesault (Alfredi)
Paul E. Burns (Tom)
Mary Newton (Martha)
Leon Lenoir (Herrera)
Frank Cody, Robert DeHaven (sailors)
Minerva Urecal (landlady)
Harry Hays Morgan (Jervis)
Cy Malis (Joe)
Wanda Perry (Flo White)
Joseph Palma (third policeman)
Ralph Linn (Officer Reynolds)
John Manning (waiter)
Stella LeSaint (woman)

70

Director William Castle, prone to the use of gimmicks for their shock value—rebuzzed theater seats, had skeletons wafting through audiences, recommended insurance policies for patrons against being scared to death—was sometimes called "the poor man's Alfred Hitchcock." Never was he more deserving of that description than for *Crime Doctor's Man Hunt* (1946). And this not well-known film was made before Castle developed his flair for exploitation.

The sixth of ten films in Columbia's Crime Doctor series, the story concerned a repressed girl (Ellen Drew) who took on the physical accoutrements of her dead sister and went around murdering people. Fourteen years later, Hitchcock had perhaps his biggest boxoffice success with the story of a repressed boy (Anthony Perkins) who took on the physical characteristics and appearance of his dead mother and went around murdering people. That movie was called *Psycho.*

In quality, however, *Crime Doctor's Man Hunt* was a far cry from *Psycho.* Rather, it merely was a workmanlike, unshocking "B" melodrama with an intriguing idea that was not always skillfully developed. Dual roles were an actress' métier in the forties (Bette Davis, Olivia de Havilland, Betty Hutton, and Eleanor Parker were among the actresses who were cast in double duty roles). While Ellen Drew was a capable player—her first film was *Sing You Sinners* (1938)—the climactic revelation of her schizophrenic masquerade came as no surprise to the audience. The bulky, patently phony, long blonde wig Drew (a brunette) wore for her homicidal spells fooled no one in the audience. Furthermore, the producer might have done better to cast an actress more physically malleable, someone without Drew's easily recognizable, square-jawed countenance.

The picture got off to an arresting start. Young Myron Healey, a shell-shocked war veteran, was shown wandering dazedly around a carnival in a section of town to which he found himself repeatedly drawn. He consulted psychiatrist Warner Baxter (the series' star), while demure fiancée Drew, who had secretly fol-

Warner Baxter, William Frawley, Ellen Drew, Francis Pierlot

lowed him, stood waiting in a nearby doorway. This first camera shot of the actress showed her body divided into two parts by the shop window; perhaps this was director Castle's way of hinting at the girl's aberration, but, since ingenuity did not occur again, it was probably a mere accident of staging.

About a week later, while investigating the neighborhood to which Healey was morbidly attracted, Crime Doctor Baxter saw two men (Bernard Nedell, Frank Sully) trying to dispose of Healey's dead body. Under treatment, Healey had told Baxter that a fortune-teller named Alfredi (Ivan Triesault) at the carnival had predicted a violent death for him several years ago; it had come true.

Meanwhile, it was learned that the deceased's fiancée, whose name was Irene, had a troublesome twin sister named Natalie who, three years before, had been thrown out of their home by their wealthy father (Francis Pierlot). When Drew, as Irene, was informed of Healey's death, she reflected weakly, "If Natalie were here she'd help me. Natalie always helped me."

In her blonde wig—obviously meant to be the same actress playing the part of the absent sister—a now cold, hard Ellen Drew murdered her two henchmen, just as she had Healey. Baxter tracked down the fortune-teller who told him that a blonde had paid him to predict Healey's death to frighten him because, she said, he was after her sister's money. It was then revealed that sister Natalie had been dead two-and-a-half years.

One night, Baxter, accompanied by Drew, visited the empty old town house that once had been inhabited by her family. As they looked around her late mother's perfectly preserved room, Baxter suddenly said he'd found some evidence, sending Drew to call the police. She quickly returned in the blonde wig, as Natalie, ready to shoot him. He was able to signal the police waiting outside, however, and she was taken into custody.

As Baxter explained to Inspector William Frawley, she was a schizophrenic, a split personality who periodically took on the identity of her stronger sister.

"Say, doctor," Frawley replied, "I'd like to have you see my wife."

"Split personality?"

"*No* personality," answered Frawley, concluding the picture on a sudden, but not unwelcome, light note.

Dignified Warner Baxter, an early best-actor Academy Award winner for *In Old Arizona* (1929), was well past his prime when he under-

Ellen Drew, Warner Baxter

Ellen Drew, player

took the quickie Crime Doctor pictures in 1943, following his nervous breakdown in the early forties. Based on the successful radio series created by Max Marcin, Dr. Robert Ordway was an ex-gangster turned psychiatrist-sleuth, but Baxter got increasingly less attention as the series wore on—none in *Crime Doctor's Man Hunt.* Baxter was content to play out his career thus, lending natty, middle-aged authority to the role until his death in 1951 at age fifty-seven.

Crime Doctor's Man Hunt was a better-than-average entry in a better-than-average series. A promising idea that unfortunately was diluted by the transparency of its dual-personality theme. It sustained interest, however, as an example of the "B" movie's answer to vehicles for some of the major actresses of the day—*and* as a harbinger of classic Hitchcock-to-come.

DANGEROUS PARTNERS

(Metro-Goldwyn-Mayer, 1945)

Credits
Producer, Arthur L. Field
Director, Edward L. Cahn
Screenplay, Marion Parsonnet
Adaptation, Edmund L. Hartmann
Based on the story *Paper Chase* by
    Oliver Weld Bayer
Music, David Snell
Art directors, Cedric Gibbons, Hubert Hobson
Camera, Karl Freund
Editor, Ferris Webster
Running Time: 74 minutes

Cast
JAMES CRAIG (Jeff Caighn)
SIGNE HASSO (Carola Ballister)
Edmund Gwenn (Albert Richard Kingby)
Felix Bressart (Prof. Budlow)
Audrey Totter (Lili Roegan)
Warner Anderson (Miles Kempen)
Horace McNally (co-pilot)
John Warburton (Clyde Ballister)
Henry O'Neill (Duffy)
John Eldredge (Farrel)
Sondra Rogers (woman)
Thomas Louden (Charles, the valet)
George Davis (waiter)
Mabel Paige (Marie Drumman)
Harry Hayden (doctor)
Edward Gargan (sergeant)
Katharine Booth (Miss Day)
George H. Reed (porter)
Grant Withers (Jonathan)
Wally Cassell (youngest brother)
John Carlyle (fourth brother)
Chester Clute (stranger)
Eddie Dunn (counterman)
Charles Wagenheim (small man)
Clancy Cooper (Ben Albee)
Teddy Infuhr (boy)
Douglas Madore (violin boy)
Jack Luden (clerk)
Sam Finn (second clerk)
Tom Dillon (captain of police)
Robert Malcolm (detective)
John Valentine (police doctor)

From any other studio, *Dangerous Partners* would have been a lesser-grade "A" by virtue of cast and excellence of production. From rich Metro-Goldwyn-Mayer, it was merely one of their glossy "B"'s, albeit an efficiently plotted and entertaining one.

Signe Hasso, the distinguished Swedish import fresh from her eye-poppingly androgynous role (especially for 1945) as the Nazi ringleader called "Mr. Christopher" in 20th-Century Fox's "A" *The House on 92nd Street,* appeared as a broke but attractive European adventuress traveling with her crooked mentor-husband (John Warburton). When their plane crashed, they searched passenger Edmund Gwenn, who had been knocked unconscious, and discovered four stateside wills, each for a million dollars, each naming Gwenn beneficiary. Hasso and Warburton set out to get the money first. After her husband was murdered, Hasso became involved with lawyer James Craig, a dangerous step. "You couldn't want a better legal mind—especially for something that ain't quite legal," said one character of him.

Reflexively, Hasso and Craig double-crossed one another along the line; but when they learned that Operation Gwenn was a Nazi scheme, their patriotism surfaced—as it did in so many unlikely film quarters in those days—and they helped apprehend the world's ene-

Matt Willis, Edmund Gwenn, Wally Cassell, Mabel Paige, Signe Hasso, James Craig, Grant Withers

mies, relinquishing the million dollars they had already managed to steal.

Actress Hasso, her eyebrows winged and her hair in a determined upsweep, was a striking looking woman, capable of some of the most chillingly villainous glares captured on sound film. She was in a particularly sinister close-up as she searched Gwenn in the crash scene, then fetched a crying baby for an injured mother (so we'd know she wasn't all bad, thereby preparing us for her about-face ending). Craig was MGM's pleasant, good-looking, second-string Gable. Also in the unusually strong cast were the promising Audrey Totter, voluptuous as a blonde nightclub singer; reliable Mabel Paige, in a rare unsympathetic role as the Ma Barker of the Nazi spy set; Felix Bressart, Warner Anderson, and Grant Withers.

Dangerous Partners had its foolish moments, such as those in which director Edward L. Cahn allowed the elderly little Gwenn only the slightest flinch after receiving punches that would have stunned a horse. (Gwenn, a beloved character actor also usually more sym-

pathetically cast, was two years away from winning the supporting actor Oscar as Santa Claus in *Miracle on 34th Street.*) Overall, the picture was a notch above the norm. "An agreeable surprise," the New York *Times* called it. "A neat package for the melodrama fans," approved *Silver Screen* magazine. There were some good touches, such as the Hitchcockian bit in which Hasso, rifling the prone Gwenn's briefcase, suddenly realized she was being stared at by an injured man leaning against the crashed plane—whereupon he fell over, dead.

But then, only at MGM could a "B" potboiler about Nazi agents have the patina of a *Weekend at the Waldorf.*

James Craig, Sjgne Hasso

James Craig, Edmund Gwenn, Signe Hasso

DESTINY

(Universal Pictures, 1944)

Credits
Associate producer, Roy William Neill
Directors, Reginald LeBorg, Julien Duvivier
Original screenplay, Roy Chanslor,
    Ernest Pascal
Music, Frank Skinner, Alexander Tausman
Camera, George Robinson, Paul Ivano
Editor, Paul Landres
Running Time: 65 minutes

Cast:
GLORIA JEAN (Jane Broderick)
ALAN CURTIS (Cliff Banks)
Frank Craven (Clem Broderick)
Grace McDonald (Betty)
Vivian Austin, a.k.a. Vivian Coe and
    Terry Austin (Phyllis)
Frank Fenton (Sam Baker)
Minna Gombell (Marie)
Selmer Jackson (warden)
Lew Wood (prison guard)
Perc Launders (sergeant, second officer)
Harry Strang (Sgt. Bronson)
Lane Chandler (patrolman)
Billy Wayne (bartender)
Bob Homans (Grogan, the watchman)
Gayne Whitman (radio announcer)
Frank Hagney (third motorcycle cop)
Erville Anderson (man, cut)
Edgar Dearing (fourth motorcycle cop)
Bill Hall (second motorcycle cop)
Mr. Bones (dog)
Dorothy Vaughn (Maggie, old woman)
Dale Van Sickel (first motorcycle cop)
Bill O'Brien (waiter)
Bob Reeves (cop)
Ken Terrell, Bud Wolfe (radio patrolmen)

78

Destiny, released by Universal for Christmas, 1944, was a peculiar film to be scheduled for the holiday season. But then, it would have been strange during any period. The production, with a notably checkered history, had at its almost literal center a story that ranked among the most hauntingly original to be found in any movie, "B" or otherwise.

It had begun as the opening segment of the star-studded Charles Boyer-Julien Duvivier production of *Flesh and Fantasy,* a film released the year before, written by Ernest Pascal and directed by France's Duvivier, with Gloria Jean and Alan Curtis in the leads. The picture itself was to contain four separate vignettes concerning the supernatural, but the Jean-Curtis curtain-raiser—about a blind girl and a criminal who died at the end—was thought too downbeat to start the already lengthy film, and *Flesh and Fantasy* became a trilogy instead. (*Fantasy's* new opening scene, however, still showed traces of the Jean-Curtis original, with Curtis' body [albeit unidentified] being washed ashore during Mardi Gras in New Orleans to commence the Betty Field–Robert Cummings episode.)

Universal didn't want to waste the Gloria Jean-Alan Curtis footage photographed by Paul Ivano (also at the camera on Erich von Stroheim's unfinished silent, *Queen Kelly,* starring Gloria Swanson). Roy Chanslor was hired to write additional material to surround the existing scenes so that they could be stretched to feature length and be released. Then Reginald LeBorg and George Robinson signed on as director and cameraman, respectively. The efforts of these late-comers cannot really be said to have worked, but they did labor on one of the most uniquely conceived pictures in the annals of Hollywood. And what remained of director Duvivier's footage—a poetically fanciful idyll culminating in supernatural violence—was extraordinary enough to obliterate the mediocrity that framed it. (Universal's still-photograph sets on *Destiny* reveal scenes that did not appear in the feature as released. Whether they belonged to the Duvivier footage or LeBorg's, or both, is a mystery.)

The shrill sound of sirens opened the picture as Alan Curtis and Frank Fenton, police in pursuit, sped along a rural highway, soon going their separate ways on foot in the woods and evading the law. That night Curtis was given a ride by sympathetic librarian Grace McDonald. When her car radio played "I'll See You in My Dreams," it reminded him that his old girlfriend (Vivian Austin) had been singing that song in a

Alan Curtis, Gloria Jean

café when he met her.

He told McDonald the beginning of his story. Austin had introduced him to Frank Fenton, who tricked him into assisting in a robbery where guard Bob Homans was shot. With Austin on his arm, he then had a lucky streak at the race track, and when he let her hold $10,000 she left town. He was arrested for the robbery and served three years in San Quentin.

Leaving McDonald, Curtis came to a roadhouse run by Minna Gombell, who immediately recognized him as the fugitive but said, "Relax, I'm no stool." She fed him and he swore he had no part in the bank robbery for which he was hunted. After his three years in prison, he explained, bringing his story up-to-date, he was working in a factory when he ran into Fenton again. Obtaining a lift from Curtis in his car, Fenton asked him to wait outside a bank while he cashed a check. Shots were fired and Fenton ran out and jumped into Curtis' car, which fled the scene.

When she thought he was asleep, Gombell phoned the police to get the reward for him, but Curtis caught her and, before escaping, told her, "Maybe one day I'll learn about women. They'll never double-cross me again."

This, evidently, was where the original Duvivier footage began (although there seemed to be inserts here and there—close-ups, especially—wrought by other hands). The whole texture of the film changed in what was now presumably Paul Ivano's exquisitely suggestive photography, low-key and moody for some scenes, brilliantly lyrical in others.

In a place called Paradise Valley, Curtis found shelter from the rain through the open door of a farmhouse. When blind girl Gloria Jean and her father (Frank Craven) returned home, Jean said, "We never close our door." They gave their uninvited guest a bed for the night. Curtis was fascinated by the sweet, smiling Jean, who moved about as easily as if sighted. Craven explained that she was "a diviner. You know, finds water. . . . She was born blind. . . . Sometimes I think she sees more than we do."

In the morning, Curtis watched Jean going about her chores singing, while birds flew to her and swarms of bees rested on her shoulders without stinging her. "Look, even the flowers lean toward her," remarked a passing crone (Dorothy Vaughn) to Curtis, who was about to abscond with valuables stolen from a desk in the house.

"So, you can make it rain, huh," he said, approaching Jean. She showed Curtis around her "little paradise," stopping for a while in a roofless church ruin. "Imagine," she mused, "having the wind for a bell-ringer. . . . I was in the city once. It was the only time I felt really blind." When he learned that the farm was doing very well, he put back what he had stolen in feigned repentence and asked her forgiveness, as well as—greed clearly his motive—permission to stay on and help with the farm.

It was becoming obvious that the Curtis of the originally filmed vignette and the Curtis of the

Gloria Jean

newer material were two different people. The destiny-buffeted, essentially straight young man of the earlier portion had little in common with the innately selfish, calculating Curtis who was ingratiating himself to Gloria Jean and Frank Craven. Clearly the initial conception had been to make Curtis a rogue in order to justify his horrible end.

One evening as Jean sat knitting in the house while a skunk frolicked on the table nearby, a shot rang out. Curtis and Craven had been out hunting a bear (nature *could* be evil); only Curtis returned.

"I thought he was the bear," he confessed lamely, going on to make sexual advances to the terrified blind girl.

Her small dog suddenly became a wild, snarling beast, attacking Curtis in bizarrely huge silhouette as Jean darted outdoors, crying for help. Gale-like winds began to blow and rain poured down. Jean ran into the storm, with Curtis in pursuit. In a beautifully staged, riveting sequence that was a technical as well as creative tour de force, tree branches seemed to grab at Curtis and trip him as he raced along, while clearing the way for Jean. Finally, he fell into a raging river. (Hence the unexplained body washed up during the Mardi Gras in the first segment of *Flesh and Fantasy* as released.)

Suddenly he woke up. Enter more non-Duvivier footage. The events of the last minutes had all been a dream (a favorite device at the time used in films such as *The Strange Affair of Uncle Harry* and *The Woman in the Window*). As he was leaving the farm, a shot rent the air once again; this time it was no dream. Craven had shot himself hunting the bear and, although Curtis knew it might mean his capture, he took him into town to the doctor. The captured Fenton then very conveniently decided to clear Curtis of the bank robbery. Jean and Curtis drove back to the farm, concluding a story which was almost transformed into just another crook-redeemed-by-goodness cliché. The original intent was exactly opposite, but, happily, enough of the offbeat character was retained.

Gloria Jean, the teenage soprano who usually appeared in lighter vehicles, drew top billing in her self-proclaimed favorite role. Winsome and unaffected, she never grew pretentious or condescending in her blind girl's near-saintliness; had her role been left in the "A" *Flesh and Fantasy,* she might have been offered more substantial parts in important films. Unfortunately, her career soon went into an unswerving decline, and the fresh little girl from Scranton, Pennsylvania, once deemed a threat to Universal's reigning songbird, Deanna Durbin, never quite made it. Today, Gloria Jean is a receptionist for a California cosmetics firm.

Alan Curtis was a handsome young man with a peculiarly mechanical, staccato line delivery that made him an unconvincing actor. Of course, the writing inconsistencies of his character in *Destiny* would have defeated any actor. He died in 1953 at age forty-three. Grace McDonald, the studio's lively in-house tap-dancer, was oddly cast as Curtis' highway pickup; she not only did not dance, she did not *walk*, playing her whole part behind the wheel of a car. The script established her character so strongly that viewers expected her to crop up again, but she did not. Frank Craven had too little to do, and Vivian Austin—a coyly obvious femme fatale—had too much.

Even the title *Destiny* had a history. It had been an all-purpose working tag for a number of Universal pictures, including *The Wolf Man* and *Son of Dracula,* until it was finally dusted off for this film.

Most reviewers did not quite understand the production. Otis L. Guernsey, Jr.'s critique in the New York *Herald Tribune* seemed a distillate of the others. "Gloria Jean is the farmer's daughter," he wrote (off to something of a gross start), "to whom all nature is kind and sympathetic in her blindness and she turns in a first-class performance. Frank Craven has his usual assignment as her father. Their hard work is generally in vain in *Destiny*. The script has a little bit of charm and a whisper of menace, but not enough of either to make an effective motion picture."

Seen today, it is startling to realize that this seriously flawed but very special little picture—with its central Grimm's fairy tale-like blending of beauty, mysticism and horror—had practically no champions in its day.

DETOUR

(Producers Releasing Corporation, 1945)
Credits

Associate producer, Martin Mooney
Director, Edgar G. Ulmer
Screenplay and original story, Martin Goldsmith
Music, Leo Ordody
Art director, Edward C. Jewell
Camera, Benjamin H. Kline
Editor, George McGuire
Running Time: 65 minutes

Cast

TOM NEAL (Roberts)
ANN SAVAGE (Vera)
Claudia Drake (Sue)
Edmund MacDonald (Haskell)
Tim Ryan (Gus)
Esther Howard (Hedy)
Roger Clark (Dillon)
Pat Gleason (Joe, the truck driver)
Donald Brodie (used-car salesman)

Although her screen career lasted only a decade and was spent almost entirely in "B"s, South Carolina-born Ann Savage was a talented, distinctively beautiful and charismatic actress who had the misfortune to sign with a bedazzled Columbia as they were building Rita Hayworth as the reigning "love goddess." (The studio paid even less attention to newcomer Shelley Winters, who was also there then, which gives one an idea of the hierarchy's awesome ability to shut out everyone but La Hayworth.) Fairhaired (sometimes), slightly aquiline of profile and authoritative, crafty, even of dangerous mien, Ann Savage became typed—in spite of her youth—as those now obsolete Golden Age regulars, the tough-nut-to-crack or siren.

Her best-remembered portrayal was in the compelling Producers Releasing Corporation "sleeper" *Detour* (filmed in six days). As Vera, "the girl of the road," she seemed a descendant of Maugham's Mildred (*Of Human Bondage*) or Cain's Cora *(The Postman Always Rings Twice)*—Savage's preceding role in *Apology for Murder* had been a first cousin to that same

Cain's Phyllis *(Double Indemnity)*. Tom Neal appeared opposite Savage to rare advantage as the traveling piano player she tried to blackmail into joining her in a criminal scheme. (Neal was also her leading man in three 1944 "B"s; *Klondike Kate, Two-Man Submarine,* and *The Unwritten Code.*)

She abandoned her usual glamorous demeanor to give a ferocious—sometimes even savage—performance. The first late shot of the young but tubercular pickup's shark-like face established in a few seconds her twisted, predatory personality. In the section on Ann Savage and *Detour* in their book *Dames*, Ian and Elizabeth Cameron remarked, "She has eyes so terrifying that one wonders how those who beheld her in the flesh managed to avoid getting turned to stone."

In an early 1960's issue of *Films in Review*, Don Miller discussed the great admiration of "new wave" French director Francois Truffaut for the Vienna-born, America-based "B" director Edgar G. Ulmer, particularly, the latter's *Detour.*

Ann Savage, Tom Neal

Wrote Miller: "[The film] was from a 1939 novel by Martin Goldsmith who also wrote the script, and apparently had been unwanted until producer Leon Fromkess thought its ironic crime-and-suspense story sufficiently like [the then fashionable] James M. Cain for it to have a chance. *Detour* was sixty-five compact minutes of straightforward cinema—lean, taut and no irrelevance. Goldsmith's script was a good one, and Ulmer enhanced it by getting good performances out of Tom Neal, whose accomplishments up to that time had not included acting ability, and Ann Savage, flamboyantly right as the femme fatale."

Writer Miller noted that Ulmer did not compromise and tack on a happy ending, citing *Detour* as "one of the few bright spots in PRC's shabby history."

This, in spite of the fact that *Detour* was, to quote the Camerons again, "a work well in the running to be the cheapest really good film to come out of Hollywood. Most of it involved just three actors and a car in front of a back-projection machine."

The story had Neal hitchiking from New York to join girlfriend Claudia Drake, a singer, in Hollywood. He was picked up in the Arizona desert by Edmund MacDonald, a dissipated socialite-turned-gambler who had not seen his family in twenty years. When MacDonald, in a pill-induced stupor, cracked his head on a rock and died, Neal, fearful he would be charged with murder, changed clothes with him and continued west in the car.

Just past the California state line, he picked up Ann Savage, who rode in hostile silence until they approached Hollywood. Suddenly she asked, "What did you do with the body?" It seemed she had hitched a ride with the dead man earlier and knew Neal was an imposter. She threatened to turn him in to the police unless he followed her orders, specifically, agreeing to pose as MacDonald and collect the inheritance from his dying millionaire father.

The theme ballad was "I Can't Believe That You're in Love with Me," written for *Detour* by Jimmy McHugh and Clarence Gaskill and sung by Claudia Drake—a standard today. Noel Coward said it in *Private Lives*: "Strange how potent cheap music is." Nevertheless, the picture's short running time plus its sudden twist-of-fate ending—Neal accidentally killed Savage, which left him hunted for two murders he didn't commit—just as the plot was thickening couldn't help suggesting the possibility that the producers had run out of money and had found it expedient simply to bring things to a close.

Ann Savage, Tom Neal

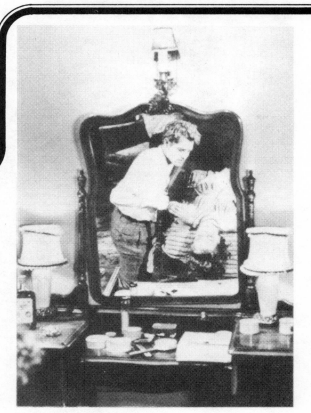

Tom Neal, Ann Savage

The Illinois-born Neal's own tempestuous life paled anything to be found in *Detour*. The many-times-married actor whose romantic escapades and brawls made tabloid headlines for years capped his career with the allegedly unintentional shooting of his last wife, Gale Bennett, in 1965. He was convicted of involuntary manslaughter and spent six years in prison. Eight months after his parole, he was found dead in bed of "natural causes."

Ann Savage, Tom Neal

EVER SINCE VENUS

(Columbia Pictures, 1944)

Credits
Director, Arthur Dreifuss
Original screenplay, McElbert Moore, Dreifuss
Music director, Mario Silva
Orchestrations, Lyle Murphy
Songs, Lester Lee and Harry Harris; Sammy
   Cahn and Saul Chaplin; Ben Raleigh
   and Bernie Wayne
Camera, Benjamin Kline
Editor, Otto Meyer
Running Time: 73 minutes

Cast
INA RAY HUTTON (herself)
HUGH HERBERT (P.G. Grimble)
ANN SAVAGE (Janet Wilson)
Billy Gilbert (Tiny Lewis)
Glenda Farrell (Babs Cartwright)
Ross Hunter (Bradley Miller)
Alan Mowbray (J. Webster Hackett)
Marjorie Gateson (Maude Hackett)
Thurston Hall (Edgar Pomeroy)
Fritz Feld (Michele)
Dudley Dickerson (Clarence)
Stewart Foster (himself)
Bill Shawn, Carol Adams (dancers)
Eddie Borden (waiter)
Muni Seroff (Pierre)
Paul Conrad (radio announcer)
Doreen Mulvey (dancer)
Ralph Dunn (policeman)
Bertha Priestly (fat girl)
P.J. Kelly (watchman)
Charles Jordan (bartender)
Kernan Cripps (waiter)
Isabel Withers (Miss Murray)
Pat Hogan (salesgirl)
Mary Gordon (Mrs. Murphy)
Jack Carr (customer)
Byron Foulger (Henley, the druggist)
Chester Clute (milquetoast customer)
Harry Depp (Taylor)
Jack Rice (butler)
Ann Loos (messenger)

86

Ever Since Venus was a pleasant surprise to come from the 1944 "B" brigade. An original musical comedy in *every* sense of that phrase, using a format—the industrial-show setting—still largely unexplored by the entertainment media. In this case, it was the American Beauty Association, and the complications attendant upon that organization's annual hotel gala, which afforded a fresh showcase not only for top-billed female orchestra leader Ina Ray Hutton, but a troupe of likable and talented players.

Corpulent Billy Gilbert, in particular, the veteran bit and supporting comic, famous for his "sneezes," had one of his larger screen parts as the songwriting waiter who submitted the tune "Glamour for Sale" to Ina Ray Hutton just as she was to star in the New York beauty show. He shared an apartment with young Ross Hunter, a research chemist, and Fritz Feld, an artist, while a new neighbor in town for the show was beauty parlor manager Ann Savage. When Hunter invented an improved, non-staining lipstick called "Rosebud," the jubilant quartet romped around the threesome's apartment for one of the movie's brighter, more exuberant musical interludes, "Rosebud, I Love You" (". . . you're so cosmetic").

Preparing to enter the show, they were told by underhanded "cosmetic king" Alan Mowbray—intent on selling lipstick buyer Thurston Hall a big order—that it would cost them $1,000 to join the association and get a booth. Meanwhile, factory owner Hugh (Woo-woo) Herbert, whom Mowbray wanted to manufacture his large order, arrived at the show incognito. A dizzy collector of penguins, Herbert was described by Marjorie Gateson, Mowbray's equally devious wife, as sounding "as if he came from a long line of squirrels."

When Gilbert's song, "Glamour for Sale," won the $1,000 beauty show theme song competition, they were able to get a booth—Number 13. "Have a little Rosebud?" asked Savage of Herbert. "Thank you very much," he replied. "Have a little penguin? Woo-woo!"

Eventually, Hall gave Hunter his large lipstick order, but, with no manufacturer yet, Mowbray convinced Feld that they were taking money

Billy Gilbert, Glenda Farrell, Thurston Hall, Ina Ray Hutton, Hugh Herbert, Ross Hunter, Ann Savage

under false pretenses and could go to jail. His solution was to buy out their business for $5,000. Glenda Farrell, Ina Ray Hutton's arranger and now Gilbert's girlfriend, got the signed document back from Mowbray. When Herbert—who had grown fond of the Rosebud contingent—revealed his identity and offered to manufacture their lipstick, they were back in business. Hunter and Savage wound up together, while Ina Ray Hutton, in the "Glamour for Sale" finale, sang and danced in a production number depicting glamour through the ages—Hutton as Cleopatra, Josephine, a belle of the nineties, and, finally, a jivey Miss 1944 ("They'll remember me in history—Miss 1944.")

Despite Hutton's stellar billing, most of the time, although spotted throughout in musical numbers, she was on the outskirts of the action. A tiny, rather plain-featured woman who did not appear in many films, as a female bandleader she was a curiosity, and her style certainly was livelier than the dominant male maestros—tap-dancing and bouncing about the podium like a stoned chorus girl contestant on *So You Want to Lead a Band.*

"The love interest is taken care of by Ann Savage," wrote the Hollywood *Reporter,* "who has developed into one of the most competent younger leading women on the Columbia contract list." She had indeed, and was a shapely eyeful to boot. Hunter was a clean-cut juvenile, but would attain greater celebrity in the next

decades as Hollywood's most successful producer of glossy films. Farrell was her usual zesty self, particularly in the duet with Gilbert entitled "Do I Need You?" ("Like a punch in the nose/ Like a stain on my clothes"); while veterans Mowbray, Feld, Gateson, and Hall rendered their expected solid support.

Variety, describing *Ever Since Venus* as "an entertaining low-budgeter," was accurate when it continued, "The buffoonery of Hugh Herbert, in the role of an eccentric factory owner, and Billy Gilbert, as a songwriting member of a trio of lipstick manufacturers who had trouble getting started, is especially commendable. The latter duo carries the film in topflight fashion."

With a little more make-up, *Ever Since Venus* might have provided a vehicle for Columbia's musical queen, Rita Hayworth. Even as a "B," it was less hackneyed and more tuneful than many of her expensive vehicles—certainly more so than the subsequent *Down to Earth,* in which "Love Goddess" Hayworth would portray not Venus but the Grecian muse of dancing, Terpsichore.

Hugh Herbert, Ann Savage

Ina Ray Hutton

EYES IN THE NIGHT

(Metro-Goldwyn-Mayer, 1942)

Credits

Producer, Jack Chertok
Director, Fred Zinnemann
Screenplay, Guy Trosper, Howard
    Emmett Rogers
Based on the novel *Odor of Violets*
    by Baynard Kendrick
Art director, Cedric Gibbons
Camera, Robert Planck, Charles Lawton
Editor, Ralph Winters
Running Time: 79 minutes

Cast

EDWARD ARNOLD (Capt. Duncan Maclain)
ANN HARDING (Norma Lawry)
DONNA REED (Barbara Lawry)
Allen Jenkins (Marty)
John Emery (Paul Gerente)
Horace McNally, a.k.a. Stephen McNally
    (Gabriel Hoffman)
Katherine Emery (Cheli Scott)
Reginald Denny (Stephen Lawry)
Rosemary De Camp (Vera Hoffman)
Stanley C. Ridges (Hansen)
Barry Nelson (Busch)
Steve Geray (Anderson)
Erik Rolf (Boyd)
Reginald Sheffield (Victor)
Ivan Miller (Herman)
Millburn Stone (Pete)
Mantan Moreland (Alistair)
Cliff Danielson (boy)
Frances Rafferty (girl)
Edward Kilroy (pilot)
John Butler (driver)
William Nye (Hugo)
Fred Walburn, Robert Winkler,
    Walter Tetley (boys)
Frank Thomas (police lieutenant)
Marie Windsor (actress)
Friday (himself)

Metro-Goldwyn-Mayer produced many crime films during its Golden Age, a number of them very good. But Hollywood's richest studio still always seemed more at home on Wimpole Street than in back alleys, and its product betrayed its uneasiness when it had to deal with punches that were more amusing than deleterious.

It was almost as if employees of MGM's sound-effects department had never heard the sound of one person belting another, which was not unlikely considering the product they were releasing—see Mrs. Miniver. Every punch thrown in a forties MGM film, whether by man, woman or child, had precisely the same sound, a muffled cross between a horse's hoofbeat and a champagne cork popping. This was never more evident than in the company's vigorous ''B'' thriller, *Eyes in the Night.*

The storyline was standard Axis spy-secret formula folderol. One gimmick, however, made all the difference: the hero, Captain Duncan Maclain (Edward Arnold), was a blind private detective—to compound the novelty, he was also middle-aged.

Arnold became involved when his distraught old friend (Ann Harding) asked his advice about her seventeen-year-old stepdaughter (Donna Reed) who was seeing much-older, self-centered ham actor John Emery. Both were acting in a local little theater-group play written by Cheli Scott (Katherine Emery, no relation to John). Reed disliked Harding (''There isn't room in this house for both of us.'') because she mistook her genuine concern for jealousy—John Emery and Harding had been lovers before she married Reed's father (Reginald Denny). When Reed discovered the actor murdered in his apartment and Harding standing nearby, she assumed her stepmother guilty. Reed informed her that she wouldn't tell the police if Harding would leave Denny in the morning. She admitted she had never really cared about Emery, adding that Harding had killed him for nothing.

Pleading innocent, Harding nevertheless agreed to go, but went first to Arnold who, arriving at the scene of the crime, found the body gone. Meanwhile, Axis agents (led by

Horace (Stephan) McNally, Allen Jenkins, Edward Arnold

Katherine Emery) were infiltrating inventor Denny's home to obtain his new World War II-related secret formula. The Denny butler (Stanley C. Ridges) was one of the spies, as was the maid (Rosemary De Camp), who was liquidated when she grew hysterical. The dead John Emery, it was explained, had been in on the plot, then tried to back out and was killed by his confederates who had stolen the body from his apartment.

Arnold came for a visit—pretending to be Harding's cranky, whiskey-loving uncle—and soon figured out the scheme. When the criminals finally declared themselves and held Arnold and the family prisoners, the detective's seeing-eye dog Friday (played, according to the credits, by himself) escaped and returned with the police. In the ensuing scramble, the sightless Arnold threw punches with the best of them and Donna Reed knocked out Katherine Emery—the MGM punch machine was never more vocal. Reed and Harding repaired their relationship.

As with so many up-to-the-finale serious quickies of the day, the film ended on a note of levity—the psychology evidently being that an audience sent home smiling was an audience more likely to recommend the picture. And who was a more surefire laugh-getter than chubby, cherubic Mantan Moreland, the talented black comedian who played Arnold's valet?

"Ah'm off to the Harlem Squash and Tennis Club to meet my dream girl," he told Arnold's dog as he opened the front door. Suddenly, the animal knocked him over to run out and off with a (presumably) female canine outside on the street. "Why, you wolf!" exclaimed a supine Moreland.

The picture, however, belonged to Edward Arnold. His hearty, realistically detailed portrayal of the shrewd blind detective, whose disability sometimes called for eccentric methods of detecting, set *Eyes in the Night* apart from run-of-the-mill private-eye adventures. It was a pleasure to observe his sleuth at work, whether he was touching the dust formation on John Emery's floor to deduce that his body had recently been removed or, later on, routing stealthy, middle-of-the-night spies at the Denny safe by suddenly blasting the Denny organ during a phony drunken foray. If Arnold, stout and aging, was less believable engaging in fisticuffs and wrestling matches (a double helped out in these scenes), the overall quality of his work was so fine he was forgiven these fleeting lapses—which, actually, were not his but

Ann Harding, Donna Reed

Donna Reed, Stanley C. Ridges, Katherine Emery,
Ann Harding, Edward Arnold

the script's. Apparently MGM agreed, because three years later there was a sequel, *The Hidden Eye,* again featuring Arnold.

Ann Harding returned to the screen after a five-year absence, a trifle theatrical in manner, her trademark-bun at the nape of her neck unmoved. But the very youthful (while obviously somewhat more than seventeen), wholesome Donna Reed—full of spiked "Dears" and "Darlings" for her stepmother—was a pretty, surprisingly convincing bitch. Almost always cast as a sympathetic young thing, Reed displayed a facility for acid characterization that should have been explored by the studio bosses.

The production's "Axis Cheli," Katherine Emery, one of the original leads in Broadway's *The Children's Hour* several years before, was among the forties' most chilling presences. Without artificial trappings, her icily neurotic, taut ladies suggested all sorts of horrific evil behind the deceptive good manners. Not taxed in *Eyes in the Night,* she still was interesting to have around.

The film was an early effort for Fred Zinnemann, later to direct such outstanding pictures as *From Here to Eternity* and *The Sundowners*. It was a promising start, and Zinnemann went on to heights beyond anyone's expectations at the time.

THE FACE BEHIND THE MASK

(Columbia Pictures, 1941)

Credits

Producer, Wallace McDonald
Director, Robert Florey
Screenplay, Allen Vincent, Paul Jarrico
Story, Arthur Levinson
Based on a radio play by Thomas Edward
    O'Connell
Music director, M.W. Stoloff
Camera, Franz F. Planer
Editor, Charles Nelson
Running Time: 69 minutes

Cast

PETER LORRE (Janos Szabo)
EVELYN KEYES (Helen Williams)
Don Beddoe (Jim O'Hara)
George E. Stone (Binky)
John Tyrrell (Watts)
Stanley Brown (Harry)
Al Seymour (Benson)
James Seay (Jeff Jeffries)
Warren Ashe (Johnson)
Charles Wilson (Chief O'Brien)
George McKay (Terry Finnegan)
Ben Taggart (Dr. Jones)
Mary Currier (Nurse Kritzer)
Sarah Edwards (Mrs. Perkins)
Frank Reicher (Dr. Cheever)
Ralph Peters (cook)
Al Hill (Horton)
Walter Soderling (Harris)
Lee Prather (immigration officer)
David Oliver (Steward)
John Dilson (Anderson)
Joel Friedkin (Mr. Perkins)
Lee Phelps (Brown)
Sam Ash (Mike Cary)
Ed Stanley (Dr. Beckett)
Claire Rochelle (Nurse Bailey)
Walter Merrill (Joe)
Al Rhein, Ernie Adams (bits)
Victor Travers (man)
Almeda Fowler (woman)
Bessie Wade (woman)
Harry Strang (clerk Stimson)
Al Bridge (Horgan)
Lee Shumway (policeman)
Jack Gardner (man at fire)
Eddie Foster (city slicker)
Chuck Hamilton (gas station attendant)
Billy Lally (Wilson)

Ostensibly only a "B" gangland melodrama, Columbia's *The Face Behind the Mask* was a gripping film. Under Robert Florey's adroit direction, Peter Lorre was brought to one of his richest roles. It was, in fact, the rare occasion when the bizarre Lorre persona was given full rein on the screen.

The star portrayed a Hungarian immigrant who turned to crime after his face had been hideously scarred in a fire. Making capital use of his expressive voice and weird features, Lorre ran the gamut of emotions: from effusive, optimistic young man, to desperate, soon suicidal freak-pariah, to sinister, embittered mob chief in a contoured rubber mask, to—when Evelyn Keyes made her tardy entrance—tender sweetheart. He was aided by superb make-up and Robert Florey's moody, sometimes expressionistic vision. The Paris-born Florey was another director with a strong sense of the visual imperative (telling close-ups were his specialty) who almost never was assigned films worthy of him. He was only an associate director on the most celebrated feature to bear his name, Charlie Chaplin's *Monsieur Verdoux* (1946).

Franz F. Planer's *Face Behind the Mask* camerawork was the perfect complement to the Lorre-Florey virtuosity. Such shots as Lorre

Peter Lorre, Evelyn Keyes

mulling suicide on a dusky dock, amid shimmering, water-reflected tentacles of light, linger in the memory.

And the leading lady was certainly not inept in her role. Southern belle Evelyn Keyes, before long graduated to such "A"s as *Here Comes Mr. Jordan* and *The Jolson Story* but never really attaining the major stardom her versatility merited, had her best part to that date. She was lovely and extremely sympathetic as the cheerful blind girl who strung beads for a living and showed the maimed Lorre the light—"Sometimes I wish I could see the world as you do," he told her. They were planning to marry when she was killed by a bomb planted in his car by his ex-gang.

When it was first released, *The Face Behind the Mask* was dismissed by critics, with *Variety*'s reviewer being especially finicky (while professing the opposite). "It's not so much likely to scare audiences as make them a little sick, between Peter Lorre in a nauseating rubber mask and the femme lead as a blind girl," he wrote. "Production, acting and story, paradoxically, are all of a high order, but it's all too unpleasant." (One wonders how this critic would react to today's unrestrained screen horrors, notably *The Exorcist*, perhaps the movie industry's all-time stomach-turner.) Nevertheless, *The Face Behind the Mask* must have done well at the box office, because two years later Columbia reissued it—something rare with "B"s.

Swift and action-packed, *The Face Behind the Mask* has become something of a classic in low-budget filmmaking, and deservedly so. Later in 1941, Peter Lorre would support Humphrey Bogart in the long-certified "A" classic, *The Maltese Falcon.*

George E. Stone

Evelyn Keyes, Peter Lorre

THE FALCON AND THE CO-EDS

(RKO Radio Pictures, 1943)

Credits

Producer, Maurice Geraghty
Director, William Clemens
Screenplay, Ardel Wray, Gerald Geraghty
Original story, Wray
Music director, C. Bakaleinikoff
Camera, Roy Hunt
Editor, Theron Warth
Running Time: 68 minutes

Cast

TOM CONWAY (Tom Lawrence, the Falcon)
JEAN BROOKS (Vicky Gaines)
Rita Corday (Marguerita Serena)
Amelita Ward (Jane Harris)
Isabel Jewell (Mary Phoebus)
George Givot (Dr. Anatole Graelich)
Cliff Clark (Timothy Donovan)
Ed Gargan (Bates)
Barbara Brown (Miss Keyes)
Juanita Alvarez (second Ugh)
Ruth Alvarez (first Ugh)
Nancy McCullum (third Ugh)
Patti Brill (Beanie Smith)
Olin Howlin (Goodwillie)
Ian Wolfe (Eustace L. Harley, the undertaker)
Margie Stewart (Pam)
Margaret Landry (Sarey Ann)
Carole Gallagher (Elsie)
Barbara Lynn (Mildred)
Mary Halsey (telephone operator)
Rosemary LaPlanche, Barbara Coleman,
    Daun Kennedy (bits)
Perc Launders (garage man)
Elaine Riley (Ellen)
Dorothy Maloney, a.k.a. Dorothy Malone,
    Julia Hopkins, Dorothy Kelly (co-eds)
Dorothy Christy (Maya Harris)
Anne O'Neal (Miss Hicks)
Ruth Cherrington (dowager)

Everybody seemed to be trying a little harder than usual in RKO's *The Falcon and the Co-eds.* The result being, according to Wanda Hale's bull's *eye,* critical assessment in the New York *Daily,* that the film still stands as "the most amusing and baffling of the series." There were ten more Falcon movies to come, for a total of sixteen.

The series began in 1941 with George Sanders in the role of the aristocratic, British-born, amateur sleuth nicknamed the Falcon. Four films later, when Sanders got the chance to graduate to regular "A" work, he turned the series over to his sound-alike brother, Tom Conway, who then appropriately played the sleuth's brother—also called the Falcon—in ten movies. The last three entries (in 1948 and 1949) found John Calvert replacing Conway, but the latter's cool, wry characterization of the dapper, unfazable ladies-man Hawkshaw remains the definitive Falcon.

Even harder to predict than this particular mystery's outcome would have been the long-inactive Conway's real-life reappearance in the mid-sixties as a destitute alcoholic. The actor died in 1967 of a liver ailment.

The Falcon and the Co-eds gave Conway a field day, surrounding him with feminine pulchritude as never before or again seen on screen. He was called to the seaside Bluecliff Seminary for girls by Amelita Ward, the daughter of an actress friend. Ward claimed that to avoid scandal, the recent murder of a professor at the school was being passed off as heart failure, and that her roommate (Rita Corday) had predicted the homicide. When dean Barbara Brown was murdered too, the school was bequeathed to fencing-dramatics instructor Jean Brooks, who consequently became the prime suspect.

Other possibly guilty parties were: George Givot, European émigré psychology professor; Isabel Jewell, timid music teacher; and student-seer Corday, whose musician father had been a suicide and who, afraid she was going insane as well, began to think that she herself might have committed the crimes.

The dénouement came when Conway learned that Givot had met Brooks on a cruise

Juanita Alvarez, Ruth Alvarez, Tom Conway, Nancy McCullum

and asked her to marry him so that he could legally enter the country. When she refused, he married spinster Isabel Jewell, a passenger on the same cruise. The school frowned on marriage between faculty members, however, so they kept it a secret. Givot continued his attentions to the pretty blonde Brooks, unbalancing Jewell, who killed the professor and the dean hoping that Givot and Brooks would be blamed. She was about to claim her third victim, Corday, by making her commit suicide from "the Devil's Ladder," an old pirate's path leading down a steep cliff to the ocean, when Conway suddenly appeared and called to her. Startled, Jewell accidentally fell to her death in the sea.

One of the niceties of the Falcon series was its sense of humor, never sprightlier than in *The Falcon and the Co-eds.* Early in the film, when Conway alighted from the bus in the little coastal town near Bluecliff, undertaker Ian Wolfe, standing in front of his establishment, asked, "Can I help you?" Responded Conway, checking the setup, "Not just yet." Later on, student Amelita Ward told the debonair Conway that Corday had predicted another murder and she feared for his safety because Corday said it would be "some elderly person."

The acting was near-exemplary, and in a bit role as a Bluecliff pupil any sharp eye could spot future Academy Award winner Dorothy Malone. One lapse was the overdrawn Brooklynese accent of co-ed Patti Brill, whose father Conway had impersonated to gain initial access to the seminary. Her bogus patois was like nothing ever heard before in that New York borough, nor, perhaps, on this earth.

The most interesting performance was probably Jean Brooks' brusque, commanding, bi-instructional young teacher—attractive and feminine in appearance at first glance, but on closer inspection possessed of large, icy-blue eyes, and the manner of a Prussian general. She was dressed accordingly part of the time in a militaristic dark dress with brass buttons up the side. In one scene she would be excoriating Corday—who had a premonition that a sword would be the next murder weapon—for fainting after refusing to take part in a fencing exhibition ("A cheap, childish bid for attention."). In another, she could be sentimental with the Falcon about the late professor's poetry and sensitivity and unrequited love for her ("I just felt sorry for him").

After Brooks apologized to Conway at an early meeting for being rude, he capsulized her intriguing, enigmatic character well when he advised her, "It takes a very unusual woman to

George Givot, Juanita Alvarez, Jean Brooks,
Tom Conway

Rita Corday, Cliff Clark

be rude and charming at the same time." *The Falcon and the Co-eds* had that woman in the person of comely, authoritative, talented Jean Brooks.

The production values were unusually good. Location scenes at the Pacific seashore, the school's musical revue, and Roy Hunt's sensitive photography (with, for a mystery in the *noir*-oriented forties, an almost daring, frequent use of daylight) evidenced a higher budget than the Falcon "B"'s generally were awarded. The screenplay by Ardel Wray and Gerald Geraghty, as well as the direction of William Clemens were also extraordinarily polished. Even the opening credits, a lovely, semi-slow-motion pounding surf against which the names fell, was indicative of the quality approach to *The Falcon and the Co-eds*.

GIVE OUT, SISTERS

(Universal Pictures, 1942)

Credits

Producer, Bernie Burton
Director, Edward S. Cline
Screenplay, Paul Gerard Smith, Warren Wilson
Original story, Lee Sands, Fred Rath
Songs, Gwynne and Lucien Denni; Walter
    Donaldson; Ray Stillwell and Ray Gold;
    Lester Lee and Zeke Manners; Al Lerner
    and Sid Robin
Dances, John Mattison
Camera, George Robinson
Editor, Paul Landres
Running Time: 65 minutes

Cast

THE ANDREWS SISTERS (themselves)
Dan Dailey, Jr. (Bob Edwards)
Grace McDonald (Gracie Waverly)
Charles Butterworth (Prof. Woof)
Walter Catlett (Gribble)
Richard Davies (Kendall)
Don [Donald] O'Connor (Don)
Peggy Ryan (Peggy)
Edith Barrett (Agatha Waverly)
Fay Helm (Susan Waverly)
Marie Blake (Blandina Waverly)
Emmett Vogan (Batterman, the costumer)
Leonard Carey (Jamison, the butler)
Jivin' Jacks: Bobby Scheerer, Tommy Rall,
    Roland DuPree, Joe "Corky" Geil
Jivin' Jills: Dorothy Babb, Jane McNab,
    Jean McNab, Dolores Mitchell
Irving Bacon (Dr. Howard)
Leon Belasco (waiter)
Robert Emmett Keane (Peabody, the lawyer)
Lorin Raker (Dr. Bradshaw)
Jason Robards, Sr. (drunk)
Duke York (Louie)
Alphonse Martel (headwaiter)
Emmett Smith (porter)
Snowflake (valet)

"We looked like the Ritz Brothers in drag," one of the Andrews Sisters once said of their 1940-45 hitch in the Universal wars. The girls made fourteen movies during those tumultuous years (one of them for Warner Brothers—*Hollywood Canteen),*and while they—and not a few reviewers—have called these productions "embarrassing," the light-of-day truth is they afforded lively, tuneful, "escapist" relaxation for a war-frantic, movie-crazy nation.

The problem, if it can be called that, was Universal's ten-day assembly-line approach to filming musicals—requiring helter-skelter musical insertions, large segments of farce and an interwoven romantic complication, all of which was compressed into an hour or so of running time. (It was remarkable how much the studio was usually able to crowd into these true quickies.) Additionally, critics have tended to regard popular recording acts in films as fish out of water, the early Sinatra not excluded, which is another reason why the press was so resistant to the Andrews Sisters' pictures. Certain supercritical, less-than-gallant fourth-estaters also dwelled on the less-than-Lamarr looks of the Greek-Norwegian sisters. Archer Winsten, discussing one of their films in the New York *Post,* wrote that "The Andrews Sisters . . . get by on sound but are still short on sight."

Give Out, Sisters, often looked on by film historians as the definitive Andrews vehicle, is the specific case in point. Jam-packed with entertainment that sometimes hit, sometimes missed, it nevertheless was always in there trying. And the film successfully cheered moviegoers during that troubled period, making a bundle for a "B" and deserving somewhat better than it got from caustic critics of the day (who perhaps could not know they were witnessing a singing act that was to prove virtually unequalled in its day).

The tone of the reviews might better have been directed toward Hitler. For example: "In spite of the priority on rubber, Universal Pictures stretches a short subject into a feature-length film by the simple expedient of combining several variety acts with a slight and ineffectual plot," growled the New York *Herald*

The Andrews Sisters

Tribune. No quarter was given in the New York *Times,* either: "There is nothing quite as exasperating as a bad musical film, and Universal appears to have missed on all beats in making *Give Out, Sisters.* The Andrews Sisters haven't come up against such weak tunes in a long while."

To be sure, *Give Out, Sisters* could have been better, and more frequent use of this most distinctive, most gifted of all popular female vocal groups, would have improved the film. The plot, on its spastic sojourns from the trunk, was inane indeed, and the girls—who were, after all, the stars and the big draw—were off the screen for long stretches. But when they did appear, it was usually to sing in their irresistible, swingy, ultra-professional manner, so movie and recording fans, at least, were lenient.

For their opening number, the sisters warbled "The New Generation," a fitting ditty to usher in the bobby-sox age. Blonde Patty Andrews, the youngest of the trio and its personality girl, characteristically took the lead, saluting and strutting pertly in her almost satirically hepcat way, while a very young Peggy Ryan mugged in ecstasy on the sidelines. The setting was a Flamingo Club rehearsal where owner William Frawley (who may have read Archer Winsten in the *Post)* remarked to assistant Richard Davies, "The Andrews Sisters are all right, but you gotta put something around them." Messenger girl Ryan had just the thing: those talented kids at her dancing school (played by the Jivin' Jacks

and Jills—plus Donald O'Connor).

The school was run by Professor Woof (Charles Butterworth), whose slogan was "Let Woof Teach You to Hoof." He had come to the school to learn the conga, he groaned, and had been given the business—in more ways than one—by his partner, previous owner Walter Catlett. In financial straits, the establishment would benefit greatly from a booking for its students with the Andrews Sisters (who were cast as themselves). The hitch came in the shapely form of the group's featured dancer (Grace McDonald), an underage heiress whose show business aspirations were anathema to her three prim spinster aunts (Edith Barrett, Fay Helm, and Marie Blake—Jeanette MacDonald's sister and best-known then for her running switchboard-operator role in the Dr. Kildare film series at MGM). Grace McDonald was secretly seeing the club's bandleader (Dan Dailey, Jr.), too.

"You have aunts in your what?" asked Catlett when she phoned the school to inform them her aunts refused to let her perform in a nightclub.

Charles Butterworth, Edith Barrett, Marie Blake, Peggy Ryan, Fay Helm

Grace McDonald, Dan Dailey, Jr.

But Frawley had bought the act on the strength of McDonald's social-register status and ordered Butterworth and Catlett to get the aunts' permission, or else. Meanwhile, Aunt Barrett, surrounded by her sisters, took to her bed with fainting spells to keep McDonald from opening that night. Masquerading as a doctor, Butterworth came to examine Barrett.

"A-ha, your tongue is coated," he informed her gravely.

"What's it look like?" she wailed.

"Imitation mink."

When Frawley arrived at the aunts' home to obtain permission from the three fuddy-duddies for McDonald to dance at the Flamingo, the Andrews Sisters—who had sneaked into the parlor disguised (well, sort of) in long, old-fashioned dresses—met him and, popping up and down to converse from behind a large floral arrangement strategically placed across the room, gave their consent. Frawley bought it and left, but when the real doctor (Lorin Raker) showed up, the angry aunts bolted for the club. Once there, the old maids began to enjoy themselves, and wound up joining the Andrews Sisters, Grace McDonald, and the rest of the cast on the nightclub floor in a chaotic but rousing finale to "Pennsylvania Polka," one of the Andrews' biggest hits (New York Times, take note).

The sisters' other numbers included the sedate, lovely "You're Just a Flower from an Old Bouquet," rendered in a huge picture frame setting, with the girls—swaying in unison—dressed as white-wigged colonial ladies; and the more typical "Who Do You Think You're Fool-ing?" In the latter number, the sisters—their quirky "jive" gestures a "camp" feast—wore horizontal-striped gowns with gigantic shoulder pads, and Patty stepped forward to prance inimitably (sporting her usual, bad blonde dye job). In their spinster costumes, especially, the in-character Patty pinching her lips tightly while sisters Maxine ("the pretty one") and LaVerne (who always looked as if she were just glad to get out of the house) tried to restrain smiles, the girls each showed a developed sense of humor that indicated they were capable of playing more demanding comedy roles.

(In recent years, Maxine, at least, has softened her stand on their work in pictures, admitting, "But now when I see those movies I think, my God, those girls are good! My God, those girls move!" LaVerne died in 1967.)

The John Mattison choreography was a little awkward, but Dan Dailey, Jr.—five years before his first big success opposite Betty Grable in Mother Wore Tights— got in a few steps with Grace McDonald that showed they too were both up to more demanding turns. Peggy Ryan had a promising comedy moment or two, but Donald O'Connor, Ryan's partner in so many Universal musical comedies of the day (they were to be called "the budget Judy Garland and Mickey Rooney") and soon to become the studio's top male star, was, surprisingly, little more than an equally youthful chorus boy.

It was the Andrews Sisters audiences came to see. And when those sisters gave out, they were—to borrow an expression from another character in the wartime movie—worth their weight in rubber.

GOOD MORNING, JUDGE

(Universal Pictures, 1943)

Credits

Associate producer, Paul Malvern
Director, Jean Yarbrough
Screenplay, Maurice Geraghty, Warren Wilson
Original story, Geraghty, Winston Miller
Music director, Charles Previn
Songs, Everett Carter, Milton Rosen
Camera, John W. Boyle
Editor, Edward Curtiss
Running Time: 67 minutes

Cast

DENNIS O'KEEFE (Dave Burton)
LOUISE ALLBRITTON (Elizabeth Smith)
Mary Beth Hughes (Mira Bryon)
J. Carrol Naish (André Bouchard)
Louise Beavers (Cleo)
Samuel S. Hinds (J.P. Gordon)
Frank Faylen (Ben Pollard)
Ralph Peters (Harry Pollard)
Oscar O'Shea (magistrate)
William Forrest (Judge William Foster)
Marie Blake (Nicky Clark)
Don Barclay (Biscuit Face—Dodgers fan)
Murray Alper (Charlie Martin)
Eddie Acuff (cab driver)
Ruth Lee (Paula)
Lee Phelps (court clerk)
Phil Warren (orchestra leader)
Ruth Warren (Katie Bevins)
Billy Newell (bartender)
Edward Earle (Ducky Evans)
Harry Strang (bailiff)
Jack Rice (hotel clerk)
Eddie Coke (reporter)
Margaret Marquis (girl)
Rebel Randell (sunbather)
Albert Ray (Tommy Bevins)
Pierce Lyden (policeman)
Hal Craig (bailiff)
Billy Bletcher (voice of radio announcer)
Charles Sherlock (waiter)
Chief Red Robe (Indian dancer)
Harry S. Smith, a.k.a. Jay Silverheels,
    Ralph Lonewolf, Byron Topetchy (Indians)
Linda Ann Bieber (little Bevins girl)
William Edritt (headwaiter)
Virginia Engels (sunbather)
Cyril Ring (Elizabeth's escort)

Good Morning, Judge would not be worthy of inclusion in any anthology except for Dennis O'Keefe. Up from the extra ranks (where he was known as Bud Flanagan), O'Keefe was one of the most comedically adept leading men in pictures, and this silly and repetitious, yet—thanks to him—frequently amusing romantic comedy gave him plenty of opportunity to dip into his hefty bag of tricks.

O'Keefe appeared as a successful music publisher who was sued for plagiarism by attractive lawyer Louise Allbritton, representing songwriters Frank Faylen and Ralph Peters. They claimed that a current hit song published by O'Keefe and sung in a Broadway show by his ill-tempered girlfriend (Mary Beth Hughes) was not written by Murray Alper, as the sheet music read, but by them. It seemed that Faylen and Peters had played their tune under another title for O'Keefe, who had turned it down only to go around the office unconsciously whistling it. Alper then "wrote" the melody.

The script proceeded on the assumption that a good gag (in this case, even a bad one) was worth repeating, and repeating, and repeating. As O'Keefe set about his unusual dual labors of both discrediting Allbritton and winning her love, he was caught in a ladies' Turkish bath and stood before Judge Oscar O'Shea. On the last occasion he had appeared before the same Judge with, and because of, Allbritton and a black-eyed Hughes, who had fought over him in a nightclub. (Observing that it was "the same bunch again," O'Shea asked, "What is this, a stock company?")

Then, in a succession of circumstances that seemed like a long commercial for the knock-out-drops industry, O'Keefe saw Allbritton felled by the drops twice. "I'd like to ask for a pone-postment," she hazily requested when their case came to court, then O'Keefe himself was slipped the "Mickey Finn" (as they were called in those fun-loving days). In the final shot, J. Carrol Naish, the French waiter at O'Keefe's and Allbritton's favorite watering hole (and the place mostly responsible for the steady flow of spiked drinks), accidentally drank his own knockout potion and keeled over.

Frank Faylen, Ralph Peters, Louise Allbritton

Noel Coward might not have approved, but *Variety* did, reporting, "A compact little package of comedy-drama, with accent on familiar but brightened comedic situations that will carry it through the program houses as a good supporter for more serious fare . . . O'Keefe competently handles his assignment of the music publisher, with Miss Allbritton catching attention in her first light role as the femme attorney."

Actually, there were two leading ladies, both pretty, dimpled, capable blondes. Allbritton, who managed the not inconsiderable feat of being alluringly feminine in suits, neckties, and a firmly upswept pompadour, was the more appealing as the vulnerable Portia, showing evidence of the superior comedienne she would soon emerge as. It was she who got O'Keefe. Hughes, taking five from relentless badgering only to sing a couple of tunes ("Spellbound/ Darling with you, I'm wedding bell-bound"), was one of the many comely girls who merely drifted through Hollywood's Golden Age.

Louise Beavers played Allbritton's inevitable husky, dusky maid, and was, as always, an endearing actress. Today, however, the image she projected in this role (and in so many others) would offend some movie-goers. Finding Allbritton unable to get out of bed after O'Keefe's secretly administered knockout drops, Beavers exclaimed, "My, my, what a man!" Later, after advising career-oriented Allbritton not to let O'Keefe get away from her, she

was told, "Did it ever occur to you that some people might want something besides matrimony?" "Sure," sallied the one-track Beavers, "if it gets 'em a husband!"

It was O'Keefe—a master of the double take—who held the picture together, though. Presentable-looking as well as droll, he was not above disguising himself as a woman to get his laughs (and he got them), nor did he eschew pratfalls (although when he got to the stepping-on-the-stray-roller skate bit, he did not take the obvious tumble but rode it upright—helplessly, dazedly—across a living room). He was funny with a little girl (Linda Ann Bieber) sitting on his lap and force-feeding him jelly bread while he tried to talk business, and he was funny in an inventive throwaway flash in the health club elevator: as he came to the gymnasium floor, where he knew he should stop, he did some spastically rapid arm exercises as he quickly sped on to the sun roof.

His supreme moment was his take after being slipped the Mickey in a nightclub. Suddenly baring teeth like a cartoon kamikaze pilot, his

Oscar O'Shea, Louise Allbritton, Dennis O'Keefe, Samuel S. Hinds, Mary Beth Hughes

Mary Beth Hughes, Samuel S. Hinds

eyes bulging, he fell over backwards with a loud thud. You will look unsuccessfully for its shameless hilarity in today's movie comedies.

Good Morning, Judge probably would not have made it without Dennis O'Keefe. With him, it became the kind of film that made the double-feature a pleasurable, fondly recalled way of life in the forties.

HIT THE ROAD

(Universal Pictures, 1941)

Credits

Associate producer, Ken Goldsmith
Director, Joe May
Screenplay, Robert Lee Johnson,
    Brenda Weisberg
Original story, Johnson
Music director, H.J. Salter
Camera, Jerome Ash
Editor, Bernard Burton
Running Time: 62 minutes

Cast

GLADYS GEORGE (Molly Ryan)
BARTON MacLANE (James J. Ryan, alias
    Valentine)
Billy Halop (Tom)
Huntz Hall (Pig Grogan)
Gabriel Dell (String)
Bernard Punsley (Ape)
Bobs Watson (Pesty)
Evelyn Ankers (Patience Ryan)
Charles Lang (Paul Revere Smith)
Walter Kingsford (Col. Smith)
Eily Malyon (Cathy Crookshank)
Edward Pawley (Spike)
John Harmon (Creeper)
Jess Lee Brooks (Rufus)
Charles Moore (Martin)
Shemp Howard (Dingbat)
Charles Sullivan (Sullivan, the chauffeur)
Grace Hayle (Mrs. Hickridge, cut from the film)
Lee Moore (second guard)
Hally Chester (Trusty)
Kernan Cripps (guard)
Ernie Stanton (O'Brien, the first guard)

The Little Tough Guys, featured in Universal's *Hit the Road,* were spin-offs of the Dead End Kids, the gang of teenage New York hooligans who had clicked in both the Broadway and movie versions of Sidney Kingsley's *Dead End.* As the Dead End Kids, they worked at Warner Brothers for a while during the late thirties, then sub-divided to go to Monogram as the East Side Kids (and later as the Bowery Boys) and to Universal as the Little Tough Guys. By the time remaining members of the troupe quit playing kids in the late 1950s, they were all into middle age.

But in 1941's *Hit the Road,* the Little Tough Guys (Billy Halop, Huntz Hall, Gabriel Dell, Bernard Punsley) were still young and able to make their mild juvenile delinquent hijinks passably amusing. In this film, which had a better cast and critical reception than most, the boys were depicted as reform-school orphans whose gangster parents had been wiped out by opposing mob chief Edward Pawley. They seemed headed for the same fate as their parents, so their parole officer (Eily Malyon) put them in the custody of Barton MacLane, the boss of their late fathers' gang who was in jail when the other gang members were gunned down.

Returning to society from prison, MacLane was determined to go straight on the lavish stock farm he shared with wife Gladys George and carefully raised, knockout daughter Evelyn Ankers, whom he now saw for the first time in years. "You've done a great job," he told George. (His daughter had been raised so carefully she had an English accent.) With his four new, young responsibilities, MacLane also took on smaller "stray orphan" Bobs Watson. Rather overbearingly aware of his "cuteness" ("Call me Slugger!"), Master Watson was nevertheless a popular child actor noted for his ability to cry realistically on cue. "Got somethin' in my lamps," he alibied on one such waterworks exhibition.

Ankers was dating Charles Lang from the district attorney's office. Introduced to MacLane, Lang said he was glad to meet him at last,

Huntz Hall, Billy Halop, Bobs Watson, Gladys George, Evelyn Ankers

adding, "I've been marking the days off on my calendar."

Replied MacLane, "Yeah, I've been doin' the same myself."

At first, the fractious boys showed no signs of rehabilitating. Tough dame supreme Gladys George, despite her new "refinement," was still able to speak their language, though, and keep them in line as much as possible. In addition, the actress *was* top-billed. When one of the youngsters tauntingly called from his doorway for her to tuck him in or he couldn't sleep, she barked, "I'll put you to sleep out here in the hallway if you don't get in that bed right now!" Later, she advised ringleader Billy Halop, "You've got a swell chance to steer your mob right. Don't muff it!"

Edward Pawley and his two henchmen (Shemp Howard and John Harmon) resurfaced to steal $50,000 George had raised to build a trade school for underprivileged youths similar to her charges, taking over MacLane's home "till the heat's off." Parole officer Malyon then showed up to check on the boys' progress, starting a free-for-all in which everybody—the boys, George, Ankers, game old girl Malyon—helped overcome Pawley and his thugs.

"You all right, kid?" Gladys George asked one of the lads after the fracas.

"I hope I am," moaned the elderly, grey-haired, stern-visaged Eily Malyon, struggling to her feet.

Joe May, a pioneer director in Germany, kept things perking, and the unsubtle doings diverted the family trade. As for the Little Tough Guys, their roistering ways often resembled the Three Stooges' physically abusive style of humor as they endlessly punched one another. Halop's continual belting of dimwitted Huntz Hall, in particular, had unintentionally sadistic overtones.

Everything considered, William Boehnel of the New York *World Telegram* was more than fair when he wrote: "Although the theme is old, the treatment is fresh and inventive, and so *Hit the Road* is one of the best of the Dead End Kids [sic] series. Chief credit for this should go, I imagine, to director Joe May, who has rearranged familiar material in such a sprightly and entertaining manner that it has all the earmarks of new stuff . . . [The Little Tough Guys'] antics are inventively amusing and their lines are frequently very funny. The adults in the cast include Gladys George, Barton MacLane and Evelyn Ankers, an attractive blonde recruit from London by way of Broadway. They are all first-rate."

Barton MacLane, Edward Pawley, Billy Halop, Bobs Watson, Bernard Punsley, Gabriel Dell, Huntz Hall, Gladys George, John Harmon, Evelyn Ankers, Shemp Howard

Charles Lang, Evelyn Ankers

I'M NOBODY'S SWEETHEART NOW

(Universal Pictures, 1940)

Credits

Associate producer, Joseph Sanford
Director, Arthur Lubin
Screenplay, Scott Darling, Erna Lazarus,
　Hal Block
Original story, Darling, Lazarus
Music director, Charles Previn
Art director, Jack Otterson
Camera, Elwood Bredell
Editor, Paul Landres
Running Time: 63 minutes

Cast

DENNIS O'KEEFE (Tod Lowell)
CONSTANCE MOORE (Betty Gilbert)
Helen Parrish (Trudie Morgan)
Lewis Howard (Andy Manson)
Berton Churchill (Sen. Henry Lowell)
Laura Hope Crews (Mrs. Lowell)
Samuel S. Hinds (George P. Morgan)
Marjorie Gateson (Mrs. Morgan)
Margaret Hamilton (Mrs. Thriffle)
Clarence Muse (Flowery, cut from film)
Tim Ryan (Judge Saunders)
Walter Soderling (Abner Thriffle)
Walter Baldwin (Elmer)
Rex Evans (Parkins, the butler)
Gaylord (Steve) Pendleton (Chuck)
Hattie Noel (Bedelia)
Gene O'Donnell (Eddie)
James Craig (Ray)
Lee Phelps (Mac, the guard)
Max Wagner (motorcycle officer)
Dorothy Moore (Elsie)
Harry Depp (judge)
Harry Strang (Harry, the waiter)
Alphonse Martel (headwaiter)
Clara Blore (fat woman)
José and Antonita de Franco (The Cansinos)

114

As the forties commenced, Universal was having much box office success with a series of low-budget quasi-musicals titled after hit songs. A bouncier entry than most was *I'm Nobody's Sweetheart Now,* thanks in no small measure to gorgeous, gifted Constance Moore, who not only sang the title tune but, at finale time, more or less enacted it as well.

Rival football quarterbacks Dennis O'Keefe, of Southern State, and Lewis Howard, of Northern U, got things off to a prophetic start when one of their periodic brawls landed them in jail. (As Judge Tim Ryan forced them to shake hands, their unenthusiastic grasp dissolved on camera into a large fish.) O'Keefe, whose senator father (Berton Churchill) was expected to be a candidate for governor of California at the next election, was going steady with Moore, a nightclub singer. His ambitious mother (Laura Hope Crews) objected to Moore, however, pushing Helen Parrish, the daughter of politically influential San Franciscan Samuel S. Hinds and Marjorie Gateson.

Meanwhile, Parrish had been seeing some-one her parents thought unsuitable. Forced to go out with O'Keefe while she and her family visited his Los Angeles home, she phoned her boyfriend and told him to bump into them while they were out at a nightclub that evening. Naturally, the rendezvous turned out to be Constance Moore's club and naturally Parrish's boyfriend turned out to be O'Keefe's football-playing archenemy, Lewis Howard.

When the smoke cleared, Parrish suggested that she and O'Keefe pretend to like each other, and, once out of their parents' sight, they could switch dates. Before long, O'Keefe and Parrish really began falling in love, and Moore, furious, prodded Howard into immediately eloping with Parrish. Waking a country justice of the peace (Walter Soderling) in the middle of the night, Howard was rebuked by Soderling's angry wife (Margaret Hamilton) who was resplendent in bathrobe and braids.

"Can't you get the justice to marry us?" he implored.

"Oh, all right," Hamilton finally relented, "but just this once."

Berton Churchill, Samuel S. Hinds, Helen Parrish,
Dennis O'Keefe, Laura Hope Crews, Marjorie
Gateson

When they didn't go right in the house, she asked what was keeping them. Parrish called back that she just wanted to be sure he could give her security.

"You take much longer and he'll give you *social* security," warned Hamilton.

The marriage did not come off, and O'Keefe and Moore caught up with them. When O'Keefe brought Parrish home at daylight, their parents assumed they were engaged and started plans for a wedding in two weeks. Moore, in the throes of another brainstorm, told them to go along with the wedding preparations, but at the last minute Parrish should elope with Howard. This, reasoned Moore, refusing to be vanquished, would get them all out of their jam and oblige Parrish's father to back the jilted O'Keefe's father for governor. But O'Keefe and Parrish now loved each other, and when the time came they went through with the ceremony, leaving the enraged Moore with a consoling wealthy sugar daddy waiting in the wings.

Although farce predominated, there was a sprinkling of tunes vivaciously sold by Moore. Especially noteworthy was her snappy, suggestive (for 1940) rendition of "Nobody's Sweetheart," waving that "bird of paradise" right under the haughty noses of the ringside families of O'Keefe and Parrish. An actress used to playing types that were more refined, Moore's performance—replete with double takes and temper tantrums—displayed unusual verve. She was among the loveliest, most talented of the forties heroines and went on to appear in Rodgers' and Hart's *By Jupiter* on Broadway and in other more important films. Like so many during this lush Hollywood period, however, she never achieved the recognition that she deserved.

Certainly the critics liked her. Especially the Hollywood *Reporter*'s man who, after calling *Nobody's Sweetheart* "a gay little musical," went on to write, with some foresight, "It has a top cast, for a budget show, has a better story than most musicals and a couple of good tunes that are certain to make the Hit Parade. The hit of the show, so far as this reviewer goes, was Constance Moore. 'Connie' looked great, gave a standout performance, in addition to tossing out a couple of song numbers that surprised even her greatest admirers. All she needs now is to be compelled to go to New York and register a hit in a stage musical to send her to the top here in one of the studios, for that seems to be the regular procedure today, as Hollywood doesn't like to pick names out of its own studio lists."

Dennis O'Keefe was the farceur extraor-

Constance Moore

Constance Moore, Lewis Howard, Helen Parrish, Dennis O'Keefe

dinaire. Some of his bits here remain in the memory: O'Keefe regaining consciousness in jail and, still groggily fighting the fight that put him there, putting up his dukes and falling out of his bunk . . . coming to life in a portrait held in Constance Moore's very hot hands and shrugging sheepishly . . . sprinting about the dance floor with Helen Parrish in his arms as he tried, unsuccessfully, to avoid the jealous Moore, who kept dancing by O'Keefe with Lewis Howard and kicking him.

Of the rest, Laura Hope Crews' flighty mother ("I did *so* want to be Mrs. Governor!")

and Margaret Hamilton's hatchet-faced yokel got the most laughs. Both had just finished two of the biggest and best movies ever made—Crews, *Gone with the Wind* (as Aunt Pittypat), and Hamilton, *The Wizard of Oz* (as the Witch).

A jarringly violent final set-to between the two male principals (Howard threw a rock through O'Keefe's car window, causing an accident) did not dispel the prevailing sense of fun. Well paced by director Arthur Lubin, *I'm Nobody's Sweetheart Now* proved itself to be the antithesis of its title: one of Universal's more popular "B"s.

Margaret Hamilton, Helen Parrish, Lewis Howard

THE MAD GHOUL

(Universal Pictures, 1943)

Credits

Associate producer, Ben Pivar
Director, James Hogan
Screenplay, Brenda Weisberg, Paul Gangolin
Original story, Hans Kraly
Camera, Milton Krasner
Editor, Milton Carruth
Running Time: 64 minutes

Cast

DAVID BRUCE (Ted Allison)
EVELYN ANKERS (Isabel Lewis)
GEORGE ZUCCO (Dr. Alfred Morris)
Robert Armstrong (Ken McClure)
Turhan Bey (Eric Iverson)
Millburn Stone (Sgt. Macklin)
Andrew Tombes (Eagan)
Rose Hobart (Della)
Addison Richards (Gavigan)
Charles McGraw (Detective Garrity)
Gus Glassmire (caretaker)
Gene O'Connell (radio announcer)
Isabelle Lamal (maid)
Lew Kelly (stagehand)
William Ruhl (stagehand)
Hans Herbert (attendant)
Bess Flowers, Cyril Ring (extras in audience)
The voice of Lillian Cornell (Evelyn
    Ankers's vocals)

George Zucco practically patented the mad doctor role in movies, but Universal's *The Mad Ghoul* offered him, if not an innovative plot, at least one with more impressive production values and cast than he was used to. The results were worth an easy three-and-a-half screams on the fright meter.

As a university professor and scientist, the middle-aged Zucco became obsessed with re-discovering a life-preserving process used by ancient Egyptians that involved gaseous vapors and a human heart substance. He was also in love with young Evelyn Ankers, the concert singer girlfriend of David Bruce, his student assistant. When Zucco had her alone one evening, he hinted that she ought to consider, instead, "a man who knows the book of life and could teach you how to read it."

When Bruce informed Zucco that he planned to ask Ankers to marry him, the professor tried out his experiment on Bruce, turning him into a shuffling, mindless zombie who had to cut out the heart of a recently deceased corpse to stay alive. Bruce then apparently reverted to his normal self, but later something else malfunctioned, and he was obliged to obtain more human hearts, often murdering to do so.

Ankers fell in love with her piano accompanist (Turhan Bey), and Zucco sent Bruce—always unaware afterward of his dark deeds—to kill Bey in an alley one night. Seeing his shadow, Ankers screamed and frightened him off. More killings. Then newspaper music critic Rose Hobart pointed out to crime reporter Robert Armstrong that Ankers had been concertizing in the same towns where the murders had been committed, "only she's been tearing their hearts out with music." Armstrong set out to trap the killer, but was himself killed while pretending to be dead in a coffin.

Eventually, Bruce realized what he had become. Zucco, following an altercation with his horrified human guinea pig, inadvertently inhaled the tragically altering gas. Whereupon

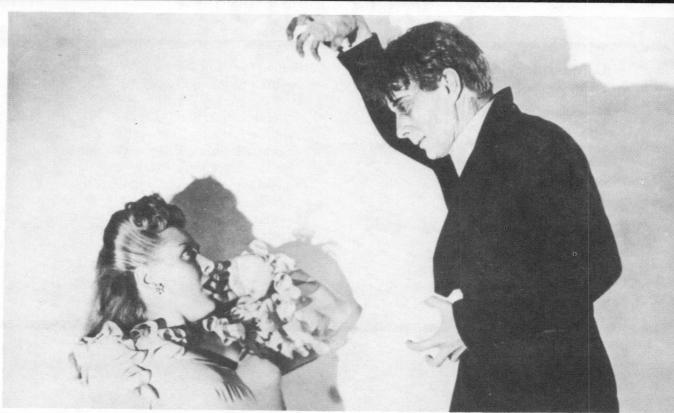

Evelyn Ankers, David Bruce

Bruce, who had been programmed again to kill Bey, ignored Zucco's pleas for help and stalked on stage during an Ankers-Bey recital. After she rendered a couple of her inimitable screams, Bruce was shot dead by the police. At the same time, the now desperate, berserk Zucco, turning into a mummy-like ghoul himself, died trying to dig up a body in the graveyard.

The courtly Zucco was, as always, flamboyantly, licentiously impeccable in his odious schemes, and young David Bruce, serious, heavy-lidded and seemingly sallow-complected even before the transformation, was a good choice for the unwilling monster. The camera-work was especially vivid: Bruce's murder instrument, a scalpel, glistening as he set about his evil business . . . artfully angled shadows on Bruce's odd juvenile's face creating as much eerie effect as the black eye make-up, the pasty complexion, the disheveled hair.

Evelyn Ankers, brightly well-lit, possessed such a stately yet warm human beauty that it must have taken no little imagination on the part of Hollywood producers to see her consigned to horror films. An incentive in this assignment was the rare opportunity to exercise her protean vocal chords not only in shriek but song. At the last minute, however, there was no time for her to record the numbers, "I Dreamt I Dwelt in Marble Halls" and "All for Love," and the studio dubbed her musical sequences with library recordings by Lillian Cornell. The unctuously exotic Turhan Bey, on the threshold of a

brief vogue (next year he would be Katharine Hepburn's leading man in *Dragon Seed),* sufficed as Ankers' amour.

And there was the predictably professional support from Robert Armstrong, who evidently hadn't learned anything from his encounter with King Kong ten years earlier. To paraphrase Armstrong's famous tagline from that classic picture, it wasn't duty that killed the reporter, it was the beast. Plus, hardies Rose Hobart, Millburn Stone as a police sergeant, Charles McGraw as a detective, and the reliably chuckle-some Andrew Tombes, appropriately (considering his surname) cast as a mortician of questionable sincerity. "For goodness sake, whatever you do, don't mar the coffin," Tombes exhorted Armstrong as he crawled into the bier to capture the mad ghoul.

A sad and rather ironic footnote: David Bruce, just hired to make his film comeback after many years out of the business, died in 1976—of a heart attack.

David Bruce, George Zucco, Gus Glassmire (on ground)

David Bruce, Millburn Stone, Turhan Bey, Evelyn Ankers

THE MAN IN HALF-MOON STREET

(Paramount Pictures, 1944)

Credits

Producer, Walter MacEwen
Director, Ralph Murphy
Screenplay, Charles Kenyon
Adaptation, Garrett Fort
Based on the play by Barré Lyndon
Music score, Miklos Rozsa
Camera, Henry Sharp
Editor, Tom Neff
Running Time: 92 minutes

Cast

NILS ASTHER (Julian Karell)
HELEN WALKER (Eve Brandon)
Reinhold Schunzel (Dr. Kurt Van Bruecken)
Paul Cavanagh (Dr. Henry Latimer)
Edmond Breon (Sir Humphrey Brandon)
Morton Lowry (Allen Guthrie)
Matthew Boulton (Insp. Garth)
Brandon Hurst (Simpson, Julian's butler)
Aminta Dyne (Lady Minerva Aldergate)
Arthur Mulliner (Sir John Aldergate)
Edward Fielding (Col. Ashley)
Reginald Sheffield (Mr. Taper, the art critic)
Eustace Wyatt (Insp. Lawson)
Forrester Harvey (Harris, a cabby)
Konstantin Shayne (Dr. Vishanoff)
Gerald Oliver Smith (clerk)
Leyland Hodgson (Dr. Albertson)
Harry Cording (first bobby)
Clive Morgan (plainclothesman)
Arthur Blake (man)
Ernie Adams (porter)
Norman Ainsley (butler)
Edward Cooper (liveried servant)
John Sheehan (expressman)
Frank Baker (plainclothesman)
T. Arthur Hughes (second plainclothesman)
Frank Moran (skipper)
John Power (guard)
Don Gallaher (ticket agent)
Bob Stevenson (guard)
Bobby Hale (deck hand)
Cy Ring (O'Hara, a plainclothesman)
Wilson Benge (official)
George Broughton (morgue official)
Robert Cory, Frank Hagney, Al
   Ferguson (bobbies)

Perhaps more than any other mad-doctor horror film of its time, Paramount's *The Man in Half-Moon Street* had a pervading sophisticated intelligence and sense of tragedy that allowed it ultimately to transcend the genre and become a haunting, moving personal drama.

Nils Asther, Swedish-born matinée idol of the silent-film days, had his best role in years as the London scientist who became engaged to young socialite Helen Walker after painting her portrait. The audience soon learned that while he looked thirty-five he was really over ninety years of age. For more than sixty years Asther, with noted endocrinologist friend Reinhold Schunzel performing the actual operations, had been transplanting rejuvenating glands into his own system at ten-year intervals. Unfortunately, the half-dozen young medical students from whom he took the glands all died.

Now, the latest decade was closing and Asther sent to the Continent for Schunzel. Meanwhile, in preparation for the operation, Asther retrieved from the river a despondent medical student (Morton Lowry) whom he took home.

An enfeebled and palsied Schunzel arrived—no longer able to perform the transplant. Furthermore, he begged Asther not to go on with their experiment: "It seems as though all we are fated to learn we know already." Asther had strayed from their original intent of benefiting mankind, however, and was determined to continue the transplants mainly to preserve his youthful appearance.

He searched for a discredited doctor to perform the operation, arousing the suspicion of Paul Cavanagh, Helen Walker's ex-boyfriend, who alerted Scotland Yard. Then young Lowry died of Asther-administered drugs. After they traced him to Asther's house, it wasn't long before the police learned, to their astonishment, that Asther was really the infamous Breslau doctor whose chain of killings had begun in the previous century.

"We are not scientists anymore. We are murderers," Schunzel continued, remorseful as he neared his own end.

The idealistic Walker never wavered in her devotion, although Asther only told her that his

Helen Walker, Nils Asther

mysterious work concerned holding back the aging of the human body. "I'll share your madness because there's grandeur in it," she assured him. "And I have faith—and love." As they were preparing to elope to Paris, where he had lined up a doctor to effect the transplant, Asther suddenly began to grow old and, running from Walker, fell dead on the train platform—a white-haired old man.

Based on the play by Barré Lyndon and directed by Ralph Murphy with unusual restraint and sensitivity, *The Man in Half-Moon Street* contained several scenes that, appropriately, have hardly aged after more than three decades and still seem fresh and vital.

One vivid early confrontation gave viewers their first inkling that there was something strange about Asther. It took place at the party for the unveiling of his portrait of Walker at her house. He was introduced to venerable, stout, titled Englishwoman Aminta Dyne, who remarked that he was "the spitting image of Julian LeStrange," whom she had known intimately many years ago—"Ah, those Shanghai nights!" Asther proceeded to give her a detailed account of their affair. She paled. "You tell it as if . . ." He extricated himself by saying that his grandfather's memory in his old age had been "embarrassingly accurate."

Then there was the reunion of lifelong friends Asther and Schunzel after ten years, to outward appearances Schunzel a doddering nonagenarian, Asther a virile man in his prime. Showing him a photo of them together as youthful blades, Schunzel sighed, "We were young then." Corrected Asther, "I'm *still* young."

Effective, too, was Asther's interview with Konstantin Shayne, a discredited, once famous European doctor reduced to working as a masseur. Asther tried to get Shayne to perform the youth-preserving gland transplant, but the declining, elderly medico explained that his ethics were not in such a poor state as that.

The scene in which Scotland Yard inspector Matthew Boulton unsuccessfully searched Asther's house for the body of medical student Lowry had a startling payoff: after Asther coolly saw the momentarily placated inspector to a foggy street corner, Asther returned to his car in front of the Half-Moon Street house in which Lowry's body was propped up behind the steering wheel, staring straight ahead.

The best scene of all was the final one between Asther and Walker on the train in Victoria Station. It recalled the fantastic moment in *Lost Horizon* (1937) wherein actress Margo, although warned that she would age

Edmond Breon, Helen Walker, Nils Asther, Paul Cavanagh

Nils Asther, Helen Walker

drastically if she left the mystical, utopian Shangri-La, departed and soon shriveled into an old hag; yet this newer version was much more moving than even that unforgettable sequence. Weakening, Asther pulled down the compartment shades and, turning away from Walker, asked her for a glass of water. When she left, his face—in a superior close-up bit of special-effects photography and make-up—began to age. When she returned, Walker sensed something amiss and took his hand, which she felt wither as she held it. Then she saw his wrinkled face. He revealed how lonely he had been through the many years until he met her. "I'll always be with you," she answered. "Dreams can't die—or love." He got up to leave, and a crooked old man lurched out of their compartment, ran a few steps on the platform and dropped dead. As a crowd gathered around the body, Walker stepped from the compartment and walked in the opposite direction. "Aren't you going, miss?" asked a conductor. "Sometime," she replied.

It was a superb ending to a tale keynoted by taste and thoughtful discourse on life and death and the ethics of man. Cheap shock tactics were taboo, and when the film's occasionally static verbosity betrayed its stage origin, it was, at least, far more meaningful dialogue than was to be found in the usual "Quick-Igor-the-shovel" horror quickie. The production was indeed, as Alton Cook wrote in the New York *World Telegram,* "a comparatively adult version of the mad scientist melodrama lifted high above average by a good cast, substantial and handsome settings and a literate script."

So sturdy was the plot that it was remade in color by Britain's Hammer Films in 1959 as *The Man Who Could Cheat Death,* with Anton Diffring and Hazel Court. The locale was switched to Paris and the protagonist's address became 13 Rue Noire. With actor Diffring striking hammy poses in the lead, the remake proved a vulgar imitation of the original.

Nils Asther, with his classic, dark good looks, smoothly designing European manner, and unique Swedish-British accent, made the desperate doctor validly ruthless but—while not quite sympathetic—somehow pitiable. Audiences almost rooted for him to consummate his "dream," even if it had become essentially the rather less-grand scheme of making off with the girl. *The Man in Half-Moon Street* should have given the veteran leading man a whole new career, yet, sadly, did not—probably because of his vehicle's "B" status.

Part of the tolerance engendered by his character was no doubt due to lovely Helen Walker's staunch loyalty opposite him. If her accent was more Boston than Blighty, she nonetheless showed again that she was one of the forties' most beguiling heroines, skilled in either comedy (*Murder, He Says*) or drama (*Nightmare Alley*). Important stardom always eluded her, though, and she died of cancer in 1968 after more than a decade off the screen and a life of great personal tragedy. She was only in her late forties.

Among the supporting players, Reinhold Schunzel scored as the conscience-stricken old doctor. In addition, the soigné, unobtrusive dignity of dependable Paul Cavanagh, as Walker's jilted beau, taken for granted by that decade's moviegoers, seems almost refreshing when viewed in these jeans-oriented days.

The Man in Half-Moon Street remains proof that the oft-disparaged horror genre can be just as creative as any other area of filmmaking. Or it could be, one long-ago foggy night in Half-Moon Street.

THE MASK OF DIIJON

(Producers Releasing Corporation, 1946)

Credits

Producers, Max Alexander, Alfred Stern
Director, Lew Landers
Screenplay, Arthur St. Claire, Griffin Jay
Original story, St. Claire
Music, Lee Zahler
Camera, Jack Greenhalgh
Editor, Roy Livingston
Running Time: 73 minutes

Cast

ERICH VON STROHEIM (Diijon)
JEANNE BATES (Victoria)
William Wright (Tony Holiday)
Edward Van Sloan (Sheffield)
Mauritz Hugo (Danton)
Denise Vernac (Denise)
Robert Malcolm (Fleming)
Hope Landin (Mrs. McGaffey)
Shimen Ruskin (Guzzo)
Roy Darmour (Mark Lindsay)
Antonio Filauri (Alex)

Erich von Stroheim was one of the authentic artists of the cinema, the director-scenarist of *Greed* (1924), which was notoriously cut to one-fourth its intended length by the studio (Metro-Goldwyn-Mayer) and yet survived as a great film. Accused of being difficult, extravagant, and decadent, his name eventually became anathema to Hollywood producers. By the 1940s he was reduced to spoofing his own intimidating Prussian image in the Broadway farce *Arsenic and Old Lace,* in supporting roles in sparse "A" films such as *Five Graves to Cairo,* and in starring parts in quickies like *The Mask of Diijon.* He had a brief resurgence when he played Gloria Swanson's butler/ex-husband in *Sunset Boulevard* (1950). He died penniless in 1957.

The Mask of Diijon, made at PRC, a definitive poverty-row studio, was a melodrama about a maniacal magician (von Stroheim) which was presented with a flair uncharacteristic of its lowly station. This suggests that von Stroheim, although credited only as the star, also advised in other areas of the production, for its underbelly show business milieu was the sort that would interest the cynical and by then thoroughly disillusioned von Stroheim.

The theatrical boarding house of the plot was inhabited not by Busby Berkeley bunnies who tapped their way to stardom overnight, nor even by catty females who cracked worldly wise but remained optimistic. These were second-rate (at best), generally hopeless acts obliged to work in minor clubs like the Romany Gardens, where the owner (Antonio Filauri), fat and far from the sleek stereotype in white dinner jacket, lolled around a cluttered backstage in his undershirt. For once, tacky poverty-row sets looked appropriate. When pianist William Wright, part of the triangle involving the middle-aged von Stroheim and his sweet young wife (Jeanne Bates), advised singer Bates that an important agent would be out front that night, somehow nobody—Bates included—really seemed to believe it.

The opening scene set a properly bizarre, ironic mood. Bates, in period costume, was guillotined, while von Stroheim, in close-up,

Erich von Stroheim, Edward Van Sloan

watched with characteristic dispassion. Suddenly her head in the basket smiled and winked. It was an illusion that she and magic store proprietor Edward Van Sloan, a neighbor, had devised to inspire her husband, a once famous vaudeville magician, to return to work.

"I've outgrown all that hocus-pocus," von Stroheim told her disdainfully, calling her "stupid." He said that he was spending his time studying something much more significant: "the power of the mind"—hypnosis.

Wright, who had known Bates before her marriage and was her own age (although some of the matured actor's close-ups refuted this), moved back into Hope Landin's New York (presumably) boarding house to work at the nearby Romany Gardens. Their rent past due, Bates convinced von Stroheim to take a job there, also. On opening night when he had his wife suspended rigidly over two chairs in a trance, she suddenly fell to the nightclub floor in a well-staged scene effected with unexpected, clumsy realism. Certain Wright had caused the mishap (although it was actually his own recent lack of practice), von Stroheim accused them of having an affair. Bates moved in with a girlfriend.

Now homicidally insane, von Stroheim used his perfected hypnotic powers to make boarding-house resident Mauritz Hugo, a dancer, commit suicide.

Bates, having obtained a solo spot at the Gardens, was singing the ballad "White Roses" when she spotted von Stroheim sitting at a table; intuitively frightened, she stepped back out of the spotlight to finish the number in enveloping shadows. Afterward, von Stroheim hypnotized her, instructing her to kill Wright. While rendering the Dietrichesque song "Disillusion" at the club, she turned toward piano accompanist Wright and said with a startling, alien hardness, "You'd better play 'Hearts and Flowers' because I'm going to kill you." She fired several shots at him, but she had taken the wrong gun and the bullets were only blanks.

(Evidently the writers didn't know—or were merely exercising poetic license—that people under hypnosis are supposed to be incapable of doing anything they would not do when conscious.)

The police trapped von Stroheim in the basement magic shop at the boarding house, where, overcome by tear gas (on one of the few occasions when an actor really seemed to be choking from this device), he fell (rather predictably and not totally convincingly) under the guillotine his wife had helped create for an act. A crouching, astonishingly dexterous cat then

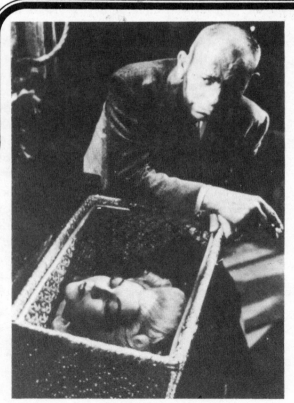

Denise Vernac, Edward Van Sloan, Erich von Stroheim

Jeanne Bates, Erich von Stroheim

George Zucco, Turhan Bey, Evelyn Ankers

stood on hind legs to unfasten the cord that sent the blade crashing down on von Stroheim.

It was a dark little story, figuratively and literally, in which practically no sunlight appeared; and every now and then—although prolific journeyman director Lew Landers had directorial credit—the master's touch seemed apparent. At one point, the audience was informed that the crazed prestidigitator had departed into the night simply by a hallway fern gently waving in the breeze from the opening door. What such a shot meant in terms of narrative may be debatable, but it and its ilk showed that someone—most likely von Stroheim—was striving for an original way of doing things.

Alas, von Stroheim was out of fashion, and PRC was never *in* fashion, so it took no feat of magic to predict reviews such as the New York *Daily News':* "Erich von Stroheim's *Mask of Diijon* is about the poorest excuse for a thriller that has come along in ages. It's slow, obvious and crudely put together, a dull account of a magician gone mad."

All repressed malice and sidelong glances (when not outright burning glares), von Stroheim's stolidity limited him as an actor; yet he was a commanding, unique presence. He gave the otherwise meretricious doings a distinction few others could match.

His co-players were less successful. In a role perhaps even more difficult than von Stroheim's, Jeanne Bates, a recent Columbia starlet, was adequate until she lapsed into her hypnotic trance, which she played mainly in a clichéd, robot-like monotone. Disturbing, too, was Hope Landin's caricatured, Irish landlady— "It's a good strong cuppa coffee I'll be getting you right away," etc., etc. Denise Vernac, von Stroheim's European-born companion during his last years, appeared to no advantage as a dancer-resident at his address who cast aside husband-partner Mauritz Hugo. "That's show business," shrugged Hugo in one of the earliest, bitterest employments of that now-popular saying.

When the dramatic black-caped Erich von Stroheim stalked out of the shadows, however, *The Mask of Diijon* seized one's attention and almost all was forgiven.

MEXICAN SPITFIRE'S ELEPHANT

(RKO Radio Pictures, 1942)

Credits
Producer, Bert Gilroy
Director, Leslie Goodwins
Screenplay, Charles E. Roberts
Original story, Goodwins, Roberts
Music director, C. Bakaleinikoff
Camera, Jack Mackenzie
Editor, Harry Marker
Running Time: 64 minutes

Cast
LUPE VELEZ (Carmelita Lindsay)
LEON ERROL (Lord Basil Epping/
    Uncle Matt Lindsay)
Walter Reed (Dennis Lindsay)
Elizabeth Risdon (Aunt Della Lindsay)
Lydia Bilbrook (Lady Ada Epping)
Marion Martin (Diana)
Lyle Talbot (Reddy)
Luis Alberni (Luigi)
George Cleveland (Chief inspector)
Marten Lamont (Arnold)
Jack Briggs (Lewis)
Arnold Kent (Don José Alamos)
Max Wagner (headwaiter)
Keye Luke (Lao Lee, Chinese magician)
Tom Kennedy (Joe, café bartender)
Neely Edwards (ship bartender)
Harry Harvey (ship steward)
Lloyd Ingraham (stage doorman)
Jack Arnold, a.k.a. Vinton Haworth
    (hotel manager)
Don Barclay (Mr. Smith)
Ann Summers (Lindsay's maid)
Mary Stuart (maid)
Ronnie Rondell (MC)

One of the leading comic sights of the forties was Leon Errol in his masquerade as the stuffy British Lord Epping, hunching his shoulders and, with his inimitable stiff, bowlegged walk, doddering to the bar for "a spot."

Australian-born Errol modeled the character after a British uncle of his. He went into this routine, and variations on it, in virtually all of RKO's popular Mexican Spitfire series, which began in 1939 and ended, eight pictures later, in 1943. Lupe Velez had the title role. She played a fiery, sometimes bombastic Mexican girl named Carmelita who married an American, Dennis Lindsay (Walter Reed), and constantly got into scrapes with him, his henpecked Uncle Matt (Errol), and his snobbish Aunt Della (Elizabeth Risdon), who disapproved of the union.

Somewhere in all of the films, for purposes of plot, Errol—donning spectacles, toupé, and bushy mustache—impersonated his look-alike, Lord Epping, who, with his wife (Lydia Bilbrook), constantly visited the Mexican Spitfire's in-laws. The in-and-out-of-disguise com-ings-and-goings of the uncle-Epping characters could get confusing, and Errol, the consummate comedian, was aware that the audience might be puzzled. Thus he usually managed to indicate character differentiation when he was portraying the uncle in Epping drag by acting slightly less British, more mystified and quizzical.

Leslie Goodwins was the director on all the Spitfire films, and he kept the farcical activities zipping along.

Mexican Spitfire's Elephant was typical of the series. The pachyderm of the title was a small glass figurine that contained a stolen precious gem. On board a ship heading for the United States, smugglers Lyle Talbot and Marion Martin spotted Errol's English lord character and decided to plant it on him to avoid the customs inspection.

Martin found him at the ship's bar, telling bartender Neely Edwards a tall story. "I was completely overcome by the white goddess," we heard Errol say.

"What did you do?" asked the bartender.

"Why, what would you do? Quick as a flash I

Leon Errol, Lupe Velez, Don Barclay, Luis Alberni

whipped out—."

The statuesque, incredibly platinum Martin interrupted him, perhaps just in time. She gave Errol the little elephant ostensibly as a token of her friendship, secretly planning to retrieve it after the ship docked. But Errol misplaced it, setting off a series of misunderstandings and mix-ups as the crooks tried to get back the elephant.

Errol's lord and his lady (Lydia Bilbrook) were in the United States to assist Elizabeth Risdon with her war-relief drive, and in short order Mexican Spitfire Velez, husband Reed, and Uncle Errol were all deeply involved in intrigue over possession of the figurine. At one point, Velez even led a spotted pink live elephant into a nightclub scene in the mistaken impression that the beast was the bone of contention. As always, it was Velez, too, who got Uncle Errol to disguise himself as the British lord: "Remember that time you put on a goat face like Lord Epping, and you look more like heem than he do?"

Inevitably there came the moment—after a dizzying series of entrances and exits by the "two" Errols—when Risdon, the uncle's wife, realized that her husband was masquerading as the titled Briton. In this case, it was in Luis Alberni's café where Velez, after a fight with husband Reed, had taken a job as a singer-dancer. Risdon described his lordship to Alberni as "a little runt" who had been annoying the women there and should be thrown out. Also inevitably, Alberni threw out the real lord, whom the livid Risdon then pushed into a gutter full of water. When she saw her husband standing nearby on the sidewalk, she fainted.

Later, after the crooks were taken into custody, Uncle Errol, masquerading as Epping again and this time fooling wife Risdon, said he'd forgive her for pushing him into the water if she'd give him "a little kiss." Horrified at first, she then realized it was her husband and chased him around the club. When she caught him, yet another switch had taken place, and it was actually his lordship whom she unwittingly thrashed.

Although given top-billing and spotted in a couple of musical numbers, the explosive, very loud Velez, as usual, acted as a foil for Errol. Her characteristic malapropisms ("artificial perspiration" and so forth) were being done more artfully by Carmen Miranda at 20th-Century Fox, but Velez attacked her role with zest. Errol was wonderful. Of *Mexican Spitfire's Elephant*, *Variety* wrote: "Latest in the Lupe Velez-Leon Errol Mexican Spitfire series is solid laugh enter-

Marion Martin, Lyle Talbot, Leon Errol

Leon Errol, Max Wagner, Luis Alberni, Elizabeth Risdon

tainment and best of the group . . . Errol catches the spotlight with another dual characterization of Uncle Matt and Lord Epping. [His] timing and delivery are tops, and he has the audience on a laugh merry-go-round with the constant switches of his two roles." Actually, Errol had a *triple* assignment—he also masqueraded as a German cop in one scene.

Expert, too, were Elizabeth Risdon and Lydia Bilbrook. The latter, upon being told by her husband that the flirtatiously aggressive Marion Martin's name was Diana, remarked imperiously, "Goddess of the chase, wasn't she?"

The Mexican Spitfire series ended tragically in 1944 when Lupe Velez, in her mid-thirties, committed suicide. The series did much for Leon Errol. It brought the aging actor a whole new, busy career in Hollywood in which he not only did many other features but innumerable short subjects.

THE MONSTER AND THE GIRL

(Paramount Pictures, 1941)

Credits
Producer, Jack Moss
Director, Stuart Heisler
Original screenplay, Stuart Anthony
Music, Sigmund Krumgold
Camera, Victor Milner
Editor, Everett Douglas
Running Time: 63 minutes

Cast
ELLEN DREW (Susan Webster)
ROBERT PAIGE (Larry Reed)
PAUL LUKAS (Bruhl)
Joseph Calleia (Deacon)
Onslow Stevens (McMasters)
George Zucco (Dr. Parry)
Rod Cameron (Sam Daniels)
Phillip Terry (Scott Webster)
Marc Lawrence (Sleeper)
Gerald Mohr (Munn)
Tom Dugan (Capt. Alton)
Willard Robertson (Lieut. Strickland)
Minor Watson (Judge Pulver)
George F. Meader (Dr. Knight)
Cliff Edwards (Leon Stokes)

Skipper (dog)
Frank M. Thomas (Jansen)
Abner Biberman (Gregory)
Corbet Morris (Claude Winters)
Edward Van Sloan (warden)
Maynard Holmes (Tim Harper)
Harry C. Bradley (Rev. Russell)
Emma Dunn (Aunt Della)
Sammy Blum (popcorn vendor)
John H. Dilson (employment clerk)
John Bleifer (janitor)
Jayne Hazard, Ethelreda Leopold (party girls)
Florence Dudley (madame)
Matty Fain (Wade Stanton)
Al Seymour, Bert Moorhouse (henchmen)
Bud Jamison (Tim, the doorman)
Paul McVey (Monarch Hotel clerk)
Oscar Smith (bootblack)
Al M. Hill (Bruhl's chauffeur)
Emmett Vogan (apartment manager)
Dave Willock (Charlie, the photographer)
Anne O'Neal (Miss Julia)
Eleanor Wesselhoeft (elderly housekeeper)
Emory Parnell (dumb cop)
Ruth Gillette (woman)
Fern Emmett (woman organizer)

Although *The Monster and the Girl* was a horror film, the screenplay by Stuart Anthony and direction by Stuart Heisler paid more attention to characterization and the human element than was the practice for this genre at the time. Sometimes, startlingly so.

As things got underway, dazed Phillip Terry was being tried for murder. He had been framed—flashbacks divulged—by racketeer Paul Lukas and his mob. A small-town church organist, he had come to the big city "to kill" Lukas henchman Robert Paige who had pretended to marry Terry's restless young sister (Ellen Drew) only to force her into a life of prostitution. When a Lukas enemy was exterminated, the blame was put on bystander Terry, who, after receiving the death sentence, vowed in some way to get all those responsible for his plight.

Pretty complicated, adult material for a "B" picture, especially a horror film, which traditionally dealt with elemental fright effects. The horror-movie fan was just about convinced he'd wandered into the wrong theater when redoubtable Dr. George ("They call me a scientist") Zucco turned up outside Terry's cell to request use of his brain after the imminent execution for "an experiment." "Help yourself!" screamed the now hysterical Terry. Zucco was shortly transferring Terry's brain into the skull of a living ape, and aficionados sat back in their seats (briefly), reassured that they were seeing the right picture after all.

One by one, the beast killed a half-dozen or so of those on whom Terry had sworn ven-

Ellen Drew, Gerald Mohr

geance ("WHO will be next?" asked a radio voice). Finally, the ape was shot dead and a sympathetic reporter (Rod Cameron) embraced Ellen Drew, obviously about to be redeemed.

There were a number of effective cinematic touches. One of the better scenes was Drew's "marriage" to Paige as a bodeful rain beats against the window. Then, after Paige paid minister Joseph Calleia and left with his "bride," the audiences saw that the sinister Reverend Calleia was wearing a shoulder-holster gun. Strong stuff, too, was the morning after Drew's wedding night. She smilingly awoke, clearly very satisfied, to find herself abandoned—except for gangster Gerald Mohr who answered the terrified girl's entreaties with "There is no Larry [Robert Paige]. There never will be," going on to virtually insist that prostitution was now her sole means of survival.

Sometimes the dialogue was banal, as when a fallen Drew began her court testimony, "What I have to say is not a new story . . ."; and the horror aspect (mad doctors, ape men, and so on), while smoothly dramatized in darkly menacing images (such as the monster stealthily trading steps along a rooftop with his next victim who strolled unawares through the night down on the sidewalk) was old goose pimples stuff even in 1941.

Overall, however, *The Monster and the Girl* was a very good example of creative moviemaking on a limited budget and with a modest (but generally capable) cast. (Phillip Terry, best-known as one of Joan Crawford's husbands, was a bit beyond his depth as the unstable young brother.) The film's ambitious intent was apparent from the very first ambient, arty shot: the usually wholesomely cast Ellen Drew, calling herself "the bad luck penny" and attired in a 1941 version of a hooker's garb (which today would look conservative on a nun), walked out of a dreamlike fog toward the camera to begin her bizarre story.

George Zucco, the monster

Robert Paige, Ellen Drew

THE MUMMY'S HAND

(Universal Pictures, 1940)

Credits
Associate producer, Ben Pivar
Director, Christy Cabanne
Screenplay, Griffin Jay, Maxwell Shane
Original story, Jay
Music director, H.J. Salter
Camera, Elwood Bredell
Editor, Phil Cahn
Running Time: 67 minutes

Cast
DICK FORAN (Steve Banning)
PEGGY MORAN (Marta Solvani/Sullivan)
Cecil Kellaway (Solvani the Great/Tim Sullivan)
Wallace Ford (Babe Jenson)
George Zucco (Andoheb)
Charles Trowbridge (Dr. Petrie)
Tom Tyler (the Mummy)
Siegfried [Sig] Arno (beggar)
Eduardo Ciannelli (high priest)
Leon Belasco (Ali)
Harry Stubbs (bartender)
Michael Mark (bazaar owner)
Mara Tartar (girl vendor)
Frank Lackteen (priest)
Murdock MacQuarrie (priest)
Eddie Foster (Egyptian)
Scenes included from 1932's *The Mummy*
   with Boris Karloff and James Crane
   (as the Pharaoh)

Pretty, dimpled Peggy Moran received the most attention during her short but prolific career when she played the feminine leads in two of Universal's biggest moneymaking "B" movies of 1940. The first released was *Oh, Johnny, How You Can Love,* titled after the popular song then sweeping the country, and the second (of moment here) was *The Mummy's Hand,* whose success ushered in a whole new horror cycle at the studio.

Somewhat of a sequel to Boris Karloff's 1932 classic, *The Mummy,* the 1940 picture had penniless young archaeologist Dick Foran and buffoon sidekick Wallace Ford on an expedition to find the sarcophagus of the ancient Egyptian Princess Ananka. Their search was financed by magician Cecil Kellaway and his skeptical daughter (Peggy Moran), both of whom went along on the trip. Instead of the Princess, they unearthed Ananka's lover, Kharis (Tom Tyler), buried alive for sacrilege but kept from death through the ages by tanna leaves administered by high priests of Karnak. His current guardian was deceptive George Zucco, who, by day, was a professor at the Cairo Museum.

At Zucco's command, the Mummy, swathed and unable to talk (his tongue had been cut out), strangled professor Charles Trowbridge and guide Leon Belasco, leaving streaks of gray dust on "the unbelievers'" throats. When Kharis abducted Moran and took her to Zucco's temple, the high priest suddenly developed more interest in Moran than the Mummy. "You and I together for eternity," he panted to the manacled heroine, preparing tanna leaves for two. Then Foran and Ford appeared, Zucco was shot and the rampaging Kharis immolated when a flaming tanna urn was thrown at him. Moran got Foran.

Not surprisingly, the studio evidently had not expected this to so take the public's fancy, because *The Mummy's Hand* was made quickly on a budget that was low even for a "B." The sets were all from previous pictures, unretouched, and the flashbacks showing Kharis' downfall more than 3,000 years earlier were borrowed from the earlier Karloff film. (Footage from *The Mummy's Hand,* showing all the

Wallace Ford, Peggy Moran, Dick Foran

principals, was used even more extensively in the next Mummy film which appeared two years later.) Even Kharis' climactic ignition was accomplished economically and with dispatch off-camera.

Kharis' sour disposition could be explained by the fact that he hardly ever heard his name pronounced the same way twice. Director Christy Cabanne either didn't notice this or didn't think it was important. "Kha-*riss* never really died," revealed aged high priest Eduardo Ciannelli to his imminent successor, George Zucco. "Kha- *reese* is still alive!" marveled Zucco. Later during the same conversation, Ciannelli pronounced it the same way Zucco had, and vice versa. Meanwhile, Charles Trowbridge was calling the Mummy "Kha-*deese.*" (This kind of carelessness was not restricted to the fictional characters, either: the name of South African-born featured player Cecil Kellaway—his English accent not a little inappropriate in his role of a Brooklynite—was misspelled twice in the credits as Kelloway.)

Another example of somebody's tin ear was the native who balefully warned the archaeologists as they prepared to break the seal to Kharis' tomb, "It mins det to whoever braigs dat sil."

Veteran of Westerns Tom Tyler—his special-effects eyes tiny, swirling black pools—was a husky, altogether acceptable, less paunchy 3,000-year-old man than Lon Chaney, Jr., who played the role in succeeding Universal Mummy features. Peggy Moran was too spirited and cute to have retired as she soon did after marrying director Henry Koster, and the others in the cast were okay, too. But Britain's George Zucco, that king of villains with the suave manner, gleamingly decadent eyes, and superb speaking voice, was more than that. His civilized perfidy was always one of the joys of moviegoing in the Golden Age; one wishes only that he had had more opportunity to display his highly cultivated acting ability in major productions.

As in most of the series of that era, the finer points of which audiences were not expected to remember from picture to picture, consistency—forget logic—was hardly a byword in the Mummy films. Shot three times at the end of *Mummy's Hand,* Zucco ("Stunt man!") fell down one of the longest flights of steps seen by man or mummy and was presumed dead. When Kharis was exhumed for the next entry, *The Mummy's Tomb* (1942), so was Zucco. Previous footage showing his bullet-riddled body taking that steep fall down the temple steps was inserted. "The bullet [sic] he fired into me only

Charles Trowbridge, George Zucco, Tom Tyler

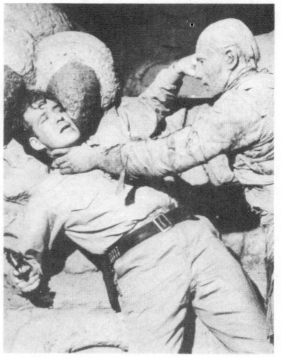

Dick Foran, Tom Tyler

Peggy Moran, George Zucco, Tom Tyler

crushed my arm," Zucco tushed in the latest installment, now doddering as the keeper of the flame who once again unleashed the Mummy and once again died. But then came *The Mummy's Ghost* (1944) wherein Zucco, without even a ludicrous explanation, reappeared as the palsied old priest to place the Mummy in John Carradine's steadier hands. This time, when he went to his rest it was for good. Not so Kharis.

If the 1940s Mummy movies also lacked the macabre poetry and ambience of the Karloff original, which was almost as much love story as horror show (although it did not want for the latter—who can forget those final close-ups of Karloff's face gradually turning to dust?), neither were they as vulgar as Britain's Hammer Films resurrections in ensuing decades. Universal's follow-ups were swift, goreless little Halloween romps. Youngsters, especially, reveled in them, and still do when they are shown on television. However, a shuffling, Kharis-trailing *schmatas* is about as frightening as Raggedy Andy. Only George Zucco seems to have found the secret of eternal life to chill viewers.

The Mummy's Hand was fun, if viewers could suspend critical acumen. But it was a real cheapie. The very short running time made Kharis the Mummy seem cut down in his prime. Of course audiences in 1940 didn't know—and maybe Universal didn't then, either—that he would be back again in a couple of years . . . and again . . . and again . . .

MY BUDDY

(Republic Pictures, 1944)

Credits

Associate producer, Eddy White
Director, Steve Sekely
Screenplay, Arnold Manoff
Original story, Prescott Chaplin
Musical director, Morton Scott
Songs, Walter Donaldson and Gus Kahn;
  Jack Elliott; Billy Baskett
Art director, J. Frank Hotaling
Camera, Reggie Lanning
Editor, Tony Martinelli
Running Time: 72 minutes

Cast

DONALD BARRY (Eddie Ballinger)
RUTH TERRY (Lola)
LYNNE ROBERTS (Lucy Manners)
Alexander Granach (Tim Oberta)
Emma Dunn (Mary Ballinger)
John Litel (Father Jim Donnelly)
George E. Stone (Pete)
Jonathan Hale (Senator Henry)
Ray Walker (Russ)
Joe Devlin (Nicky Piastro)
Matt McHugh (Happy)
Jack Ingram (Charlie)
George Humbert (Albert)
Gayne Whitman (young senator)
Edward Earle (Chairman)
Emmett Vogan (second senator)
Jimmy Zaner (messenger)
Jack Baxley (Jim)
Connie Leon (housekeeper)
Milton Kibbee (Pa Manners)
Almeda Fowler (Ma Manners)
Sam Bernard (salesman)
Constance Purdy (woman)
Blake Edwards (prison kid)
Sven-Hugo Borg (German sniper)
George Lloyd (Hendricks)
Lee Shumway (Jim, the guard)
Harry Strang (first detective)
Jack Gardner (Mike)
Russ Whiteman (Tommy)
Boots Brown (kid)
Robert Middlemass (judge)
Marshall Reed (second detective)
Nolan Leary (lawyer)
Ralph Linn (jury foreman)
Roy Darmour, Lynton Brent (detectives)
Frank Marlowe (Joe)
Charlie Sullivan (loudmouth mug)
Larry Steers (prosecuting attorney)
Jack Rockwell (jail attendant, in shadows)
Charles P. Sherlock (policeman)
Kid Chissell (second mobster)
John Bagni (first mobster)
Jay Norris (Spats)
Poison Gardner Trio (prison singers)
Arthur Loft (warden)
Jack Mulhall (announcer at convicts' show)
Larry Burke (singer at convicts' show)

Two years before producer Samuel Goldwyn and director William Wyler dealt with returning World War II veterans in the monumental *The Best Years of Our Lives* (1946), farsighted Republic Studios got there first with a Donald Barry vehicle titled *My Buddy.*

Not nearly as ambitious nor as effective as the Goldwyn-Wyler masterpiece, *My Buddy* was a well-intentioned ''B.'' Its fast-moving script by Arnold Manoff was the melodramatic story of one particular ill-fated World War I veteran (Barry). Through the use of flashback technique, priest-friend John Litel told Barry's tale to a 1944 Washington Post-War Planning Committee to help prevent it from happening again. Essentially, the plot was quite similar to a James Cagney vehicle *The Roaring Twenties* (1939), and star Barry—although best known for his Western films as Red Ryder—had long been compared to Cagney. Both were shortish redheads with hair-trigger tempers. The Houston, Texas-born Barry, however, rarely rose above ''B'' films except to play small parts, yet he was competent and certainly one of the most convincing actors who regularly appeared in quickie Westerns.

Returning to civilian life in 1918 Chicago, Barry's veteran (named Eddie Ballinger— Cagney's in *Roaring Twenties* had been Eddie Bartlett) was unable to find work and so postponed marriage to long-time sweetheart Lynne Roberts. He was soon picking up cigarette butts in the street. When he saw his mother (Emma Dunn) taking in washing, and his girl helping her, he accepted a job offer from bootlegger Alexander Granach. Eventually, Barry, taking a rap for Granach, went to prison where he formed his own mob.

Roberts visited him, telling Barry she had another boyfriend but adding, ''I'll wait for you if you want me to.'' Thoroughly embittered now, he would not promise to go straight when he got out, so she married the other man.

After Barry served his five years, Granach gave him a welcome home party at his nightclub where the singing star was Ruth Terry. Terry, a Republic leading lady and second-billed in *My Buddy,* made her first appearance about 15

Donald Barry, Lynne Roberts

minutes before the film was over. She proceeded to do one of the lamest Charlestons ever (the camera kept a polite distance) but atoned for this by—starting with a piercing scream from the darkened club floor—rendering a more characteristic, nose-crinklingly cute vocal of a Jack Elliott novelty song called "Whodunit?" By the finish of the number, she had sidled over to Barry and decided that he "dunit." She switched affections from Granach to Barry ("You're going places and I'd like to be with you"), who was also encroaching on Granach's protection racket territory.

When Granach's mob killed three of Barry's men, he shot Granach. Terry, for whom Barry had shown only contempt in an obviously sex-only relationship surprisingly unsweetened for its cinema time and station, informed on him to the police. Barry was killed in a roof-top gun battle.

Litel concluded his tale by telling the Post-War Planning Committee that Barry had left all the stolen money with him, along with a note begging him to pass along his story, if the need arose, so that other war veterans might be spared his tragic end.

The sentimental title ballad, Walter Donaldson and Gus Kahn's World War I standard, was sung in a prison show scene by Larry Burke, reminding the incarcerated Barry of his old friends in the trenches. Under Steve Sekely's direction, a number of sensitive touches indicated that, the low budget notwithstanding, its people cared. I remember the felicitous way the film showed time passing: a close-up cornerstone with the changing dates engraved on it surrounded by, according to the season, snow or flowers, etc. And the careworn Emma Dunn, departing after visiting Barry in prison, tremulously reaching out to touch her son but realizing there was a screen partition between them.

Donald Barry, also known as Don (Red) Barry and still working today, was thoroughly credible, as well as unexpectedly moving in the early duologue with John Litel in which Barry's desperate veteran said he wasn't asking for much, only a job. Lynne Roberts was a pretty, dainty girl; the undeniably talented Ruth Terry was more at home in lighter vehicles such as *Pistol Packin' Mama*, and chunky Alexander Granach, strutting about wearing a white carnation and twirling a key chain, was a bit of a caricature. Its manifest imperfections aside, *My Buddy* was a decently made, timely little movie with its heart in the right place.

Donald Barry, Ruth Terry, George E. Stone

Donald Barry

MY NAME IS JULIA ROSS

(Columbia Pictures, 1945)

Credits

Producer, Wallace MacDonald
Director, Joseph H. Lewis
Screenplay, Muriel Roy Bolton
Based on the book *The Woman in Red*
   by Anthony Gilbert
Music director, Mischa Bakaleinikoff
Camera, Burnett Guffey
Editor, Henry Batista
Running Time: 65 minutes

Cast

NINA FOCH (Julia Ross)
DAME MAY WHITTY (Mrs. Hughes)
GEORGE MACREADY (Ralph Hughes)
Roland Varno (Dennis Bruce)
Anita Bolster (Sparkes)
Doris Lloyd (Mrs. Mackie)
Leonard Mudie (Peters)
Joy Harrington (Bertha)
Queenie Leonard (Alice)
Harry Hays Morgan (Robinson)
Ottola Nesmith (Mrs. Robinson)
Olaf Hytten (Rev. Lewis)
Evan Thomas (Dr. Keller)
Marilyn Johnson (nurse)
Milton Owens, Leyland Hodgson (policemen)
Reginald Sheffield (McQuarrie)
Charles McNaughton (gatekeeper)

My Name is Julia Ross (1945) had the kind of thriller plot that was a boon to forties movies. It concerned a young girl held captive by villains who, for their own evil ends, tried to make her appear incompetent. Ingrid Bergman, for one, starred in at least two celebrated variations on this theme, *Gaslight* (1943) and *Notorious* (1946). Though only a "B," *My Name is Julia Ross* could still hold its own in this collection of women-in-jeopardy films.

Thanks to augmented promotion by Columbia, which was experiencing a temporary paucity of product, the film was lavishly and laudably reviewed and became one of the decade's most highly regarded low-budget productions. Time and the increasing familiarity of its story somewhat dim its luster when viewed today; nevertheless, James Agee's notice in *The Nation* still goes: "The film is well planned, mostly well played, well directed and, in a somewhat boom-happy way, well photographed—all around, a likable, unpretentious, generally successful attempt to turn good trash into decently artful entertainment."

One of the picture's biggest assets was succinctness. A mere 65 minutes short, it contained not an unessential character or action; everyone and everything contributed significantly to the Gothic suspense yarn at hand, a model of pithy screenwriting by Muriel Roy Bolton. Nina Foch played the title role, a London lass who obviously didn't go to the movies much. Arrears in her rent and feeling dejected after her boarding house boyfriend (Roland Varno) left to marry someone else, she took a live-in secretarial position that required a girl with no romantic or familial ties. Her employers were George Macready and his mother (Dame May Whitty), who, after interviewing Foch, remarked ominously, "She's perfect. There's even a small resemblance." Meanwhile, Varno returned to his old residence, the wedding off and anxious to resume with Foch. Because of her new job, she asked him to wait.

Foch moved into her employers' town house, which the camera moved in to show had a demon's head for a door-knocker. Sure enough, that evening she was drugged and

Nina Foch, Harry Hays Morgan, Ottola Nesmith,
Olaf Hytten, Dame May Whitty

awoke at their sprawling seaside mansion in Cornwall. The initials "M.H." peered at her from everywhere in the bedroom; she wore a wedding ring and the door was locked. After making a disturbance in front of the maid (Queenie Leonard), who insisted that Foch was someone named Marian Hughes and married to Macready, Foch was confronted by her "husband": "You haven't forgotten us again, have you, Marian?" To which Foch replied, "You know perfectly well I'm Julia Ross!"

She next glimpsed the housekeeper (Anita Bolster), whom she protested was the employment agency woman who had obtained the job for her.

Leaving Foch's room, Bolster informed the maid, just hired and innocent of the conspiracy, "Last week she thought I was the queen."

"Comin' down in the world, aren't you?" was maid Leonard's rejoinder.

Spying through secret doors, Foch, who was being held prisoner and made to look mad to the community, discovered that she was to be murdered and buried in the name of Macready's wife. It seemed he had married Marian Hughes for her money, then killed her in a fit of rage and thrown her body into the sea.

After a visit from the village vicar (Olaf Hytten), Foch managed to hide on the floor in back of his car. Not far from the house, she was observed and turned over to her captors. "Now everyone knows she's not responsible for anything she does," Whitty gloated. A phony doc-

tor (Leonard Mudie) sent for by Whitty and a real doctor (Evan Thomas) sent for by the maid got into the fray, too.

One night Macready removed a couple of steps near the top of the staircase and called to Foch from the shadows below, pretending to be Varno. She realized the situation just in time, ran to her room and screamed. When Macready entered, he saw her open window and outside her still figure on the faraway rocks. Standing over her body by the surf, he was about to finish the job with a poised rock when the police appeared and shot him. A letter Foch had managed to mail had reached Varno. Furthermore, she was not dead but stood up to explain that she had just tossed the robe down, let herself out through a secret door and, donning the robe again, assumed the prone position on the rocks.

As Foch and Varno drove back to town, she vowed, "The next time I apply for a job I'll ask for *their* references!"

Director Joseph H. Lewis and cinematographer Burnett Guffey refined the straightforward

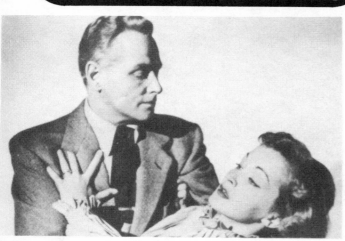

George Macready, Nina Foch

Dame May Whitty

narrative with some effective cinematic touches, including—for a film sans stars—a large number of tension-heightening close-ups. (The close-up erroneously has been called mainly an ego-flattering service for stars.) Notably expressive were a couple of shots focusing on the eyes of Foch and Macready—Foch's seen growing wider and wider from over his shoulder as he told her how he met his late wife, then attemped to kiss the girl; Macready's glistening in the dark at the bottom of the stairs as he waited for Foch to fall to her death.

Nina Foch, an unconventionally attractive, robust blonde with an intense intelligence about her sharp features, was a proficient dramatic actress. Born in Holland and raised in the states, she was also one of the rare contract girls of that era who managed to survive industry turmoil of ensuing years and become a respected actress in both California and New York. Today, she also teaches acting. Not many forties starlets can make that statement.

So memorably held captive herself in Alfred Hitchcock's *The Lady Vanishes* (1938), Dame May Whitty was always welcome, even in an unsympathetic role such as this treacherously charming, scheming mastermind-mother. In all honesty, though, her bustling little old lady seemed less dangerous than quaint.

More like it was the distinctive, ripe menace of George Macready, with his scarred right cheek, whispery voice, and decadent suavity—Columbia's all-purpose degenerate in the forties. *My Name is Julia Ross,* which had him uncontrollably playing with knives that his mother had to keep taking away from him and filing in a crowded drawer, was right up his dark alley. It was sort of a dress rehearsal for possibly his best-known part, the cane/knife-carrying, bisexual husband of Rita Hayworth in *Gilda* (1946).

Among the lesser players, Anita Bolster had an unforgettably devious, slightly cracked look, while Doris Lloyd offered a nice if familiar bit as Foch's venal landlady who nonetheless saved the day when she had Leonard Mudie, a Whitty-Macready henchman, arrested while trying to steal Foch's letter-cry of help to her boyfriend.

Some of the picture's passages seemed overly contrived, unlikely expediences. Such as Whitty and son permitting Foch to mail her letter (even though at first they thought—mistakenly—they had removed the message) and Foch's climactic escape through the secret door to play dead on the beach (why hadn't she just kept going?). Quibbling aside, *My Name is Julia Ross,* with its taut suspense and extensive and favorable critical reception, brought a new respectability to the "B" movie.

MY PAL WOLF

(RKO Radio Pictures, 1944)

Credits

Producer, Adrian Scott
Director, Alfred Werker
Screenplay, Lillie Hayward, Leonard Praskins,
  John Paxton
Original story, Frederick Hazlitt Brennan
Music, Werner R. Heymann
Art directors, Albert S. D'Agostino,
  Carroll Clark
Camera, Jack MacKenzie
Editor, Harry Marker
Running Time: 76 minutes

Cast

SHARYN MOFFETT (Gretchen)
Jill Esmond (Miss Munn)
Una O'Connor (Mrs. Blevins)
George Cleveland (Wilson)
Charles Arnt (Papa Eisdaar)
Claire Carleton (Ruby)
Leona Maricle (Mrs. Anstey)
Bruce Edwards (Mr. Anstey)
Edward Fielding (Secretary of War)
Olga Fabian (Mama Eisdaar)
Larry Olsen (Fred)
Jerry Michelsen (Alf)
Bobby Larson (Karl)
Marc Cramer (Sgt. Blake)
Victor Cutler (Wolf's trainer no. 1)
Carl Kent (Wolf's trainer no. 2)
Bryant Washburn (commanding officer)
J. Louis Johnson (butler)
Joan Barclay (Willie)
Chris Drake (bit)
Tom Burton (reporter)
Bert Moorhouse (cop)
Alan Ward (truck driver)
Grey Shadow (Wolf)

RKO's *My Pal Wolf* is a good example of a basically tired story (a girl and her dog) given new life by a charming and talented lead player (newcomer Sharyn Moffett), painstaking direction (Alfred Werker), and tasteful production values.

Little Miss Moffett was the film's flywheel, a gifted, natural-acting child with an almost uncanny affinity for the camera who was chosen from among fifty applicants for this demanding role. No blonde and ringletted Shirley Temple, Sharyn was brown-haired and slightly gap-toothed but plumply sweet-faced and, with her infectious laugh, enormously appealing. Born in 1936 of performing parents who had done some minor movie work, she was actually the RKO studio's answer to reigning MGM moppet Margaret O'Brien, and while a comparison is really unnecessary, in my opinion Sharyn—a born film actress—just may have had the edge on the much-honored Margaret.

Regrettably, RKO's shaky status then prohibited the kind of build-up and "A" vehicles she deserved, so she spent the rest of the decade working mostly in "B"s (after *My Pal Wolf,* most notably in *Child of Divorce)* and then disappeared. Today remembered mainly by movie buffs, she was the rare child performer to whom even the ultra-sophisticated warmed.

In *My Pal Wolf,* Sharyn played the wealthy but lonely child of Leona Maricle and Bruce Edwards, busy, working parents who seemed merely visitors at their estate in Virginia where Sharyn lived. As the picture opened, stern new governess Jill Esmond arrived to take care of the little girl. Left by grizzled handyman George Cleveland to carry her own bag, Esmond found the bell didn't work and upon walking in beheld cook Claire Carleton disheveled and wrestling a broken vacuum cleaner, grumbling, "Miss Pruneface is coming!" She was next met by housekeeper Una O'Connor, who also horrified the rigid British woman. Briefing her, O'Connor added, "You can get yourself a passable husband around here, if you work at it."

Esmond likewise was aghast at her unkempt little charge who stepped from behind portieres in scruffy long pants and dirty face, wiping her

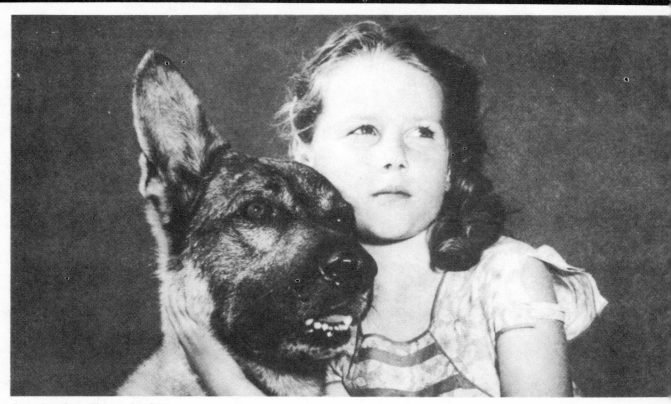

Grey Shadow, Sharyn Moffett

nose on her sleeve. After Sharyn suffered the first of many scoldings from Esmond, O'Connor returned saying, "Dearie, you can come up and get out of your girdle now."

"Is she old?" a little friend asked Sharyn later, referring to Esmond.

"Uh-huh."

"Is she older than Miss Carlson [the previous governess]?"

"She's older than anything," sighed Sharyn, whose free-spirited ways of amusing herself the new governess persistently aborted.

Soon wearing a dress and hair ribbons, Sharyn was trapped in an abandoned well trying to help a German shepherd dog she called Wolf (played, the credits informed, by Grey Shadow) who had fallen in a while before. He managed to get out, though, and brought help. When Sharyn asked if she could keep the apparently homeless dog, O'Connor, glaring at Esmond, said, "Of course you can. Anybody says you can't, send 'em to Mrs. Blevins. I'll give 'em a run for their money. Twice around the whiskey jug, with a head start!"

The animal's harmlessly frisky behavior upset Esmond even more than the outspoken unconventionality of the staff. She gave notice to her employers, but a $20 raise convinced her to stay. The dog and Sharyn grew inseparable, frolicking with other children at the old swimming hole where Sharyn delightedly was pulled through the water hanging onto her pal Wolf's tail.

When Esmond learned that the animal was a runaway Army dog and sent him back, a heart-broken Sharyn hitchhiked to Washington to get the Secretary of War (Edward Fielding) to release Wolf from service. There, she was made to realize that Wolf was needed to help win the war and so, returning home, put a service flag with one star in the window. Esmond was fired and Sharyn's parents decided to spend more time with her. As the family was leaving for a vacation together, a baby German shepherd arrived from the Secretary of War to keep Sharyn company while Wolf was away.

The skilled art direction of Albert S. D'Agostino and Carroll Clark in *My Pal Wolf* rates a paragraph of its own. The coziness of a neighboring farmhouse with several children, for instance, warmed by a crackling fireplace as well as by its inhabitants, was creatively contrasted with the cavernous austerity of the little girl's plantation-like mansion. The Secretary of War's dark study, lit mostly by flickering light from the hearth, at once suggested both the entering child's trepidation and the warm reception that ultimately would be hers within.

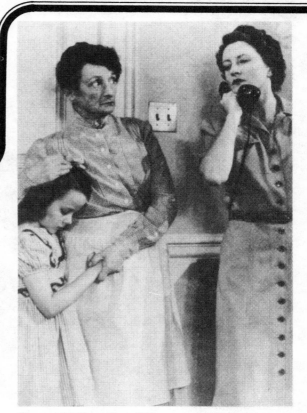

Sharyn Moffett, Una O'Connor, Jill Esmond

Jerry Michelsen, Grey Shadow, Larry Olsen, Charles Arnt, Sharyn Moffett, Bruce Edwards, Bobby Larson, George Cleveland

Werner R. Heymann's nursery rhyme-inspired music score was appropos, and director Alfred Werker showed a remarkable understanding and control of his material, handling his inexperienced child star with great sensitivity. The large, handsome dog named Grey Shadow, too, actually seemed to enjoy romping with Sharyn and the other children, something not all that common in animal pictures. Actress Jill Esmond, the ex-Mrs. Laurence Olivier, with the stride of a Storm Trooper, was unrelieved malevolence as the cold-hearted governess—the last job in the world for which this character was equipped. "A divil in skirts" was how Una O'Connor described her. And wonderful little O'Connor—her hair dyed ink-black while looking like she'd forgotten to put in her bottom teeth, and late of Ireland's famed Abbey Players, mind—stole scenes from everyone, man, woman, child and beast, as the heroically insolent, coarse housekeeper.

I could have done without some of the Secretary of War's jarringly ugly war propaganda lecture to the already distraught small girl about children overseas being set afire. On the whole, though, *My Pal Wolf* managed to brighten up an old story so that it sparkled touchingly—and entertainingly—anew.

Una O'Connor, Claire Carleton, Jill Esmond, player, George Cleveland, Sharyn Moffett

NINE GIRLS

(Columbia Pictures, 1944)

Credits
Producer, Burt Kelly
Director, Leigh Jason
Screenplay, Karen deWolf, Connie Lee
Based on the play by Wilfrid H. Pettitt
Music director, John Leopold
Camera, James Van Trees
Editor, Otto Meyer
Running Time: 75 minutes

Cast
ANN HARDING (Grace Thornton)
EVELYN KEYES (Mary O'Ryan)
Jinx Falkenburg (Jane Peters)
Anita Louise (Paula Canfield)
Leslie Brooks (Roberta Holloway)
Lynn Merrick (Eve Sharon)
Jeff Donnell ("Butch" Hendricks)
Nina Foch (Alice Blake)
Shirley Mills ("Tennessee" Collingwood)
Marcia Mae Jones (Shirley Berke)
Willard Robertson (Capt. Brooks)
William Demarest (Walter Cummings)
Lester Matthews (Horace Canfield)
Grady Sutton (photographer)

154

The original *Nine Girls* was a mystery-comedy, with the emphasis on the latter. Its makers were clearly bent more on being funny than mysterious, evidence of which was the revelation of the murderer's identity quite a while before the ending—whereas the wise continued to crack right to the very last line. Most of the humor leaned toward bitchy repartée. While the nine girls of the title were supposed to be students at a smart California college, they sounded more like chorus girls, and with the obvious heavy call for the peroxide bottle, they also looked like it. I might mention, too, that most of them were a bit past college age—in my place, *they* would.

Practically the whole distaff contract list at Columbia Pictures was hired to play the girls. For the occasion, the on-screen billing cleverly broke routine:

Nine Girls
With Ann Harding as chaperone to:

1. Evelyn Keyes
2. Jinx Falkenburg
3. Anita Louise
4. Leslie Brooks
5. Lynn Merrick
6. Jeff Donnell
7. Nina Foch
8. Shirley Mills
9. Marcia Mae Jones.

William Demarest and Willard Robertson as police investigators were the most prominent among the few males employed.

Anita Louise was immediately pegged as the sour apple of the bunch—nine sorority sisters—insulting everyone in sight in the first few minutes. Without taking a breath, she tried to steal medical student Jinx Falkenburg's boyfriend ("Suppose I pick you up and we do something gay?") and to blackmail neurotic brain Nina Foch into writing her thesis by threatening to tell Foch's poor family that she had borrowed a lot of money from Louise. When Evelyn Keyes, who was working her way through college, caught Louise in action and chided, "Confidentially, you slink," Louise cautioned that it could cost Keyes her promised teaching position at an

Evelyn Keyes, Lynn Merrick, Jeff Donnell, Shirley Mills, Anita Louise, Marcia Mae Jones, Nina Foch, Jinx Falkenburg, Leslie Brooks

exclusive school if it were made known that her brother had been in trouble (unspecified in the script). As they prepared for an initiation weekend at their sorority lodge in the mountains, favorite teacher Ann Harding as chaperone, all these "finished" young ladies could talk about was killing Anita Louise.

The other sorority members were Leslie Brooks, who had been raised with Louise; Lynn Merrick, the drama major; Jeff Donnell, a physical fitness fiend because her mother had been an Olympic champion ("What would you do," asked Foch, "if your mother had been a bearded lady?"); and terrified new pledges Shirley Mills and Marcia Mae Jones.

At the lodge, the group learned that Louise had been murdered, cueing the arrival of Robertson and Demarest with instructions not to leave the premises. "No one thought more of Paula [Louise] than I did, and I hated her," admitted Keyes. The girls began to suspect one another as the weekend wore on, and bungling detective Demarest made himself at home.

"That certainly was a good meal," he said after dinner, no small portion of same having settled on his clothes.

"Yeah, and on you it looks good," snapped Donnell.

Each of the nine girls was clearly minoring, at least, in wisecracks.

When we saw Harding burn the shoes worn at the scene of the crime, the unstartling mystery—but not the movie—was over. Later, she tricked Keyes into writing a self-incriminating letter which Harding kept. She next saw to it, as everybody was leaving after the weekend, that Keyes' car would not start. Trapping her alone in the house, the spinster teacher confessed she had murdered Louise because she had tried to keep Harding from marrying her wealthy father (Lester Matthews). She was about to shoot Keyes when the police returned and arrested her. Keyes, Harding, and the law drove grimly by the other girls on the highway, causing them to speculate that Keyes might be in trouble. But not to worry, because their dear teacher was there, as always, to comfort her. "She's such a kind, thoughtful soul," smiled Shirley Mills.

Actress Harding, a major star in the thirties, was her usual patrician, dignified self even when preparing to murder Keyes. And she subsequently looked genuinely stunned that the police:

1. Would presume to talk to her
2. Would arrest her.

Only a slight eyebrow twitch in time of stress hinted at the deep-rooted psychological aberra-

Leslie Brooks, William Demarest, Shirley Mills, Willard Robertson, Marcia Mae Jones, Evelyn Keyes, Ann Harding, Jinx Falkenburg, Lynn Merrick, Nina Foch, Jeff Donnell

Ann Harding, Evelyn Keyes

tion we were told was responsible for her perfidy.

The charming, eminently utilitarian Evelyn Keyes proved, as I'd always suspected, fine company on a weekend. While the lighter side of her talent was not exercised as much in the strongly comic proceedings as her admirers would have liked, she admirably registered bug-eyed horror and incredulity in the closing scenes as her character's mentor turned homicidally against "teacher's pet."

As the obsessively athletic but not too skilled "Butch," Jeff Donnell stood out. "Do you have a tough, stubby beard that defies your razor?" a voice asked when she turned on a radio, leaving her to wonder for an instant if she had. William Demarest—translating the double take into head bumps, as well as falling in mud and getting caught in his union suit by medical student Jinx Falkenburg, who then fainted (good luck to her patients)—was a master at slapstick comedy, and was given ample opportunity here.

Most amusing of all, perhaps, was attractive blonde starlet Lynn (earlier, Marilyn) Merrick, who gave a blanketly funny characterization of a Katharine Hepburn-imitating aspirant actress. Affected and supercilious much of the time, when caught off guard, she lapsed into an argot considerably lower on the social scale than that of the Boston Brahmin she claimed to be.

Doing her exercises before bed, Donnell asked her, "Do you think I'll ever have an athlete's arm?"

Gibed Merrick, "Why don't you settle for athlete's foot?"

As the girls prepared to leave the lodge, Leslie Brooks sat on her overstuffed suitcase to close it. "That's using your head, old girl," approved a passing Merrick—yet another actress from Hollywood's halcyon years who deserved a better break.

The picture was directed with wily persuasion by Leigh Jason, the sudden all-out suspense and peril of the closing scenes heightened by the preceding concentration on levity. Exceptional, too, was James Van Trees' photography, lush for a "B" that was obviously made with more care than most. Especially so was his handling of the climactic confrontation between Ann Harding and Evelyn Keyes, the dim room seemingly lit by glistening sheets of rain battering the windows behind the murderess.

Nine Girls was a highly entertaining little movie and one of the era's brighter ideas for mass employment of contract ingenues. These worldly wise college sorority sisters were a lot more fun than Mary McCarthy's subsequent "Group."

THE PEARL OF DEATH

(Universal Pictures, 1944)

Credits
Producer-director, Roy William Neill
Screenplay, Bertram Millhauser
Based on *The Six Napoleons* by
    Sir Arthur Conan Doyle
Music director, Paul Sawtell
Camera, Virgil Miller
Editor, Ray Snyder
Running Time: 69 minutes

Cast
BASIL RATHBONE (Sherlock Holmes)
NIGEL BRUCE (Dr. Watson)
EVELYN ANKERS (Naomi Drake)
Dennis Hoey (Insp. Lestrade)
Miles Mander (Giles Conover)
Ian Wolfe (Amos Hodder)
Charles Francis (Digby)
Holmes Herbert (James Goodram)
Richard Nugent (Bates)
Mary Gordon (Mrs. Hudson)
Rondo Hatton (The Creeper)
J. Welsh Austin (Sgt. Bleeker)
Connie Leon (Ellen Carey)
Charles Knight (bearded man)
Al Ferguson (third guard)
Colin Kenny (second guard)
Audrey Manners (teacher)
Billy Bevan (constable)
Lillian Bronson (housekeeper)
Leslie Denison (Constable Murdock)
John Merkyl (Dr. Boncourt)
Harry Cording (George Gelder)
Eric Wilton (chauffeur)
Harold de Becker (boss)
Arthur Mulliner (Sandeford)
Wilson Benge, Arthur Stenning (stewards)
Leyland Hodgson (customs officer)

157

Since some of Universal's most successful pictures in the early forties were horror stories, it was probably inevitable that their goose-pimply presence would be felt elsewhere in the lot's product. Eventually, of course, it was carried to extremes when Frankenstein met Abbott and Costello. Before this, though, the influence of these films was evident in several of the Sherlock Holmes features, notably *The Pearl of Death*, which introduced the hulking, hideous acromegalic actor Rondo Hatton as the back-breaking "Creeper."

Britons Basil Rathbone and Nigel Bruce once again presided as, respectively, the sleuth indefatigable—but, as this version of the Sir Arthur Conan Doyle adventure of *The Six Napoleons* proved, not infallible—and his live-in companion, Dr. John H. Watson. As other actors who have taken on these characters can attest, Rathbone, whose profile paled those of the ancient Romans, and the fumfering Bruce became almost indivisible from these roles after fourteen Holmes movies (this was the ninth) from 1939 to 1946, and they were in top form in *The Pearl of Death*. It was one of the popular series' most effectively plotted entries, produced and directed—as was almost always the case—by Roy William Neill.

From an actor's standpoint, the film was a particular lark for Rathbone and featured players Evelyn Ankers and Miles Mander, who went through such a maze of disguises that, other possibilities exhausted, they wound up beginning to imitate each other.

The handsome and, as was proved here, versatile Evelyn Ankers portrayed Naomi Drake, a kind of surrogate Irene Adler, the adventuress from Conan Doyle's fiction who was the rare woman to arouse the interest of the cerebral, deductive, crusty Holmes. As the film began, she was seen as a beautiful young traveler on the boat to Dover, England, who in short order had stolen the fabulous Borgia pearl from a museum agent on board. Hiding it in her camera, she asked the elderly clergyman in the deck chair next to her to take it through customs for her—she was afraid, she said, that they would ruin the exposed film she had in it. The stranger obliged, then returned the camera to Ankers, who darted off to meet brains-behind-the-theft

Nigel Bruce, Ian Wolfe, Evelyn Ankers, Basil Rathbone

Miles Mander, essaying master criminal Giles Conover. After somewhat perversely telling her that her old "friend," the Creeper, was back in London, which caused her to shudder, he opened the camera to observe the gem missing and a slip of paper signed "S.H." The old clergyman actually had been, as Mander exclaimed, "Sherlock Holmes of Baker Street!"

The giant pearl was turned over to the Royal Regent Museum, where the visiting Rathbone called it "a miracle of horror," recounting its bloody history through the ages. To test the electrical burglar system protecting the gem, Rathbone surreptitiously (and rather foolishly) disconnected the wires at, coincidentally, the precise moment that Mander, disguised as a museum cleaning man, overheard him. Mander easily made off with the pearl but was collared a few minutes later in the street and brought back—without it.

Rathbone was discredited, Mander sent briefly to prison for breaking a window while running from the museum. Suspecting that he would try to get a message out via the food served him in jail, Dennis Hoey, as Inspector Lestrade, searched Mander's tray as it was being returned. Finding a piece of paper stuffed into the teapot's spout, Hoey said, "A note to one of his accomplices or I'm a Dutchman." It read, "You are a great fool," and was signed "Giles Conover."

Ankers' first disguise was a Cockney dishwasher in the restaurant that sent the food. Hair disheveled and dangling a cigarette from her lips, she washed leftover gravy from Mander's plate, found the real message underneath, and quit the job.

When a retired major was murdered, his back broken and his body surrounded by broken china, Rathbone got his first lead toward recovering the pearl—and his reputation. He immediately thought of the Creeper, "with the chest of a buffalo and the arms of a gorilla" and always Mander's right arm when it came to murder.

Ankers' disguise Number Two. "Buy a box of matches, gentlemen?" whined a poor old match woman in the street as she followed Rathbone and Bruce. Suddenly, Ankers pulled the shawl from her head and whistled for the henchmen who then drove by and shot at, but missed, the detective and his friend.

It was Mander's turn again. Disguised as a feeble old man, he gifted Rathbone with a book containing a lethal spring-knife device. Rathbone saw through it, and set off the mechanism harmlessly.

Two more people had their backs broken and were found amid a litter of shattered china. Rathbone had found, mixed in with the bric-a-brac from all the murder scenes, pieces of

Rondo Hatton

Evelyn Ankers

plaster which he was able to deduce were from small busts of Napoleon. "Something was hidden in these busts—precisely: the Borgia pearl!" Rathbone announced. He checked the plasterer's shop which the fleeing Mander had briefly entered when he bolted the museum with the pearl, and learned that there had been six wet plaster Napoleon busts on the workbench the day Mander burst in. All had been delivered to an art shop run by Ian Wolfe, who explained to Rathbone that two of the busts had been broken in the shop, three went to the murder victims, and the last one had gone to a doctor.

Wolfe's clerk, in disguise Number Three, was Evelyn Ankers, wearing spectacles and a prim hairdo and now suggesting a Scotch accent. As Wolfe read the name and address of the recipient of the sixth Napoleon to Rathbone, he realized they had been tampered with and were incorrect. Meanwhile, in the other room Ankers phoned Mander to tell him it was safe to rob the doctor in question now because Rathbone would be in another part of town. Rathbone picked up the extension, and, cutting him off, disguised his voice as Mander's and tricked Ankers into giving him the doctor's real whereabouts.

Ankers was arrested. When she asked the charge, Rathbone said, "Peddling matches without a license."

The doctor, wearing a surgical mask, was busy in his laboratory when Mander arrived to get the last bust—which had to contain the pearl. The doctor whipped off the mask, and—voilá—Rathbone. On the spot (Mander had a gun), Rathbone turned the Creeper against him by revealing that Ankers, whom the Creeper worshipped, had been arrested, that Mander had gotten her into all this, that she would hang "by that soft, white neck." The Creeper killed Mander and was then shot by Rathbone. And the pearl was indeed in the sixth Napoleon.

As was often the case with the wartime, contemporized Sherlock Holmes adventures, the picture wound up with Rathbone giving a brief patriotic speech. This time he likened the greed of men for pearls to the greed for world domination.

Everyone was in fine fettle: the unflappable, incomparable Basil Rathbone, born to play Holmes; Nigel Bruce, his Watson, pasting clippings on the case in a scrapbook and misplacing some on the back of his sleeve, a virtuoso at well-intentioned bumbling; reliables Evelyn Ankers and Miles Mander (each cast as totally different characters in two earlier, separate Holmes episodes) in two of their best showings as the chameleonesque criminals; Dennis Hoey, perfect as the thick Inspector Lestrade; and loveable Mary Gordon, the motherly, rotund Baker Street landlady.

Not to forget Hatton, the Creeper, who got considerable attention for this effort which actually had him, until the end, obscured by shadows most of the time. Perhaps producer-director Roy William Neill was borrowing a page from the notebook of RKO producer Val Lewton, whose specialty was *suggested* horror. Or maybe Neill was simply worried that Hatton's grotesqueness might be too much for some audiences. There were chilling previews dropped here and there, however: the close-up of the Creeper's gross fingers caressing Ankers' vanity case . . . the Creeper stalking a victim in a dark house to a cat's persistent meow . . . the close-up of the Creeper's massive digits suddenly seen grasping the side of an archway as he entered a room. And, of course, the final revelation of his swollen, tragic ugliness.

Hatton had played a number of screen parts before this, but *The Pearl of Death* endeared him to horror fans and Universal, which quickly used him in similar parts.

Bert McCord applauded in the New York *Herald Tribune*: "[*The Pearl of Death* is] a pleasant surprise . . . the Universal offering will succeed in diverting most murder mystery addicts . . . Rondo Hatton plays [the Creeper] and if he goes to the right Hollywood parties with the right people, Boris Karloff had better look to his horrors."

Rondo Hatton died in 1946, two years after *The Pearl of Death* was released. And while he was hardly in a class with Karloff, not to mention Lugosi or the Chaneys senior and junior, he is remembered as—to quote another critic—"the only film star to play monsters without make-up."

REVEILLE WITH BEVERLY

(Columbia Pictures, 1943)

Credits

Producer, Sam White
Director, Charles Barton
Original screenplay, Howard J. Green,
　　Jack Henley, Albert Duffy
Music director, M.W. Stoloff
Art director, Lionel Banks
Camera, Philip Tannura
Editor, James Sweeney
Running Time: 78 minutes

Cast

ANN MILLER (Beverly Ross)
WILLIAM WRIGHT (Barry Lang)
DICK PURCELL (Andy Adams)
Franklin Pangborn (Vernon Lewis)
Tim Ryan (Mr. Kennedy)
Larry Parks (Eddie Ross)
Adele Mara (Evelyn Ross)
Walter Sande (Canvassback)
Wally Vernon (Stomp McCoy)
Andrew Tombes (Mr. Smith)
Eddie Kane (medical officer)
Boyd Davis (Gen. Humphrey)
Eddy Chandler (Top sergeant)
Doodles Weaver (Elmer)
Eugene Jackson (Jackson)
Harry Anderson (Sgt. Anderson)
Si Jenks (Jenks)
David Newell (sentry)
Jack Rice (Davis)
Irene Ryan (Elsie)
John T. Murray (director)
Virginia Sale (Mrs. Browning)
Herbert Rawlinson (announcer)
Ernest Hilliard, Jean Inness (Mr. and
　　Mrs. Oliver)
Shirley Mills (Laura Jean)
Maude Eburne (Maggie)
Bobby Barber (Collins)
Lee and Lyn Wilde (singing twins)
Bob Crosby and His Orchestra, Freddie Slack
　　and His Orchestra, with Ella Mae Morse,
　　Duke Ellington and His Orchestra, Count
　　Basie and His Orchestra, Frank Sinatra,
　　the Mills Brothers, the Radio Rogues
　　(themselves).

Reveille with Beverly was not another *Singin' in the Rain.* In fact, with its vaudeville-styled musical inserts and time-tired gags, it almost wasn't even another *movie.* Viewed today, the enthusiastic performance and patriotic fervor make it a quintessential—and campy, if you must—WWII home-front movie morale-booster. As well as one of the earliest tributes to the disc jockey, whose wartime contributions I had never given much thought before (outside of Tokyo Rose).

Reveille with Beverly was roasted by the critics but proved a "sleeper," Columbia's biggest moneymaking "B" of 1943. Discussing the several quickies she did for the studio during the war years in her autobiography, *Miller's High Life,* Ann Miller, who played the title role, wrote, "Among my most notable ones was a happy-hearted little film called *Reveille with Beverly,* which really cleaned up at the box office, racking in millions more than the $40,000 which Columbia spent to make it."

Although Miller's character was the picture's cynosure, she was billed, curiously, *after* the many musical specialty interludes (and in smaller type)—Bob Crosby and His Orchestra, Freddie Slack and His Orchestra, with Ella Mae Morse, Duke Ellington and His Orchestra, Count Basie and His Orchestra, the Mills Brothers, the Radio Rogues and, in his third feature movie appearance, the fast-rising Frank Sinatra. (Later that year, Sinatra would have a lead in *Higher and Higher.)*

Miller played a radio-struck record shop clerk who dreamed of becoming a radio star. Getting a job at the switchboard of a local station (where the cooking expert was carried out with ptomaine poisoning), she got her chance by convincing early morning classical music broadcaster Franklin Pangborn that he was ill and needed a rest. (Shades of his enforced siege of biliousness as the ill-timed bank examiner in W.C. Fields' *The Bank Dick.)*

It was wartime. Miller's father (Douglas Leavitt) was an air raid warden, her mother (Barbara Brown) saved kitchen grease, her brother (Larry Parks—three years before *The Jolson Story)* was a soldier, and her sister (Adele Mara) was a

Frank Sinatra

riveter ("She *is* a little jumpy, isn't she?" noticed a guest after she had shaken his hand numb). So Miller decided to dedicate her popular early bird music program to the armed services, calling it—*Reveille with Beverly.* An immediate hit ("I feel like a new broom," she remarked on the premiere broadcast), Columbia said it was inspired by an actual radio show of the time.

Complicating matters were two Miller suitors: William Wright, the playboy "chocolate king," and his chauffeur (Dick Purcell), both new Army recruits but an old movie gimmick—see Abbott and Costello's earlier *Buck Privates* for one example.

The major part of the film's musical program was introduced as dj Miller put on her records. The label on each disc expanded, showing more and more of the spotlighted act until the performance took over the full screen. The tunes were big hits of the day, although their flat, short subject, chintzy staging left much to be desired. Duke Ellington's "Take the 'A' Train" was ostensibly performed aboard a speeding Super Chief—not exactly the train composer Billy Strayhorn had in mind. (This title recalls the now infamous time Lawrence Welk introduced "Take the 'A' Train" on his television program as "Take thee a Train.") One surprise in the Bob Crosby "Big Noise from Winnetka" number was the unbilled singing appearance of the pretty Wilde twins, Lee and Lyn, soon to give Andy Hardy blonde trouble and to be featured in their own films.

The best of these "guest" shots was Frank Sinatra's. Film critics, though, had not yet been informed that they were listening to possibly the greatest male pop voice of all time. For instance, John T. McManus in *PM* wrote, "I am convinced there has been nothing like him since goldfish-eating. He even out-manias the chain-letter rage and the Rudy Vallee crush of 15 years ago. And for the life of me, I can't tell you why. He is a slight young man given to violent sport jackets. He sings, yes—with an almost studied affectation of zombie mannerisms. His voice is pleasant enough—a kind of moaning baritone with a few trick inflections that involve going off-key at turning points in the melody."

In *Reveille with Beverly,* the startlingly young, thin singer, almost swallowed up by his soup-and-fish finery, gave a smooth, expressive reading of "Night and Day" (puzzlingly sans close-up) in a budget Busby Berkeley-type production number surrounded by girl violinists and pianists.

Ann Miller's pyrotechnic tap-dancing was kept under wraps, along with her shapely gams,

Ann Miller, Irene Ryan, Franklin Pangborn, Tim Ryan

Ann Miller

Walter Sande, Dick Purcell, Wally Vernon, Larry Parks, William Wright

until the Army camp show finale, "Thumbs Up for V for Victory." Dressed in a microminiskirted "military" costume and backed by waving Allied flags and servicemen chorus boys, her taps ignited a huge flaming V for Victory on the stage floor for an effective finish.

The humor in the script was sometimes weary but, under Charles Barton's seasoned direction, never wearily rendered. Tim and Irene Ryan, old married pros (she of later fame as Granny on TV's *Beverly Hillbillies*), got the worst of it as, respectively, Miller's harried radio station boss and a nitwit switchboard operator who had to have been one of the relatives Gracie Allen always joked about. Example: after one of their frequent office set-tos, Irene sweetly asked Tim for his picture for a scrapbook she kept on important people. "I'm simply dying to paste you," she said innocently.

Miller, fresh and attractive and obviously thor-

oughly sold on her material, which had to count for something, had one surprisingly sophisticated bit when doing a radio commercial in which she told her "husband" he needed a shave. "It's the palm of your hand that has the whiskers," he suavely retorted—it was a hand lotion blurb.

The biggest laugh, however, came from an unbilled character actress. Maude Eburne had a fleeting, almost lineless scene or two as the station cleaning woman, and the viewer began to think that this great old character comedienne was about to be completely wasted. But when the fussy, effeminate, overage Franklin Pangborn (also very funny) suddenly received his draft notice and pranced away, she came through. Leaning on her mop, with faultless timing she sighed out of the corner of her elastic crone's mouth, "God bless America!"

Disarming was the word for *Beverly*.

SAN DIEGO I LOVE YOU

(Universal Pictures, 1944)

Credits

Producers, Michael Fessier, Ernest Pagano
Director, Reginald LeBorg
Screenplay, Fessier, Pagano
From a story by Ruth McKenney,
    Richard Bransten
Music director, Don George
Camera, Hal Mohr
Editor, Charles Maynard
Running Time: 83 minutes

Cast

JON HALL (John Caldwell)
LOUISE ALLBRITTON (Virginia McCooley)
Edward Everett Horton (Philip McCooley)
Eric Blore (Nelson)
Buster Keaton (bus driver)
Irene Ryan (Miss Jones)
Rudy Wissler (Walter McCooley)
Gerald Perreau, a.k.a. Peter Miles
    (Joey McCooley)
Charles Bates (Larry McCooley)
Don Davis (Pete McCooley)

Florence Lake (Miss Lake)
Chester Clute (Percy Caldwell)
Sarah Selby (Mrs. Lovelace)
Fern Emmett (Mrs. Callope)
Mabel Forrest (Mrs. Fresher)
George Lloyd (moving man)
Jack Rice (hotel clerk)
Bill Davidson (general)
John Gannon (soldier)
Jerry Shane (sailor)
Clarence Muse (porter)
Jan Wiley (receptionist)
Matt McHugh (man on street)
Harry Barris (clarinetist)
George Meader (Mr. Applewaite)
Almira Sessions (Mrs. Mainwaring)
Leon Belasco (violinist)
Sarah Padden (Mrs. Gulliver)
Vernon Dent (Mr. Fitzmaurice)
Harry Tyler (Mr. Carruthers)
Victoria Horne (Mrs. Allsop)
Hobart Cavanaugh (Mr. McGregor)
Esther Howard (mother)
Teddy Infuhr (brat)
Gene Stutenroth, a.k.a. Gene Roth (stevedore)

165

Blithe Louise Allbritton was one of the nice things about "B" movies in the forties. Under contract for seven years to Universal, her parts generally were too big for the ever-supporting Eve Arden of that day, yet lacked the "A" values to lure Rosalind Russell. Like those ladies, the elegant, Oklahoma-born, Texas-raised Allbritton excelled in comedy, low and high. To these roles she brought a special, unique combination of slightly distracted wit, poise, and charm.

An homage to 1930s farce with leveling doses of forties warmth, *San Diego I Love You* presented her in a diverting showcase. She portrayed the oldest sister caring for a wild family of motherless youngsters, while she kept trying to sell a collapsible life raft invented by her father (Edward Everett Horton).

The reviews were interestingly divergent.

Starting at the top, the Hollywood *Reporter* rhapsodized that it was "the kind of movie that people go back to see more than once. As a matter of simple fact, *San Diego I Love You* comes dangerously close to being Academy Award material, for it has all the charm, zany gayety and greatness that made box-office smashes out of *It Happened One Night and You Can't Take It with You* . . . Producers Michael Fessier and Ernest Pagano, who double in brass and write their own screenplays, prove themselves a decided asset to Universal with this picture, and they verify the judgment of whoever was responsible at Universal for inaugurating the policy of producers-writers . . . Jon Hall has never been better, or more human . . . Louise

Louise Allbritton

Allbritton is a threat to any light femme comedienne in pictures."

In *The Nation*, reserved James Agee termed it "A coarse-weft, easygoing little farce about an inventor (Edward Everett Horton), his daughter (Louise Allbritton), a girl-shy financier (Jon Hall) and some pleasant comics (notably Buster Keaton). I can't exactly recommend it, but if you see it by accident it will cause no particular pain."

Then there was Bosley Crowther in the New York *Times:* "Louise Allbritton, who could play rough-house comedy if the right sort were given her, carries the embarrassing burden of the focal girl in this case." He did not like the film at all.

Each of these critiques seemed to fall short of the mark to me. *San Diego I Love You,* from a story by Ruth *(My Sister Eileen)* McKenney and Richard Bransten, was neither great nor painless, but it certainly wasn't embarrassing. It simply was very enjoyable family entertainment that, furthermore, remains Allbritton's own favorite of her movies. And rightly so. Appearing in almost every scene, the blonde star kept the picture afloat with her energetic, airy performance in a role with overtones of one of her professed idols, the late Carole Lombard.

An outstanding bit was a beguiling, whimsical bus ride along the beach at night after the driver (Keaton) had been convinced by Allbritton that he was in a rut driving the city streets. She even got to hum a song through in this interlude.

Affectionately directed by Reginald LeBorg, *San Diego I Love You* was choice Louise Allbritton, and it can still be viewed as agreeable proof that the actress rated, although did not get, important stardom. (Allbritton would have made a sensational Auntie Mame.) She chose instead to concentrate on her enduring marriage to newsman Charles Collingwood, who was himself the kind of dashing reporter that inspired so many vintage movie heroes. Thus, Allbritton became a forties heroine in real life— except that these values were definitely "A."

Jon Hall, Louise Allbritton

Rudy Wissler, Gerrald Perreau, Charles Bates, Donald Alan Davis, Louise Allbritton

SAN FRANCISCO DOCKS

(Universal Pictures, 1941)

Credits
Associate producer, Marshall Grant
Director, Arthur Lubin
Original screenplay, Stanley Crea Rubin,
    Edmund L. Hartman
Music director, H.J. Salter
Camera, Art Lasky
Editor, Bernard W. Burton
Running Time: 60 minutes

Cast
BURGESS MEREDITH (Johnny Barnes)
IRENE HERVEY (Kitty Tracy)
Raymond Walburn (Admiral Andy Tracy)
Robert Armstrong (Father Cameron)
Lewis Howard (Sanford)
Barry Fitzgerald (The Icky)
Ed Gargan (Hank)
Esther Ralston (Frances March)
Edward Pawley (Monte March)
Floyd Criswell (traffic cop)

William B. Davidson (District Attorney Craig)
Don Zelaya (Felipe)
Joe Downing (Cassidy)
Colin Campbell (Dr. Conway)
Ralf Harolde (Hawks)
Esther Howard (Jean)
Harold Daniels (cab driver)
Ken Christy, Lou Hicks (cops)
Billy Mitchell (black man)
Harry Cording (Collins)
Glenn Strange (Mike)
Kernan Cripps (first guard)
Max Wagner (second guard)
Ed Cassidy (dock foreman)
Minerva Urecal (landlady)
Ralph Dunn (guard)
William Ruhl (Forkild)
Harold [Hal] Gerard (interne)
Charles Sullivan (first longshoreman)
Tom London (second longshoreman)
Branford Hatton, Charles McMurphy, Jimmy
    O'Gatty, Art Miles, Jimmie Lucas, Charles
    Sherlock (longshoremen)

San Francisco Docks was typical of Universal's low-budget action fare, which means that it unwound with dispatch, had a crackerjack cast and a serviceable if unexceptional story. In short, the essential "B" movie.

One atypical aspect, perhaps, was casting Burgess Meredith in the male lead. A serious young character actor, Meredith, shortly before appearing in this film, had starred in John Steinbeck's *Of Mice and Men* and soon after would win Ginger Rogers in *Tom, Dick and Harry*. In *San Francisco Docks* he made one of his infrequent "B"-melodrama appearances, and—while he was given top-billing—more screen time was devoted to his co-star, Irene Hervey, than to him.

With almost dizzying economy, the first minute of the movie—depicting an in-progress lovers' quarrel on the waterfront—told just about everything there was to tell about the two principals. Meredith and Hervey portrayed dockside sweethearts, he a longshoreman studying aviation mechanics at night, she the barmaid daughter of saloon owner Raymond Walburn, a bogus ex-admiral constantly boasting of his naval exploits. When Edward Pawley escaped from Alcatraz and killed a man (Joe Downing) with whom Meredith had just fought, Meredith was arrested for the crime. His story about accidently meeting three men who could provide him with an alibi for the night of the killing, was not believed. The men did not come forth—for good reason: they were Pawley himself, whom the police thought dead, and two dock men who had helped him escape from prison (Harry Cording, Don Zelaya).

Assisted by priest Robert Armstrong, barfly Barry Fitzgerald, and her father, Hervey set out to unearth the men Meredith had seen. She finally traced Pawley's platinum blonde wife

Barry Fitzgerald, Irene Hervey, Robert Armstrong, Raymond Walburn

(Esther Ralston) to a beauty parlor owned by that unfailingly delightful character actress Esther Howard, who looked at Ralston's picture and said, "Looks familiar, but dearie, these blondes all bleach alike." After Hervey had staked out the place for several days, Ralston showed up ("Can I still get a finger wave?"). She and Hervey had a lengthy hair-pulling match. Meanwhile, after a street shoot-out, Pawley was brought to justice. Again, it was not Meredith, the hero, who caught the heavy but priest Armstrong who felled him in an alley.

More predictable were the humorous lines given Barry Fitzgerald, who two years later would win the best supporting actor Oscar for his role as the old priest in *Going My Way* and become one of Hollywood's most in-demand character actors. Although always a skilled scene-stealer, his somewhat dragged-in comic interest in this film made for a part that was scarcely of award caliber. For example:

Fitzgerald: "I was a spy once. They sent me on a secret mission."

Ed Gargan (a pal of Meredith's): "What was the mission?"

Fitzgerald: "I don't know. It was so secret they didn't tell me."

Still, despite the dank, foggy backlot appropriate for this waterfront, there was an atmosphere of warm camaraderie that made the picture stand out a bit from the pack. The dock denizens, aside from the villains capably headed by the deliciously shifty Pawley and veteran actress Ralston in her last film appearance, were unusually likable. There was the always welcome Irene Hervey's plucky girl ("My, she's pretty!" wrote another Irene—Thirer—in the New York *Post* review), Meredith's ambitious boy, Walburn's gassy but ultimately heroic, wounded pub owner, Armstrong's two-fisted priest, Lewis Howard's novice legal counsel for Meredith, and Esther Howard's gilded, elderly beautician.

Irene Thirer summed up *San Francisco Docks* nicely: "The plot is reminiscent, but the picture nevertheless is actional, performances are all good, and atmospherically the film seems sound."

Robert Armstrong, Irene Hervey, Burgess Meredith,

Irene Hervey, Burgess Meredith

THE SEVENTH VICTIM

(RKO Radio Pictures, 1943)

Credits

Producer, Val Lewton
Director, Mark Robson
Original screenplay, Charles O'Neal,
    DeWitt Bodeen
Music, Roy Webb
Music director, C. Bakaleinikoff
Art director, Albert S. D'Agostino,
    Walter E. Keller
Camera, Nicholas Musuraca
Editor, John Lockert
Running Time: 71 minutes

Cast

TOM CONWAY (Dr. Louis Judd)
KIM HUNTER (Mary Gibson)
JEAN BROOKS (Jacqueline Gibson)
Hugh Beaumont (Gregory Ward)
Erford Gage (Jason Hoag)
Isabel Jewell (Frances)
Chef Milani (Mr. Romari)
Marguerite Sylva (Mrs. Romari)
Evelyn Brent (Natalie Cortez)

Mary Newton (Mrs. Redi)
Jamesson Shade (Swenson, the cop)
Eve March (Mrs. Gilchrist)
Ottola Nesmith (Mrs. Lowood)
Edythe Elliott (Mrs. Swift)
Milton Kibbee (Joseph, a devil worshipper)
Marianne Mosner (Miss Rowan)
Elizabeth Russell (Mimi)
Joan Barclay (Gladys)
Barbara Hale (young lover)
Mary Halsey (bit)
William Halligan (Radeaux)
Wheaton Chambers, Ed Thomas (men)
Edith Conrad (woman)
Lou Lubin (Irving August)
Bud Geary, Charles Phillips, Howard
    Mitchell (cops)
Lloyd Ingraham (watchman)
Dewey Robinson (conductor)
Ann Summers (Miss Summers)
Tiny Jones (news vendor)
Adia Kuznetzoff (ballet dancer)
Sarah Selby (Miss Gottschalk)
Betty Roadman (Mrs. Wheeler)
Eileen O'Malley, Lorna Dunn (mothers)

173

When *The Seventh Victim* was first released, it was trounced by the press, especially by the New York *Times'* Bosley Crowther and the New York *Herald Tribune'*s Howard Barnes. Crowther thought the film might make more sense if run backwards, and Barnes said it put him to sleep. So much for the state of film criticism during the last decade of the screen's Golden Age.

In his book *An Illustrated History of the Horror Film,* Carlos Clarens wrote that *The Seventh Victim* could be considered Lewton's masterpiece. "Rarely has a film succeeded so well in capturing the nocturnal menace of a large city, the terror underneath the everyday, the suggestion of hidden evil," Clarens went on. "The anti-heroine (well-played by Jean Brooks in a cryptic sort of way) has defected from a secret society of Palladists. She endangers the safety and secrecy of the adepts by mysterically murdering an informer and is condemned by the society to death by execution or suicide. She takes the latter as the way out, hanging herself, alone and dejected in her dismal rented room while a consumptive neighbor (Elizabeth Russell) goes out into the night for one last fling. A hauntingly oppressive work, *The Seventh Victim* seemed to draw its inspiration from the John Donne sonnet that closed it: "I run to Death, and Death meets me as fast, and all my Pleasures are like Yesterdays."

Somewhat over-written, incomparably unnerving, and original, *The Seventh Victim* began with a schoolgirl (Kim Hunter, in her screen debut) journeying to a rather stylized Greenwich Village in search of the older sister (Jean Brooks) who, following her altercation with the devil-worshippers, had disappeared. The younger sister met a few weird ones on her own, including the missing girl's remarkably unconcerned husband (Hugh Beaumont), an unfrocked psychiatrist (Tom Conway) and an unproductive poet (Erford Gage—who was to die in service during World War II at age 32). Hunter soon learned that her sister had gone into hiding because she was to be the seventh victim of the evil cult.

The film had a strange, dreamlike ambiguity.

**Jean Brooks, Ben Bard, Milton Kibbee (at right),
Mary Newton (seated)**

One explanation for it all could be that the schoolgirl, repressed and naive, lost her grip on reality at her first contact with a complex adult world and fantasized the macabre events. Perhaps she was literally, as one character put it, "half-crazy with anxiety." This seemed particularly likely in light of Kim Hunter's almost somnambulent performance and her delivery of her lines in a hushed monotone. Everything she saw took on a seemingly bizarre quality, including her sister.

When Jean Brooks finally made her belated entrance, she was indeed something to see. "Anyone who sees her never forgets her," said Brooks' former beautician employee (Isabel Jewell), a line also echoed by a couple of other actors. Crowned by a black Cleopatra wig and photographed with either a dazzling key light or in the suggestion of shadows, Brooks was every inch the "sensationalist" described by Tom Conway—and perhaps seen as her (?) disturbed younger sister would have her look.

Although used sparingly, the normally blonde, intense Jean Brooks proved again that she was a forceful and attractive actress who should have attained big-time stardom but never did. For a few years during the forties she was the resident neurotic in RKO "B"'s. She deserved a better fate than her succession of roles with—almost exclusively, it sometimes seemed—Tom (the Falcon) Conway. Earlier, Brooks—Texas-born/Costa Rica-raised—had been a nightclub singer and entered pictures in

the thirties as Jeanne Kelly. Apparently, she changed her name professionally when she married director Richard Brooks, who is today wed to actress Jean Simmons.

One of Jean Brooks' most evocative bits in *The Seventh Victim* was the almost silent sequence in which she sat deep into a large chair, methodically tapping her finger, while outside the window, day changed to night and the clustered secret society tried to make her drink a glass of poison which had been set before her.

Other moments to remember:

The terrified, pursued Brooks, hiding in dark alleys, suddenly encountering a group of costumed, reveling actors on the way to the stage door; the shower confrontation between Kim Hunter and her sister's ex-beauty parlor "partner" (Mary Newton), the latter appearing only in silhouette outside the shower curtain, wearing a hat that seemed as if she were sporting horns while she warned the schoolgirl to go home; and Hunter, riding in a lonely subway car, seeing the body of the man (Lou Lubin) whose murder she had inadvertently caused as he was being

Evelyn Brent, Tom Conway

Jean Brooks

dragged by two men passing him off as a drunk. (Incidentally, the train scene had an unbilled walk-on by Barbara Hale, who had just come to RKO and before long would be playing leads and eventually Della Street in the Perry Mason television series.)

The Seventh Victim was the first—and possibly best—directorial credit of one-time film editor Mark Robson, who went on to helm *Champion* and *Peyton Place.* It was co-written by DeWitt Bodeen, whose work on several Val Lewton productions helped to establish their high level of literacy.

In a 1963 article on the late producer in *Films in Review,* Bodeen described the making of *The Seventh Victim.* "My second assignment for Val (after *Cat People*) was an original called *The Seventh Victim,* which I again wrote as a long short story," he reported. "This time an orphaned heroine is caught in the web of murder against a background of the Signal Hill oil wells. Gradually she realizes she will herself be the murderer's seventh victim if she does not discover his identity in time." But Val Lewton decided on a different approach, Bodeen went on to explain, the one ultimately used, and

Charles O'Neal (Ryan's father) signed on to develop the new scenario with Bodeen. "Val himself dictated the good taste which graced his pictures," noted Bodeen.

He told this writer that considerable material had been cut after filming to get the picture down to bottom-bill length. For instance, the minor character of the one-armed devil-worshipper played by Evelyn Brent was originally more prominent as a concert pianist who had turned to the evil society in bitterness over the loss of her arm. This was not explained in the film, nor even suggested, causing some viewers to think veteran actress Brent, not as active then as she once was, actually had had her arm amputated.

Despite some pseudo-poetic heavy-handedness (a schoolgirl's romantic fondness for poetry?) and the sudden love between Jean Brooks' husband and Kim Hunter (a schoolgirl's romantic dream of conquest?), *The Seventh Victim,* a seventy-one-minute quickie, remains one of the most absorbing, creative chillers of any day. As an adventure in stylish diabolism, real or unreal, it makes *Rosemary's Baby* look like *Blondie's Blessed Event.*

SHE GETS HER MAN

(Universal Pictures, 1945)

Credits

Producer, Warren Wilson
Director, Erle C. Kenton
Original screenplay, Wilson, Clyde Bruckman
Music director, Frank Skinner
Gowns, Vera West
Camera, Jerome Ash
Editor, Paul Landres
Running Time: 73 minutes

Cast

JOAN DAVIS (Jane "Pilky" Pilkington)
LEON ERROL (Officer Mulligan)
WILLIAM GARGAN (Breezy Barton)
Vivian Austin (Maybelle Clarke)
Millburn Stone (Tommy Tucker)
Russell Hicks (mayor)
Donald MacBride (Henry Wright)
Paul Stanton (Dr. Bleaker)
Cy Kendall (Police Chief Brodie)
Emmett Vogan (Hatch)
Eddie Acuff (Boze, the photographer)
Virginia Sale (Phoebe)
Ian Keith (Oliver McQuestion)
Maurice Cass (Mr. Fudge)
Chester Clute (Charlie, in play)
Arthur Loft (Waldron)
Sidney Miller (boy)
Al Kikume (Joe, in play)
Leslie Denison (Barnsdale, in play)
Bob Allen (song specialty)
Vernon Dent (doorman)
Charles Sherlock (Moe)
Jerry Jerome (Bat)
Nan Brinkley (girl)
Pierre Watkin (Johnson)
George Lynn (sinister cameraman)
Syd Saylor (waiter/tour guide)
William Hall (Bill, the policeman)
Richard Hirbe (newsboy)
Ruth Roman (glamour girl)
Sam Flint (dignified man)
Howard Mitchell (train announcer)
George Lloyd (town character)
Hank Bell (Clem)
Billy Newell (bettor)
Claire Whitney (landlady)
Harold Goodwin (winning companion)
Olin Howlin (Hank)
Bobby Barber (trombone gag, short man)
Sid Troy (trombone gag, tall man)
Max Wagner (mailman)
Perc Launders (hot dog man)
Charles Sullivan (cigar gag man)
William J. O'Brien (painted suit gag)
Kit Guard (bootblack gag)
Charles Hall (painter gag)

"I'll be hovering over you like a hawk," officer Leon Errol promised Joan Davis, marked for death by an unknown fiend in Universal's *She Gets Her Man*.

Gulped Davis, "I'm glad you didn't say buzzard."

Not Ernst Lubitsch comedy, but at a Joan Davis movie (she alone was starred above the title) you didn't look for sophistication. A slapstick comedienne of unsurpassed ability, Davis received her basic training in vaudeville where she had headlined since childhood. She became a master at wresting laughs from weak film scripts, and her wellspring was heavily tapped in this opus that had a promising premise that some tired writing kept from reaching full potential. Still, there was plenty to enjoy in the little farce—with Joan Davis and Leon Errol on tap, both known for their supple legs, and two of the finest comic actors the screen has ever presented, it could scarcely have been otherwise.

As Leonard Maltin wrote in a *Film Fan Monthly* career study of Errol, "If they had been more alert, the Universal executives might have done well to team Davis and Errol in a series of comedies."

Their vehicle, co-written by veteran comedy writer-director Clyde Bruckman and directed by the equally practiced Erle C. Kenton, was so full of visual comedy that it sometimes seemed to be the first talking silent comedy. If the soundtrack had been shut off, the picture probably would have been almost as easily comprehended. Fortunately, it wasn't, because Davis and Errol (who was not getting any younger) were as deft with a quip as a flip.

When a rash of mysterious blowgun murders broke out in a small midwestern town, Joan Davis, klutzy daughter of the community's legendary crime-smasher, the late Ma Pilkington, was called into service. A huge banner proclaimed, "Ma Pilkington Rides Again." It was obvious that the ride would be bumpy, however, when at a press conference the daffy Davis uttered, among other gaffes, "That was a very intelligent question. Has anybody got any stupid ones?" Leon Errol, an arthritic cop, was ap-

Vivian Austin, William Gargan

pointed her assistant in crime detection.

Local officials were invited by the brazen killer to the Neptune Club that evening to witness Davis' murder. "Good evening, Miss Pilkington," said club manager Arthur Loft as she arrived. "It's so nice to have you with us—for a while." There was another murder, but it wasn't Davis, and the trail led Davis and Errol to a theater where Vivian Austin, girlfriend of reporter William Gargan (on whom Davis had a crush), was starring in a play called *The Voodoo Princess*. The sight comedy really got underway then, with Davis repeatedly interrupting the actors on stage to retrieve an inadvertently loaded prop blowgun, then accidentally turning the rain and snow effects on the sweltering jungle inhabitants in the drama.

The theater prop room provided a number of the film's heartiest laughs. Davis had a superbly timed bit of nonsense pantomime as she stealthily investigated things backstage: a balloon became attached to her clothing and kept bouncing up to tap her on the head every couple of steps, but swerving out of eye range every time she turned around. The lifesize dummy of a man on the floor terrified her when it kept sitting up and lying down. Then she saw that it was over a trap door that her partner kept raising from below. Bumping into a skeleton, Errol cracked, "Oh, another crooner." (Frank Sinatra had not yet been deified.)

One of their zaniest episodes occurred as the dejected duo, Davis and Errol, walked deserted, dark streets. Suddenly a sound effects gismo Davis didn't know was in her pocket began to sound off with footsteps, dogs barking, babies crying, horses stampeding, train whistles and gun fire, scattering the pair with each new outburst. "Just missed me," groaned Davis at last, sighted near the top of a telephone pole.

This time to get only her *morale* up, Errol explained that three people were taught in the town's schools, George Washington, Abraham Lincoln and Ma Pilkington. "If you make them lose faith in Ma Pilkington," he reasoned, "they're liable to lose faith in Washington and Lincoln."

Finally, she uncovered the murderer, who turned out to be Paul Stanton, a reputable town doctor who, Davis explained, first drugged his victims and then while pretending to examine them, punctured them with the poison darts palmed in his hand. Yes, someone said, but *why* had he killed all those people? Davis shrugged, "Murder was just his hobby." That was it. No

Joan Davis, Leon Errol

Joan Davis, Leon Errol

further explanations. Anyway, it saved the writers—already obviously pooped—a lot of exposition.

There were a couple of interesting casting footnotes. Ruth Roman, who would later become a well-known leading lady, had a cute one-line walk-on as she entered the Neptune Club (which had just put up a poster outside boasting "Another Blowgun Murder"). Approached by a guard, she threw open the fur coat that covered her tight-fitting gown and exclaimed, "I assure you, officer, I'm not concealing anything!" Another bit player, comic Syd Saylor, had an unusual dual assignment: early in the picture he was seen as a waiter at the Neptune and toward the end popped up again as a tour guide in the street. Davis actually had two roles, too: her own character, nicknamed "Pilky," and her formidable mother, Ma Pilkington, glimpsed only in a scene where her portrait came to life to advise her daughter.

That was the kind of movie *She Gets Her Man* was. Wacky—and often funny, thanks to the comic genius of Davis and Errol. Leon Errol died in 1951 at the age of 70, a prolific comedian; Joan Davis passed away in 1961 at 53, perhaps the more tragic loss—she had so many more years of pleasure to give audiences. But as Liza Minnelli said in *That's Entertainment!*, "Thank God for film!"

SIS HOPKINS

(Republic Pictures, 1941)

Credits
Associate producer, Robert North
Director, Joseph Santley
Screenplay, Jack Townley, Milt Gross,
  Edward Eliscu
Based on the play by F. McGrew Willis
Music director, Cy Feuer
Songs, Frank Loesser, Jule Styne
Camera, Jack Marta
Editor, Ernest Nims
Running Time: 99 minutes

Cast
JUDY CANOVA (Sis Hopkins)
SUSAN HAYWARD (Carol Hopkins)
Bob Crosby (Jeff Farnsworth)
Charles Butterworth (Horace Hopkins)
Jerry Colonna (Professor)
Katherine Alexander (Clara Hopkins)
Elvia Allman (Ripple)
Carol Adams (Cynthia)
Lynn Merrick (Phyllis)
Mary Ainslee (Vera de Vere)
Charles Coleman (butler)
Andrew Tombes (mayor)
Charles Lane (Rollo)
Byron Foulger (Joe)
Betty Blythe (Mrs. Farnsworth)
Frank Darren (Jud)
Joe Devlin, Elliot Sullivan, Hal Price,
  Anne O'Neal (bits)
The Bob Crosby Orchestra with the Bobcats

After appearing in 1940's *Scatterbrain* for Republic, Judy Canova, the homely but ingratiating hillbilly comedienne who sang with a factory whistle trill, became the unlikely first lady of that action-specializing "B" lot. (Until the hovering ice skater-"actress" Vera Hruba Ralston married the boss, Herbert Yates, and deposed her.) The follow-up picture to her initial surprise hit was one of Canova's vervier vehicles, *Sis Hopkins,* bolstered no little bit by the pre-stardom presence of firebrand Susan Hayward in a major part.

The property had been an early stage vehicle for Rose Melville as well as a silent film with Mabel Normand, and if 1941 viewers looked too closely they could see things literally coming apart at the seams. Essentially, it provided a springboard for the slapstick newly devised for Canova and company. The star was cast as (what else?) a pigtailed, amiably gauche bumpkin, with Hayward as her snobbish city cousin, the daughter of wealthy plumber Charles ("I know my bathrooms") Butterworth. When Canova's farm burned down, she moved in with Hayward in college. Many of the resulting jokes, possibly because of the dusty original source, sounded antique even then. For example:

When Canova uttered her trademark expression, "You're tellin' I," college employee Elvia Allman (of Brenda and Cobina radio fame) remarked, "Your syntax is irregular."

"Where?" cried Canova, quickly examining herself.

Somewhat more palatable were Canovaisms

Susan Hayward

such as this:

"Why," exclaimed Sis Canova arriving at her uncle's mansion, "it couldn't be purtier if it were a gas station!"

Hayward, whipping that incredible red mane about, was an extraordinarily attractive menace. Scornful of her country cousin, she achieved her moment of supreme treachery when she obtained the guileless Canova a spot in a burlesque show ostensibly as a sorority initiation.

Hayward: "But you musn't tell a soul."

Canova: "I'll be a real dummy."

Hayward: "You're tellin' I."

Backstage at the burlesque, Hayward phoned the police to report an "indecent performance," then pulled a thread that caused her cousin's dress to fall off on stage just as the theater was being raided.

Canova sang a remarkably diverse program, from "Wait for the Wagon" to excerpts from *La Traviata* to some new tunes by Jule Styne and Frank Loesser. One of the latter, a pleasant ballad titled "Look at You, Look at Me," was sung by the normally dramatic Hayward and film boyfriend Bob Crosby, her voice throatily, credibly dubbed. Their setting was a Ziegfeldian *Fall Frolics* school revue, with Hayward and Crosby at opposite ends of a split stage duetting over the telephone. Otherwise, Hayward's role, almost as big as that of star Canova, was among the future Academy Award winner's most physical. She got drenched with a pan of water, ran in a track meet, with hurdles, and, in what may stand as an unparalleled instance of indignity for any actress, nearly impaled herself walking over a perpendicular plunger.

Pop-eyed "Professor" Jerry ("Ah, yessss . . .") Colonna made Judy Canova a suitably irrepressible foil. At one point rising from a bubble bath in a bathing suit, he informed the camera, "The Hayes Office made me do it." Ex-child actor Joseph Santley directed—although refereed seems a more apt word. He was now fully ready to helm Republic's *Remember Pearl Harbor* (1942).

Charles Butterworth, Bob Crosby, Susan Hayward

Charles Butterworth, Judy Canova, Charles Coleman

SO DARK THE NIGHT

(Columbia Pictures, 1946)

Credits
Producer, Ted Richmond
Director, Joseph H. Lewis
Screenplay, Martin Berkeley, Dwight Babcock
Story, Aubrey Wisberg
Music, Hugo Friedhofer
Music director, M.W. Stoloff
Camera, Burnett Guffey
Editor, Jerome Thoms
Running Time: 75 minutes

Cast
STEVEN GERAY (Henri Cassin)
MICHELINE CHEIREL (Nanette Michaud)
Eugene Borden (Pierre Michaud)
Ann Codee (Mama Michaud)
Egon Brecher (Dr. Boncourt)
Helen Freeman (Widow Bridelle)
Theodore Gottlieb, a.k.a. Brother
    Theodore (Georges)
Gregory Gay (Commissaire Grande)
Jean Del Val (Dr. Manet)
Paul Marion (Leon Achard)
Emil Ramu (Pére Cortot)
Louis Mercier (Jean Duval, Prefect)
Billy Snyder (Philippe, the chauffeur)
Frank Arnold (Antoine, the police artist)
Adrienne d'Ambricourt (newspaper woman)
Marcelle Corday (shop proprietor)
Alphonse Martel (bank president)
André Marsaudon (postmaster)
Francine Bordeaux (flower girl)
Esther Zeitlin (peasant woman)
Cynthia Gaylord (French bootblack)

Columbia Pictures' *So Dark the Night* was one of the forties' finest "B" movies, as well as one of the unlikeliest.

Based on an actual 19th century murder case, the film had little in common with any of its bottom-bill brethren. The cast—led by stocky, middle-aged Steven Geray, a heavily accented minor player of Continental waiters and (notably in *Gilda)* men's room attendants—was virtually unknown to filmgoers, at least by name, and its crime-and-passion story of an aging man led to murder by a woman was then usually the domain of Edward G. Robinson in "A" pictures. Under the guidance of Joseph H. Lewis, who directed many pictures but none better, it became an affectingly offbeat, moody, "artistic" production that startled moviegoers expecting formula filler.

Its distinction did not go unrecognized. In a rare review of a "B" in *Time* magazine, their unsigned critique read, "Director Joseph H. Lewis has turned out a neat little job. It is more entertaining than most of the better-advertised movies it will get paired with on double feature

bills . . . It just goes to show that thoughtful direction and handsome camera work can lift a mediocre movie a long way above its humble beginnings."

The atmosphere so beautifully captured the French ambiance that it often had the texture of a foreign-made film, a realism few Hollywood productions have been able to achieve. (Even the title had a rather awkward English-translation lilt.) Nowhere—except in the hiring of unfamiliar actors, which contributed further to the tale's credibility—did it look as if the usual "B" corners had been cut. Taste and skill were evident at all times, in every female bootblack, every chicken-strewn country yard, every melancholy landscape. The characters' inevitable torrent of verbal "monsieurs," then thought by California filmmakers to be the definitive suggestion of the Gallic milieu, for once did not jolt, either.

Geray appeared as Henri Cassin, the Paris sureté's foremost detective, a relentless sleuth who, ventured a colleague, "would turn in his own mother if he were sure of her guilt." On his

Paul Marion, Steven Geray, Micheline Cheirel

first vacation in 11 years, he went to a rural inn. His arrival was observed in a trenchant moment by innkeeper's daughter Micheline Cheirel: from behind her wash on the line, the young woman's eyes flashed from one brilliant chrome fixture to another on Geray's impressive automobile. In this briefly eloquent, silent footage, audiences were saved several pages of script explaining Cheirel's character plus given a portent of things to come.

Encouraged by her mother (Ann Codee), whose creed was "Love has its place—but it puts no butter on the bread," Cheirel set her cap for Geray and got him, enraging her childhood sweetheart (Paul Marion).

"Leon [Marion] thinks only of his farm. But we—we could have a wonderful time in Paris—you and I," she urged her aging swain.

Her father (Eugene Borden) disapproved, and on the night Geray and Cheirel were to announce their engagement, he grimly advised him, "A man your age isn't meant for marriage."

Marion showed up, vowed he would get her back and stormed out of the inn, followed by Cheirel.

She never returned.

Geray brooded in his room for a week—"I knew it was too good to be true. That much happiness just wasn't meant for me." Then the boy and girl were found murdered, and Geray methodically set about solving the crime. Stumped for the first time in his career, he was next confronted by the murder of Cheirel's mother—dead in the kitchen, unseen on the floor by the camera, the tragedy punctuated by her unattended steaming tea kettle on one side of the screen, a dripping faucet on the other.

When a footprint found at the scene of Marion's murder indicated that the perpetrator fit Geray's general description, the detective realized that, suffering from schizophrenia, he had himself committed the homicides. Now apparently completely unhinged (the psychological fine points here did not seem to bear scrutiny), he killed his police guard and returned to the inn to murder Cheirel's father—"So I wasn't good enough for Nanette. I was too old, too old . . ." The constabulary arrived in time to save the father and Geray was shot, hallucinating as he died that through a window he saw his own image, happy and expectant, arriving at the inn on an earlier day.

His last words: "Henri Cassin is no more. I caught him. I killed him."

Director Joseph H. Lewis and cameraman Burnett Guffey—both just coming off another

Steven Geray, Micheline Cheirel, Emil Ramu, Ann Codee, Eugene Borden

Theodore Gottlieb, Louis Mercier, Eugene Borden, Steven Geray, Paul Marion

188

Billy Snyder, Steven Geray, Eugene Borden, Ann Codee

acclaimed "B," the same studio's *My Name is Julia Ross*— composed a stunning series of pertinent cinematic images, among the most efficacious of their epoch. Besides those already mentioned, there were the authentic looking provincial French lakeside on a dying summer's day, ducks gliding by as the older man and the young girl made love on the bank . . . the long shot of Geray, pondering his growing attraction to Cheirel, peering into that same lake's waters by twilight . . . his features just before he murdered the guard, distorted by suddenly darkening shadows into a gargoyle's countenance . . . Geray's own tormented face through the window of the train that was carrying him to his death, the rain lashing against the glass.

Although some felt that the Hungarian-born Steven Geray's performance lacked the desperate passion necessary to the role, a recent viewing showed that he was thoroughly accept-

able. Unfortunately, the actor quickly went back to supporting parts in a lengthy career in films. French import Micheline Cheirel looked a bit long in the tooth as the peasant seductress, a quickly dispatched Madame Bovary who never got to taste the sweet life she craved; but her coal-black eyes conveyed a believable selfishness. She could say "I love you, Henri" while the windows of her soul opened on dreams of Paris. Eugene Borden, as the simple, grief-stricken father and widower, perhaps the most sympathetic person in the story, did the next most creditable job. Interesting, too, was Helen Freeman as a smilingly sinister, middle-aged, widowed employee of the inn who discovered Geray's guilt and tried in vain to blackmail him into taking her to Paris.

These, then, were not your average quickie types. And few of Columbia's "A" pictures in that year of 1946 equalled the bright achievement of *So Dark the Night*.

SOMEONE TO REMEMBER

(Republic Pictures, 1943)

Credits
Associate producer, Robert North
Director, Robert Siodmak
Screenplay, Frances Hyland
Original story, Ben Ames Williams
Musical director, Walter Scharf
Camera, Jack Marta
Editor, Ernest Nims
Running Time: 80 minutes

Cast
MABEL PAIGE (Mrs. Freeman)
Harry Shannon (Tom Gibbons)
John Craven (Dan Freeman)
Dorothy Morris (Lucia Stanton)
Charles Dingle (Jim Parsons)
David Bacon (Ike Dale)
Peter Lawford (Joe Downes)
Tom Seidel (Bill Hedge)
Richard Crane (Paul Parker)
Chester Clute (Mr. Roseby)
Elizabeth Dunne (Timid Miss Green)
Vera Lewis (Aggressive Miss Green)
John Good (Charlie Horne)
Susan Levine (Patricia)
Buz Buckley (Roger)
Harry Bradley, Edward Keane, George Lessey
   (college trustees)
Flo Buzby (Mrs. Marston)
James Carlisle (Mr. Marston)
Wilbur Mack (Mr. Thurber)
George Reed (John)
Jesse Graves (elevator operator)
Virginia Brissac (Mrs. Parsons)
Jimmy Butler (Bob Edgar)
Michael Owen (Pete Myrick)
Selmer Jackson (Mr. Freeman)
Irene Shirley (Mrs. Freeman)
Frank Jaquet (man in store)
Ann Evers (girl)
Lynette Bryant (Mary Ann Mayberry)
Ada Ellis (governess)
Russell Hicks (Mr. Stanton)
Madeline Grey (Mrs. Stanton)
Edward Earle (Mr. Fielding)
Leona Maricle (Mrs. Fielding)
Georgia Davis (girl in café)
Henri De Soto (headwaiter)
Leo White (waiter)
Broderick O'Farrell (gentleman)

Someone to Remember was a remarkable film in many ways, not the least of which was the fact that it came from Republic Studios. As Wanda Hale put it in her favorable New York *Daily News* review, "Offhand, I can't think of any other picture this studio has turned out that is comparable to this one."

Republic was an outfit whose stock-in-trade was the serial or low-budget action picture. *Someone to Remember,* a moving story of mother love before we learned that such phrases were sexist, did not fit into either of these categories. It was an amazingly sensitive script by Frances Hyland from Ben Ames Williams' original story that, a decade earlier, probably would have been a vehicle for loveably grumpy old May Robson, by this time deceased. Robson, however, of "Apple Annie"-*Lady for a Day* fame, was not an actress given to moderation, to put it mildly, and *Someone to Remember* in her hands might have turned sticky and maudlin. With Mabel Paige giving a tenderly beautiful performance in the lead, it evoked its

prescribed tear or three as well as a modicum of smiles, and under the controlled direction of Robert Siodmak—interestingly, about to make his reputation as a director of fine thrillers such as *The Spiral Staircase* and *The Killers*—it was a picture that eschewed excess for excellence.

Paige, a white-haired old darling who looked as if she had stepped off a pie truck illustration, in reality had come from Broadway recently to establish herself immediately as a top Hollywood character actress in such films as Alan Ladd's *Lucky Jordan,* in which she gave a hilarious—yet ultimately tragic—performance as a boozey old Times Square moocher. It was probably this unexpectedly touching 1942 characterization that won her the fat role of the steadfast Mrs. Freeman in 1943's *Someone to Remember.*

The story found Paige as the sweet, elderly widow who lived on the fourth floor of an old apartment building just purchased by the local university for their boys' dormitory, and which she adamantly refused to vacate. Her husband

Mabel Paige, Dorothy Morris

dead 20 years, she lived there alone in the hope that her long-missing son, expelled from the university, would return to her. When her lease proved unbreakable, she was permitted to stay in her apartment, and that fall—after the renovation of the rest of the building—the college youths moved in all around her. The youngsters were enchanted with the quaint little woman who gave them a standing invitation to tea. They rigged up an alarm bell to clear the floor of unclad boys whenever she was to appear and devised a sort of sedan chair to carry her up and down stairs.

Paige quickly took a special interest in freshman John Craven, who bore the same name as her lost son and whom she came to believe was actually his child—her grandson. Never divulging her presumption, she assisted the lad with his studies, and, after encouraging his elopement with Dorothy Morris, even arranged for the couple to live with her. As she was about to meet Craven's father in the certainty that he would be her own long-absent son, Paige passed away smilingly in her sleep. It was then revealed that her son actually had died in prison 20 years before, the shock of which had killed her husband.

"All this may have a tragic sound to you, but the story isn't presented that way," observed critic Wanda Hale. "It's so very natural, amusing and charming that you can readily forgive the film's few coincidences." (Someone to Remember, which was called The Prodigal's Mother during production, was remade in 1957 as Johnny Trouble, starring Ethel Barrymore in her last role. It did not equal the original's success.)

The acting was uniformly fine, with second honors, perhaps, to veteran Harry Shannon as Paige's taxi driver friend for many years who knew the true story of her son all along but kept it from the old lady.

It was in Mabel Paige's glowing work, however, that the film found real distinction. "Someone to Remember has no marquee names, but it is an absorbing sentimental drama. A grand performance by Mabel Paige (remember Lucky Jordan?) lifts it above average," wrote Frank Quinn in the New York Daily Mirror. If the production had not been a "B," a species normally ignored by the film Academy, Paige would almost surely have had an Oscar nomination for her restrained, never-cloying valentine to maternal devotion.

Mabel Paige, Harry Shannon

Mabel Paige, John Craven, Dorothy Morris

STRANGER ON THE THIRD FLOOR

(RKO Radio Pictures, 1940)

Credits
Producer, Lee Marcus
Director, Boris Ingster
Original screenplay, Frank Partos
Music, Roy Webb
Camera, Nicholas Musuraca
Art director, Van Nest Polglase
Editor, Harry Marker
Running Time: 64 minutes

Cast
PETER LORRE (Stranger)
JOHN McGUIRE (Michael)
MARGARET TALLICHET (Jane)
Charles Waldron (district attorney)
Elisha Cook, Jr. (Joe Briggs)
Charles Halton (Meng)
Ethel Griffies (Mrs. Kane)
Cliff Clark (Martin)
Oscar O'Shea (judge)
Alec Craig (defense attorney)
Otto Hoffmann (police surgeon)
Charles Judels (Nick)
Frank Yaconelli (Jack)
Paul McVey (Lieut. Jones)
Robert Dudley (postman)
Frank O'Connor (officer)
Herbert Vigran (first reporter)
Robert Waldon (second reporter)
Terry Belmont, a.k.a. Lee Bonnell
  (third reporter)
Gladden James (fourth reporter)
Harry C. Bradley (court clerk)
Greta Grandstedt (chambermaid)
Katherine Wallace (bit)
Bud Osborne (bartender)
Lynton Brent (taxi driver)
Broderick O'Farrell (minister)
Emory Parnell, Jack Cheatham, Dell
  Henderson (detectives)
Don Kelly (cop)
Henry Roquemore (Boss McLean)
Jane Keckley (landlady)
Bess Wade (charwoman)
Ralph Sanford (truck driver)
James Farley (cop)
Betty Farrington (stout woman)
Ray Cooke (drug store attendant)
Don Kerr (bit)
William Edmunds (janitor)
Lee Phelps (first taxi driver)
Bobby Barber (Italian man)
Frank Hammond (second janitor)
Max Hoffman (second taxi driver)

RKO's *Stranger on the Third Floor* is a "B" melodrama that has acquired a lofty reputation not entirely deserved. But it is still an engrossing hour, broodingly well photographed by Nicholas Musuraca with, in its jabs at an insensitive society, a more provocative Frank Partos original scenario than most of its class.

The plans of New York star reporter John McGuire and secretary Margaret Tallichet to marry were interrupted when McGuire was called upon to be star witness against Elisha Cook, Jr., charged with the murder of a lunchroom proprietor (Charles Judels). In court, Cook said he had gone there to pay a debt of 30¢, found the owner dead, and ran away. McGuire testified that he had seen him bolt.

"All they want is to get it over with and go home," remarked McGuire's appalled fiancée, observing the terrified, innocence-protesting little man's incompetent lawyer (Alec Craig) and the dozing judge (Oscar O'Shea) and jury. She was upset further, she explained to McGuire, by the fact that it would be his testimony that would send Cook to the chair.

"There's too many people in the world already," shrugged Cliff Clark, a reporter friend of McGuire.

Cook was sentenced to death, and there ensued a long sequence in which McGuire wrestled with the soundtrack voice of his conscience, wondering if Cook actually was guilty. ("Why did I have to live across the street? A lot of people live in Brooklyn. Why couldn't I?") An imaginative, surreal dream sequence then showed him meeting Cook's fate—this arty segment alone has done much toward acquiring advocates among film historians.

Shortly after McGuire spotted stranger Peter Lorre sneaking around the hall of his boarding house ("What an evil face!"), he discovered

Peter Lorre, Margaret Tallichet

next-door neighbor Charles Halton dead, his throat slashed just like the lunch room proprietor. McGuire had once threatened in public to kill the obnoxious Halton, so the police, realizing McGuire had discovered the bodies of both recently murdered men, took him into custody.

Tallichet then began to scour the neighborhood for Lorre, the stranger with the long white scarf, "thick lips and bulgy eyes" described by McGuire as being the probable real murderer. Relaxing in a lunch room after a fruitless search, she heard someone order two raw hamburgers, sans buns, and turned to face the man McGuire had seen. She followed him outside, where he gave the meat to a stray dog.

As they walked off together chatting, Lorre revealed to Tallichet that he had run away from a place where they had put him in a binding jacket and poured ice water on him. Finally, he admitted the two murders and, chasing the young woman into the street, was about to make her the third when a truck ran him down. Dying, he confessed to the police, adding, "But I'm not going back."

The top-billed Lorre, allotted surprisingly little footage, was appropriately creepy, even slightly sympathetic, despite appliance teeth later inherited by comedian Jerry Lewis; but McGuire and Tallichet, with the largest roles, were painfully inadequate. In an unusually demanding part for a quickie production, McGuire

appeared a dimpled, obtuse caricature of the stalwart hero, posturing like a third-rate silent film ham. And Tallichet, while possessing a seemingly sweet personality, delivered her lines as if she hadn't heard those that preceded them, indeed sometimes looked over the shoulders of co-players with whom she was deep in conversation in the manner of today's television sketch actors reading "idiot cards." Then recently married to director William Wyler, she soon retired.

Stranger on the Third Floor, directed with flair by Boris Ingster, should be remembered less for its arty melodramatics than for a sense of human awareness evident amid the mayhem. It had a social conscience, rare in "filler" product, dramatizing an apathetic judicial system and taking a well-aimed shot or two at the sometimes cruel, anything-but-therapeutic therapy visited on mental patients.

Ethel Griffies, Charles Halton, John McGuire

John McGuire, Peter Lorre

THERE'S ONE BORN EVERY MINUTE

(Universal Pictures, 1942)

Credits
Associate producer, Ken Goldsmith
Director, Harold Young
Screenplay, Robert B. Hunt, Brenda Weisberg
Original story, Hunt
Art director, Jack Otterson
Music director, H.J. Salter
Gowns, Vera West
Camera, John W. Boyle
Running Time: 60 minutes

Cast
HUGH HERBERT (Lemuel P. Twine/Abner Twine/Col. Claudius Zebediah Twine)
PEGGY MORAN (Helen Barbara Twine)
Tom Brown (Jimmie Hanagan)
Guy Kibbee (Lester Cadwalader, Sr.)
Catharine Doucet (Minerva Twine)
Edgar Kennedy (Mayor Moe Carson)
Scott Jorden, a.k.a. William Henry (Lester Cadwalader, Jr.)
Gus Schilling (Prof. Asa Quisenberry)
Charles Halton (Trumbull)
Elizabeth Taylor (Gloria Twine)
Renie Riano (Aphrodite Phipps)
Carl [Alfalfa] Switzer (Junior Twine)
Jack Arnold, a.k.a. Vinton Haworth (photographer)
Ralph Brooks (man at meeting)
Frankie Van (busboy brawler)
Melville Ruick (radio announcer at election)
Barbara Brown (club woman)
Claire Whitney (Mrs. Barstow)
Harlan Briggs (Luke Simpson, the grocer)
Jack Gardner, Ted Oliver (reporters)
Bess Flowers (luncheon extra)
Nell O'Day (Antoinette)
Maude Eburne (Agatha)

197

Although it was Elizabeth Taylor's film debut, *There's One Born Every Minute* has been seen by very few. The last assignment on his contract for the movie's star, Hugh Herbert, it was thrown away by Universal. There were virtually no trade reviews, and the New York press didn't bother either.

Even some of its players do not seem to have seen it. When in a recent interview I asked feminine lead Peggy Moran, now retired, what nine-year-old Elizabeth Taylor had been like in those days, Moran replied, "I never worked with Elizabeth Taylor. Your information is wrong." And in Taylor's 1964 autobiography, she referred to the film only by its working title, *Man or Mouse,* describing her part inaccurately: "All I did was run around and shoot rubber bands at ladies' bottoms." In the version that finally was released, no such mischievous activity took place (although plenty of others did). Nor, as best as can be discerned, have any of Taylor's many biographers actually sought out the 1942 film for viewing.

The object of this colossal indifference was a fast screwball comedy that, while certainly no *You Can't Take It With You,* was still a genial lunatic romp with a cast of well-practiced movie madcaps.

The nabob nut, of course, was Herbert, portraying the henpecked owner of Twine's Tasty Pudding Powder, the recipe for which an ancestor bought from the Indians for $24. Currently, he was being run for mayor of Witumpka Falls. Wife Catharine Doucet was his motivation for social-climbing ("If it takes the last breath I take," she vowed haughtily, ferociously devouring a sandwich left over from an Historical Society meeting in her parlor, "I'm going to bring this family up to snuff.") Herbert's two small children (Carl Switzer, Elizabeth Taylor) were brats, but nubile daughter Peggy Moran was relatively normal, although she had her moments, too. After her car knocked boyfriend Tom Brown into a pile of dry leaves, she pounced on him and proceeded to give the uninjured young man violent artificial respiration, which pushed his face sputteringly deeper and deeper into the leaves. A recent advertising

Elizabeth Taylor, Catharine Doucet, Carl Switzer

graduate, Brown was forced to work in the local shoe store owned by town boss Guy Kibbee.

Kibbee, only backing Herbert "to keep a better man out of the field," was behind incumbent mayor Edgar Kennedy, whom he nevertheless continually brushed off. "I demand a little respect," said Kennedy. "You're getting it," retorted Kibbee, "very little." Also courting Moran was Kibbee's overbearing son (Scott Jorden, a.k.a. William Henry), whom Moran definitely did not favor—"The big heel—and shoe man!" she called him during a row.

Although the pudding business was poor, Herbert gave Brown a job in advertising. Trying to come up with a new merchandising gimmick in the form of an undiscovered vitamin contained in the Twine pudding, Brown said no to "O" ("That's for Oomf") but yes to brainstorm "Z"—"Oomf is out and Zumf is in!" he proclaimed. Vitamin Z, corroborated wacky scientist Gus Schilling, had the power to endow "the frail sex with that certain bloom." Herbert's pudding sales soared, and before long the town was celebrating Zumf Day. When Kibbee's secret tests proved Vitamin Z a fraud, Herbert, asserting himself, stayed in the mayoralty race anyway. "What do you want for a mayor," he asked, "a pudding or a man?"

The campaign grew heated—and perhaps more relevant to the seventies than the forties.

"The other side has been robbing us for 20 years. Why not give us a chance?" orated Herbert.

"I want tax reform, school reform," bellowed Kennedy.

"Give him chloroform," stage-whispered Herbert.

Things looked grim, however, until the ghosts of his great-grandfather, a colonial skirt-chaser, and his father, a Southern gentleman (all played by Herbert), materialized to help. With them was protesting ancestral crone Maude Eburne (clock-stopping in colonial gown and white wig)—"Since when have we become troubleshooters for dimwit mortals?" They revealed that Kibbee's pudding tests were made with old powders, which information Brown passed on to the voters. Herbert won the election and Brown won Moran.

In many ways, *There's One Born Every Minute* looked like it might have been conceived originally as a vehicle for W. C. Fields, then under contract to Universal. The pretentious wife (played by Catharine Doucet, Fields' nemesis in *Poppy)*, the nasty children, the winsome daughter, the jaundiced view of society, the free-form style—all were Fieldsian staples.

Tom Brown, Catharine Doucet, Gus Schilling, Peggy Moran, Hugh Herbert, Edgar Kennedy

Hugh Herbert, Catharine Doucet, Carl Switzer, Elizabeth Taylor

Herbert's name, Lamuel P. Twine, might have made him a first cousin to Fields' Cuthbert J. Twillie (*My Little Chickadee),* and his town, Witumpka Falls, could have been within walking distance of Fields' beloved Lompoc. The title, too, sounded as if it had come out of the same hopper as Fields' *You Can't Cheat an Honest Man* and *Never Give a Sucker an Even Break.* One wonders, therefore, if Fields, who did so much of his own writing, had had anything to do with the screenplay (credited to Robert B. Hunt and Brenda Weisberg, from an original story by Hunt).

The main Fields element missing (and it was an essential one) was malice. As silly as these characters were, they never became quite as disagreeable as they would have in a Fields vehicle. Nor, it has to be added, quite as funny.

The guiding force became Herbert, a highly gifted clown with a unique addled style of his own that did not exclude warmth. He is unjustly neglected today. With his strategically placed, trademark outbursts of "Woo-woo!", Herbert was a delight in this multiple assignment. Perhaps his biggest moment in the film was one of his smallest. At a luncheon in his honor, he suddenly found himself holding a dish of Twine's Tasty Pudding which wobbled disconcertingly. Surreptitiously, he steadied it with his hand. A worthy mayor for sure.

Peggy Moran was both lovely and lively, making a stock ingenue part unusually attractive. The front office must have been blind not to see that she deserved much better breaks than she got. But then, these were the same people who let Elizabeth Taylor—her dark, ringletted beauty already lighting up the screen—sign with MGM right after this one-and-only picture at Universal. Little Elizabeth showed spunk in her role, too, pulling Carl (Alfalfa) Switzer's cap down over his face during Zumf Day festivities, thus causing a riot, as well as winding up a saccharine campaign song duet with her brother with a sneer that appeared almost cinéma vérité. She ought to see the picture; it is nothing to be ashamed of; she has appeared in far worse in recent years.

Trust Maude Eburne as the cantankerous colonial phantom (and a transparent one at that) to sock across the film's best line, though. "Very well," she barked to another of Herbert's clustering ancestral wraiths, "if you can't keep a civil tongue in your mouth, I'll thank you for my trumpet and be gone."

THUNDERHOOF

(Columbia Pictures, 1948)

Credits
Producer, Ted Richmond
Director, Phil Karlson
Original screenplay, Hal Smith
Additional dialogue, Kenneth Gamet
Music, Mischa Bakaleinikoff
Art director, Walter Holscher

Camera, Henry Freulich
Editor, Jerome Thoms
Running Time: 77 minutes

Cast
PRESTON FOSTER (Scotty)
MARY STUART (Marguerita)
WILLIAM BISHOP (Kid)
THUNDERHOOF (himself)

Few Westerns, "B" or otherwise, crowded as much into their brief running time as Columbia's *Thunderhoof*. And with only three people on view throughout. It was equal parts allegory, melodrama, love triangle, psychological drama, and outdoor action film—an extremely ambitious stew for any Western and, happily, largely an effective one. Little noticed when it was released in 1948, the picture holds up today as an absorbing and unusual Western adventure.

The actors, Preston Foster, Mary Stuart and William Bishop, played roles exceptionally complex for their primitive setting. Foster was Scotty, a hearty, middle-aged rancher who had brought his young wife, Marguerita (Stuart), with him to the wilds of Mexico for the second time in a year to catch the elusive, near-legendary wild horse known as Thunderhoof. "That beautiful head, with fire in his eyes—his stride must be twenty feet long, and when he runs his hooves sound like thunder," said Foster, almost as obsessive about the black and white stallion as Captain Ahab was about the great white whale, Moby

Dick. As the film began, Foster returned to camp with the unconscious "Kid," played by Bishop, whom he had fetched from the nearest town.

"He's dead. Dead drunk," laughed Foster to his wife. "He's young and wild, but he'll grow up, just like you did."

He had taken the then very young Stuart out of a cantina to marry her, and she was grateful; but Bishop, rescued by him from a quicksand bog at the age of fifteen and raised as a son, resented always having to do "what Scotty wants." And the malcontent young man was very much against Preston's latest trek through no man's land to capture Thunderhoof.

As the two men left camp for the hunt, Foster remarked, "There's a story they tell that whoever catches him gets what's coming to him, his judgment right here on earth." After a while, Bishop said he was quitting the search. The men fought, the sudden appearance of Thunderhoof uniting them briefly—"That's not a horse, it's a devil," groused Bishop. In the scuffle to secure him, Foster's leg was broken. Thunderhoof in

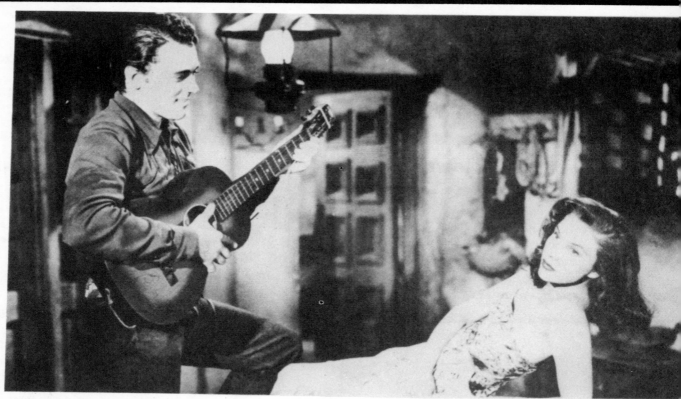

William Bishop, Mary Stuart

tow, they returned to camp where Bishop set his leg.

"Look at Thunderhoof, Marguerita. He's the beginning of our ranch . . . Ten days from now we'll be under our own roof, your own house," said Foster, who had put a down payment on a horse ranch in Texas.

The rugged journey out of the wilderness was hampered not only by Foster's infirmity but by Thunderhoof's obstreperousness, aggravated by the periodic appearances of his mate. Bishop tried to shoot the mare, and subsequently mistreated Thunderhoof as well. With the food running out, Stuart began to get edgy, too.

"That jackass bray of his—don't you ever get tired of it?" Bishop asked her, referring to Foster's neurotic laugh. A few years before there had been something between her and Bishop, who now renewed his attentions. "You'll find yourself married to an old man," he warned the girl, telling her she should see more of life. "But I reckon you'd rather herd horses." He vowed he was going to take her away from Foster as soon as they got out of Mexico.

Then Foster came down with a fever, forcing them to stay at a deserted house where they found food. Stuart and Bishop grew closer; Foster only watched. "Why doesn't he say something?" complained Stuart. "Speak out what's on his mind?" The next day Foster and Stuart discovered that the family living there had fled because their little girl had died from typhoid contracted from contaminated water on

the property. The trio departed.

After a mountain lion killed Foster's horse and stampeded Stuart's, he forced Bishop to break Thunderhoof so Foster could ride him. "You thought he'd be killed, didn't you?" Stuart asked her husband accusingly.

Off by themselves, Foster and Bishop brawled again. When Thunderhoof ran away, Bishop knocked Foster out and rolled him down a ravine. He told Stuart that Foster had deserted them on Thunderhoof, and the young couple went off together. Before long, Bishop came down with a fever, admitting he had drunk from the contaminated waterhole and divulging what had really happened to Foster. He died, leaving Stuart to wander off alone on foot in the desert. Thunderhoof returned to Foster, however, and that night he caught up with his wife, who at first thought the thundering hoofbeats she heard coming closer and closer were her imagination. "He wasn't a bad kid. Just young, wild. He never grew up because I wouldn't let him," said Foster as he and Stuart rode away.

Phil Karlson, who ten years later would direct

Preston Foster, Mary Stuart, William Bishop

Preston Foster, Mary Stuart

another corrosive, Western father-son type relationship in the same studio's *Gunman's Walk,* with Van Heflin and Tab Hunter, deftly vivified the diverse elements in Hal Smith's extraordinarily thoughtful, fibrous screenplay. Between them, they managed to create a good deal of suspense regarding the plight of the three tormented characters, and there was even some question which of the men would wind up with Stuart. The indoctrinated moviegoer, though, knew that no cowboy who was unkind to a horse ever got the girl—at least not in a forties Western, no matter how offbeat. Well-photographed mostly out of doors by Henry Freulich, the production's original gold-like sepia tinting gave the stark proceedings an appropriate scorched look.

Few actors of the day had more demanding roles than the three lone players in *Thunderhoof.* Their enactments were generally good. The veteran Foster, while leaning a little heavily on the laugh button, probably fared best in one of the most challenging assignments of a generally pedestrian career. He made the grizzled rancher's double-leveled drive comprehensible; when he swore of Thunderhoof, "I'll follow him clear across Mexico," we got the message that the stallion was not simply a horse but a symbol of Foster's striving to capture, too, his young wife's love along with her gratitude and—on a larger scale, if you like—*man's* striving for love. Thunderhoof's somewhat improbable return to the abandoned Foster in the desert was almost exactly coincidental with Bishop's revelation to Stuart of his treachery, which made her realize that she loved Foster after all.

Stuart, a hat-check girl discovery of MGM producer Joe Pasternak who would become one of television soap opera's first ladies with her long-run record on *Search for Tomorrow,* had her largest screen part in *Thunderhoof.* A sexy, pouty starlet, she displayed a definite screen presence and acting ability; one of her best bits here, a soggily bedraggled "Whew!" while riding into camp after a desert foray (stationed a little behind the central action of the scene), looked realistic enough to have been filmed unbeknownst to the actress. Bishop tried but never really got inside his complicated, ambiguous character, and especially toward the end seemed to turn self-consciously toward the camera when his turn came to emote. He, too, was best known for a television series, the fifties situation comedy *It's a Great Life.* Bishop died in 1959 at 41.

Thunderhoof was a far piece from Roy Rogers or Gene Autry. Perhaps therein lies the reason it went unheralded in its time. People—reviewers included—just may not have known what to make of such an anomaly, a "wild West" saga of its humble station, that eschewed barroom battles, shoot-outs and Indian massacres in favor of character development, yet did not sacrifice action.

WEIRD WOMAN

(Universal Pictures, 1944)

Credits
Associate producer, Oliver Drake
Director, Reginald LeBorg
Screenplay, Brenda Weisberg
Adaptation, W. Scott Darling
From the novel *Conjure Wife* by Fritz Leiber, Jr.
Music director, Paul Sawtell
Camera, Virgil Miller
Editor, Milton Carruth
Running Time: 62 minutes

Cast
LON CHANEY, JR. (Norman Reed)
ANNE GWYNNE (Paula Reed)
EVELYN ANKERS (Ilona Carr)
Ralph Morgan (Prof. Millard Sawtelle)
Elizabeth Risdon (Grace Gunnison)
Lois Collier (Margaret)
Elizabeth Russell (Evelyn Sawtelle)
Harry Hayden (Prof. Septimus Carr)
Phil Brown (David Jennings)
Jackie Lou Harding (student)
Hanna Kaapa (Larqua)
John Hudson (student)
Chuck Hamilton (carpenter)

Elegant and able Evelyn Ankers, Universal's screaming Mimi mauled by most of the studio's rebounding stable of monsters, got the chance to get in her own licks in *Weird Woman*. And she gave an exhibition that put her old pals Frankenstein and the Wolf Man on their mettle.

As character woman Elizabeth Risdon sized her up in this picture, one of Ankers' several in the company's series inspired by the *Inner Sanctum* mystery books of the day, "Ilona, there's something about your smile right now that makes me think of Jack the Ripper." Indeed, *Weird Woman* provided Ankers with one of her showiest roles, as well as a better story than usual—if no better dialogue (Professor Lon Chaney, Jr., during one crisis: "Aw, honey, you're gonna drive us both mad with these foolish superstitions of yours"). The basis for a television drama in the fifties, the story was re-filmed in England in the sixties as the highly thought-of *Burn, Witch, Burn*, starring Janet Blair, of all musical comedy people, in Anne Gwynne's part and Margaret Johnston in Ankers'.

Ankers essayed the college librarian jilted by Chaney for an islands-reared Gwynne (an always appealing actress who was no babe in these cinematic woods, either). Chaney advised

Evelyn Ankers, Elizabeth Russell

the distraught loser, who—don't ask how come—practiced black arts, that they had merely enjoyed "a pleasant flirtation . . .Oh, Ilona, for Pete's sake! The worst I could've done was—puncture your ego."

Whereupon she drummed out word in their crowd that the new bride was a witch whose jungle-learned voodoo had caused a couple of mysterious deaths, actually brought about by Ankers' own evil machinations. The climax saw the tables turned by a wife whom Ankers had helped to make widow (cat-eyed Elizabeth Russell, the weirdest-looking woman of all, moonlighting from the Val Lewton horror unit at RKO). Made to think dark powers were being used against *her,* weird woman Ankers then got to give out with one of her juiciest screams (one of her specialities), go crazy, fall off a roof and, for an encore, hang herself from a grapevine.

Ankers' beauty played down for obvious reasons, she was still sufficiently—in the vernacular of the islands—hubba-hubba to make viewers wonder why Chaney had looked elsewhere for a spouse. Maybe it was those little images she liked sticking needles into. A malevolent, tree-

rustling nocturnal atmosphere was well-maintained by Reginald LeBorg, Vienna-born director who, with a journeyman's ease, was shuttling back and forth between "B" horror and comedy (a trip some might call short). His *Weird Woman*—from the Fritz Leiber, Jr., novel *Conjure Wife*—stood out among Universal's fright flicks.

Even the high-toned New York *Herald Tribune* bestowed approval. "A neat little murder tale all souped up with black magic," wrote Otis L. Guernsey, Jr. "Universal has produced it with more taste and effort than is usual with a thriller of this type."

Player, Harry Hayden, Anne Gwynne, Lon Chaney, Jr., Evelyn Ankers, Elizabeth Risdon

WHISTLING IN THE DARK

(MGM Pictures, 1941)

Credits
Producer, George Haight
Director, S. Sylvan Simon
Screenplay, Robert MacGunigle, Harry Clork,
    Albert Mannheimer
Based on the play by Laurence Gross,
    Edward Childs Carpenter
Camera, Sidney Wagner
Editor, Frank E. Hull
Running Time: 76 minutes

Cast
RED SKELTON (Wally Benton)
ANN RUTHERFORD (Carol Lambert)
VIRGINIA GREY (Fran Post)
CONRAD VEIDT (Joseph Jones)
"Rags" Ragland (Sylvester)
Eve Arden (Buzz Baker)
Don Douglas (Gordon Thomas)
Don Costello (Moose Green)
Paul Stanton (Jennings)
William Tannen (Robert Graves)
Reed Hadley (Beau Smith)
Lloyd Corrigan (Harvey Upshaw)
Henry O'Neill (Phillip Post)
George Carleton (Deputy Commissioner
    O'Neill)
Mariska Aldrich (Hilda)
Will Lee (Herman)
John Piccori (gatekeeper)
Joe Devlin (taxi driver)
Ruth Robinson (Mrs. Robinson)
John Wald (announcer's voice)
Ken Christy (inspector)
Betty Farrington (Mrs. Moriarity)
Paul Ellis (captain)
Dora Clement (Mrs. Upshaw)
James Adamson (attendant)
Inez Cooper (stewardess)
Emmett Vogan (producer)
Barbara Bedford (local operator)
Lester Dorr (dispatcher)
Mark Daniels (co-pilot)
Leon Tyler (Gerry)
Mel Ruick (engineer)
Dorothy Adams (Mrs. Farrell)
Jenny Mac (Mrs. Kendall)
John Dilson (Vanderhoff)
Billy Bletcher (effects man)
Larry Steers (studio manager)
Ronnie Rondell (waiter)
Brick Sullivan, Al Hill, Robert Homans
    (policemen)

Red Skelton had made a few films before *Whistling in the Dark* (1941), but this one—from an old play and movie starring Ernest Truex—was his first starring vehicle. Returning a considerable amount of money on a miniscule initial investment by MGM, it was also the picture that made him a star. Skelton, who had left home at thirteen to join a traveling stock company and was now in his late twenties, was ready.

The public so liked the comedian and his character of Wally Benton, the zany radio sleuth known as "The Fox" ("Ah-wooooo, I'm the Fox!"), that the studio made two sequels, *Whistling in Dixie* (1942) and *Whistling in Brooklyn* (1944). All were directed by S. Sylvan Simon. The series was discontinued when Skelton became a major star, outgrowing the small-budget concept of the *Whistling* films.

Whistling in the Dark was an amusing, swift, even suspenseful farce-melodrama bolstered by the still-fresh clowning of a youthful, attractive Skelton. He was supported by a sterling cast that included the accomplished Berlin-born Conrad Veidt as head heavy; Ann Rutherford, borrowed from the Andy Hardy series in which she played Andy's girlfriend, as Skelton's radio-actress girlfriend; Virginia Grey as the daughter of Rutherford's sponsor and as Rutherford's competition for Skelton; Eve Arden as Skelton's manager; "Rags" Ragland and Don Costello as dumb Veidt henchmen; and Lloyd Corrigan as an heir in jeopardy.

Eve Arden, although only on the fringe of the action, had the best lines, delivering them with her incomparable dry panache.

"How many?" asked a waiter as she and Grey entered a nightclub to wait for Skelton.

"Three," Arden replied.

"You said three?" repeated the waiter.

"Yes, I hope we're being followed."

She told the waiter to send the gentleman they were expecting right over to their table when he arrived, adding that he might be bringing another lady.

Virginia Grey, Red Skelton

"One gentleman for three ladies?" queried the relentless waiter.

"Oh, it's all right," Arden assured him. "I'm just going to watch."

Later on she told the same waiter, "I feel like a new woman. In fact, I feel like a new man. Bring me a telephone book."

The picture opened arrestingly. Veidt, the leader of a phony religious cult at an estate called Silver Haven, presided over the moonlit, outdoor funeral rites for one of its members before a white-robed congregation of middle-aged women. (If the picture had been filmed six months later, they would probably all have become Nazis.) Veidt had expected to receive the dead Mrs. Upshaw's million dollars, but learned that her nephew (Lloyd Corrigan) from Kansas City controlled the money until his death. As Veidt and his men pondered a solution, "Rags" Ragland suggested murdering the nephew. Knocking Ragland down, Veidt exclaimed, "Silver Haven stands for a refuge for peace and contentment!"

Murder was very much on his mind, though, and he soon kidnapped Skelton, "the master brain of murder" on radio, to help devise the most effective, clueless way. Also abducted to the cult's castle-like, suburban New York headquarters were Rutherford and Grey, whom Veidt hoped would influence the unwilling Skelton to come up with a plan to eradicate Corrigan.

Beset by secret passageways, sinister Veidt accomplices (such as grim, oversize house-keeper Mariska Aldrich, whom Skelton asked, "Aren't you wrestling somewhere tonight?") and two scrapping girlfriends, he relented and had their chemist make up an undetectable poison for the nephew's toothpaste. His plan to substitute a harmless substance was thwarted. Veidt cohort Don Douglas immediately obtained a seat on Corrigan's New York-bound plane where he put the poison in his toothpaste. Connecting the cut telephone wires to the radio, the captive Skelton managed to call the police as well as broadcast his Fox radio program right from Silver Haven, thereby reaching Corrigan on the plane with his warning.

"Do not . . . brush . . . your teeth!" he instructed.

"Don't worry," answered the shaken Corrigan in one of the biggest and best-timed laughs, "I won't even take 'em out!"

Among the principals, Skelton was funny and likable, vulnerable but not moronic (something that could not be said of many later roles),

Red Skelton, Eve Arden

Virginia Grey, Red Skelton, Ann Rutherford

Rutherford was cute and spirited, Grey a delicate-looking, pretty girl who packed a longshoreman's wallop with a quip, Arden a joy, and Veidt a perfect villain who did not take himself too seriously—led away by the authorities at the end, he uttered the cult's standard farewell, "We part in radiant contentment."

So did viewers of Red Skelton's first big hit.

Virginia Grey, Red Skelton, Conrad Veidt, Ann Rutherford

THE WOLF MAN

(Universal Pictures, 1941)

Credits

Producer-director, George Waggner
Original screenplay, Curt Siodmak
Make-up, Jack P. Pierce
Music, Charles Previn
Art director, Jack Otterson
Camera, Joseph Valentine
Editor, Ted Kent
Running Time: 71 minutes

Cast

CLAUDE RAINS (Sir John Talbot)
LON CHANEY, JR. (Larry Talbot)
EVELYN ANKERS (Gwen Conliffe)
Ralph Bellamy (Capt. Paul Montford)
Warren William (Dr. Lloyd)
Patric Knowles (Frank Andrews)
Maria Ouspenskaya (Maleva)
Bela Lugosi (Bela)

Fay Helm (Jenny Williams)
Leyland Hosgson (Kendall)
Forrester Harvey (Victor Twiddle)
J. M. Kerrigan (Charles Conliffe)
Kurt Katch (gypsy with bear)
Doris Lloyd (Mrs. Williams)
Olaf Hytten (villager)
Harry Stubbs (Rev. Norman)
Tom Stevenson (Richardson, the
    graveyard digger)
Eric Wilton (chauffeur)
Harry Cording (Wykes)
Ernie Stanton (Phillips)
Ottola Nesmith (Mrs. Bally)
Connie Leon (Mrs. Wykes)
La Riana (gypsy dancer)
Caroline Cooke (first woman)
Margaret Fealy (second woman)
Jessie Arnold (gypsy woman)
Eddie Polo (churchgoer)
Gibson Gowland (villager)

Even a man who is pure in heart
And says his prayers by night
May become a wolf when the wolf-bane blooms
And the autumn moon is bright.
　　　　　—Gypsy folk rhyme.

What is it about *The Wolf Man*—a horror film made more than three decades ago—that has intrigued each new generation of film goers? Although blessed with an outstanding cast, it is tame indeed by today's violent standards. Nary a drop of blood was spilled on the screen. Most of the killings were accomplished almost discreetly behind marshland tree trunks. And yet *The Wolf Man* has become a landmark of the genre.

Why do nationwide television stations play it again and again, like Bogart and Bergman's *Casablanca*, or, "ad infinitesimal," like *Jungle Gents*, with those language-mangling Bowery Boys?

Why does it endure?

Why has it inspired jokes? Such as, Wolf Man to barber: "Just a light trim around the legs."

Why has it inspired television commercials? Such as the one showing a man turning into a werewolf for want of a Butterfinger candy bar.

Why is this monster truly immortal?

With respect for veteran "things-that-go-bump-in-the-night" make-up expert Jack P. Pierce's wet-nosed, whiskery vision of the werewolf, it seems to me that the artisan who so craftily cranked the always-active Universal fog machine deserved billing right up at the top. (And he may have gotten it—as director, cameraman, art director . . .) Rarely has fog been used so creatively and with such virtuosity to evoke an atmosphere of foreboding. Sometimes chokingly heavy. Occasionally only a light mist. Sometimes sneaking up on a scene. Occasionally whooshing on like gas warfare. I contend it is really *this* "fuming around," and not the monster's, that has made *The Wolf Man* survive all the horrors of Hammer (Films). The picture could have been subtitled *The Attack of the Vapors*.

The production values, in general, were a major asset, excepting the inexplicably tacky opening shot of Lon Chaney, Jr., returning to

Claude Rains, Lon Chaney, Jr., Evelyn Ankers

his ancestral estate after being away eighteen years. The rural England unspooled behind his car was glaringly obvious rear projection and led even more regrettably to a child's primer rendering of the exterior of Talbot Castle.

Otherwise, there was a sharp visual awareness everywhere. The clean lines of the castle observatory designed by Chaney's titled scientist father (Claude Rains). The clutter of the local antique shop where Chaney met heroine Evelyn Ankers, who first recited the rhyme about "the beasties" as she sold him a walking stick with a silver werewolf's head. Maria Ouspenskaya's shadowy Gypsy camp, from whence her werewolf son (Bela Lugosi) bit Chaney, turning him into a werewolf, too. A small but lively detailed glen carnival ending with an eerie mental collage of people, canes and wolf-bane that preceded Chaney's initial "change." The cavernous, echoing Talbot mansion, in which he felt the first signs—shoes and socks off, trouser leg lifted: hair, great clusters of *hair!* The celestially lighted village church where, following the forest murder of Ankers' girlfriend (Fay Helm), latecomer Chaney stood in the rear while the camera panned down the aisle to catch face after face turning to stare at him.

And, most of all, the fog-shrouded marsh, pinioned by grasping, almost intertwined trees. This semi-stylized setting recalled the woodland nightmare through which Disney's Snow White fled the wicked queen.

Joseph Valentine's photography was no small credit to *The Wolf Man,* either, with both animate and inanimate subjects bathed throughout in an unearthly silver moonglow—for both day and night scenes.

The treatment of the story was direct and economical, without fuss or feathers—*if* fuzz. It was straightforward monster stuff, with no fudging to make Chaney more squirrelly than werewolf—a split personality and/or victim of his own imagination. A couple of characters, like Dr. Warren William, did hint at schizophrenia, a 1940s staple at the old Bijou; but our fellow clearly *physically* changed, certainly as far as the audience was concerned.

At the end, while the Wolf Man was being tracked, Ankers suddenly turned up in the dark mire looking for Chaney, to whom, though engaged to castle gamekeeper Patric Knowles, she was attracted. When they inevitably collided, he was sans mufti and lunged hairily for her. She rent the fog with one or two of her soon-to-be familiar screams and was rescued by Rains, who beat him to death with his own silver cane. (Need I mention, at this late date, that only silver weapons can kill werewolves?) Rains then

Lon Chaney, Jr., Maria Ouspenskaya

Warren William, Claude Rains, Gibson Gowland (in derby), Lon Chaney Jr., (on ground), Ralph Bellamy

watched his son revert to his normal, clean-shaven self. Chief constable Ralph Bellamy finally arrived and concluded (perhaps disbelievingly), "The wolf must have attacked her and Larry came to the rescue. I'm sorry, Sir John."

Again, there should be no minimizing of what its talented cast did for *The Wolf Man*. Evelyn Ankers, who after this hit became the studio's "Queen of Horrors" in a succession of weird vehicles, was not only healthily beautiful but wholly convincing. She refreshingly managed to suggest a blithe personality behind the flustered exterior of a conventional monster-menaced miss. Her appearances often underscored by abrupt but apt switches in the first-rate Charles Previn score from portentous to lyrical, Ankers ideally complemented, even offset Chaney's forehead-pounding style which was further larded by a facial wart that resembled a huge tear. The latter blemish was especially evident in the shooting gallery scene where, now infected, he broke down when his target popped up: a wolf's figure. Following in Chaney pére's outsize footsteps, he was much more effective in wolf's clothing, stalking tiptoed with a forward list and howling the gingerbread village to life in the wee hours of the full moon at the thought of death.

Surprisingly few later film authorities have been of a single mind about the monster portion of this basically sympathetic characterization. In *An Illustrated History of the Horror Film*, Carlos Clarens likened Chaney's Wolf Man to "a hirsute Cossack," while in *Horror in the Cinema*, Ivan Butler said he more closely resembled an ape. Actually, it was all done with yak hairs glued onto Chaney's face by Jack Pierce a few frames at a time, each complete transformation taking a full day to shoot. (Chaney, Sr. usually had created and supplied his own make-up, but union rules now prohibited this.)

Rains, that mellifluous voice, hands characteristically in jacket pockets, that shock of hair, was a five-foot-five tower of strength, as usual. This Briton was one of the medium's most consistently dynamic and pleasurable actors, no matter the milieu—often uneasily a far piece from Blighty. Mme. Ouspenskaya, of the Moscow Art Theater, was fun as Maleva, a Gypsy "camp" if there ever was one. Weighted with babushka, long print skirts, jangly necklaces that hung the short distance to her knees and a 1941 version of the caftan, the shriveled but miraculously mobile little Slav—also given to reciting gloomy folk ballads—not only looked but sounded like the house mother in a modern day commune. Nobody else had a great deal to do, including Lugosi, who arose in the graveyard in a couple of scenes, but the presences were formidable.

When first released, *The Wolf Man* was dismissed by critics as "just another horror movie." It became Universal's biggest moneymaking attraction that season, cueing the return of Chaney's Larry Talbot for several sequels. (Until, oh ignominy! he was finally interred by Abbott and Costello, with a brief resurrection effected for a *Route 66* television segment years later.) With its longevity and a new perspective has come respect from horror chroniclers, too.

There was incalculable help from that fog which, unlike Mr. Sandburg's, crept in on little *wolf* feet. But one thing else gnaws: the sad story of George Murphy, who made a picture in the 1930s that also obliged the cast to be misty-eyed most of the time. "In those days 'fog' was manufactured by shooting Nujol on an electric hot plate which threw up incredibly thick oily clouds," wrote Murphy in his autobiography. "As a result my two fine Earl Benham suits became oil cloths, and I acquired through inhalation a slight case of diarrhea."

For the sake of everybody involved, let's hope the process of fog simulation had been improved by the time *The Wolf Man* bloomed.